CREDO SERIES

God's Word Revealed in Sacred Scripture

Based on the Curriculum Framework
Course I: The Revelation of Jesus Christ in Scripture

TEACHER'S RESOURCE

VERITAS
www.veritasreligion.com

The Subcommittee on the Catechism, United States Conference of Catholic Bishops, has found this catechetical text, copyright 2011, to be in conformity with the Catechism of the Catholic Church.

Veritas would like to thank all those who contributed to the development of this text:

CREDO SERIES CONSULTANT AND CONTRIBUTING WRITER: Maura Hyland
CONTRIBUTIONS FROM:
Joseph F. McCann, Thomas H. Groome, Hosffman Ospino, Susan Morgan, Brendan O'Reilly
TEXT CONSULTANTS:
Ed DeStefano, Annette Honan, Ailís Travers
TEXT EDITOR: Elaine Campion
DESIGN: Lir Mac Cárthaigh

INTERNET RESOURCES
There are internet resources available to support this text. Log on to www.credoseries.com

IMPRIMATUR
Most Reverend Kevin J. Farrell
Bishop of Dallas
January 12, 2011

The Nihil Obstat and Imprimatur are official declarations that a book or pamphlet is free of doctrinal and moral error. No implication is contained therein that those who have granted the Nihil Obstat or Imprimatur agree with the contents, opinions, or statement expressed.

Copyright © 2011 by Veritas Publications

All rights reserved. No part of the material may be reproduced or transmitted in any form or by any means, electronic or mechanical, including photocopying or by any information or retrieval system, adapted, rented or lent without written permission from the copyright owner. Applications for permissions should be addressed to the publisher.

See page 287 for copyright acknowledgments.

SEND ALL INQUIRIES TO:
Veritas
P.O. Box 789
Westerville, OH 43086
Tel. 866-844-0582
info@veritasreligion.com
www.veritasreligion.com

ISBN 978 1 84730 279 3 (Student Edition)
ISBN 978 1 84730 288 5 (Teacher Resource Edition)

Printed in the United States of America
1 2 3 4 5 6 7 / 11 12 13 14 15

CONTENTS

INTRODUCTION 5

CATECHESIS FOR YOUNG PEOPLE: JOSEPH F. MCCANN CM 8

A SHARED CHRISTIAN PRAXIS APPROACH: THOMAS H. GROOME 10

CULTURAL AWARENESS IN RELIGIOUS EDUCATION: HOSFFMAN OSPINO 14

CHAPTER 1	**God's Desire for Us; Our Desire for God**	**17**
	Introduction	17
	Notes and Guidelines for Student Activities	20
	Worksheets	25
	Review of Chapter 1	38
CHAPTER 2	**God Reaches Out to Us in Many Ways**	**41**
	Introduction	41
	Notes and Guidelines for Student Activities	44
	Worksheets	48
	Review of Chapter 2	61
CHAPTER 3	**God's Revelation through the Bible**	**64**
	Introduction	64
	Notes and Guidelines for Student Activities	67
	Worksheets	71
	Review of Chapter 3	72
CHAPTER 4	**The Bible: The Inspired Word of God**	**83**
	Introduction	83
	Notes and Guidelines for Student Activities	85
	Worksheets	88
	Review of Chapter 4	99
CHAPTER 5	**The Bible: God's Living Word for Our Lives**	**103**
	Introduction	103
	Notes and Guidelines for Student Activities	106
	Worksheets	109
	Review of Chapter 5	118
CHAPTER 6	**The Bible: A Blueprint for Living**	**122**
	Introduction	122
	Notes and Guidelines for Student Activities	124
	Worksheets	127
	Review of Chapter 6	137

CHAPTER 7	**The Bible Is the Book of the Church**	**140**
	Introduction	140
	Notes and Guidelines for Student Activities	143
	Worksheets	146
	Review of Chapter 7	151
CHAPTER 8	**Interpreting the Word of God in the Bible**	**154**
	Introduction	154
	Notes and Guidelines for Student Activities	156
	Worksheets	159
	Review of Chapter 8	169
CHAPTER 9	**The Old and New Testaments: God's Faithfulness over Time**	**173**
	Introduction	173
	Notes and Guidelines for Student Activities	176
	Worksheets	179
	Review of Chapter 9	191
CHAPTER 10	**The Gospel Is Good News**	**195**
	Introduction	195
	Notes and Guidelines for Student Activities	198
	Worksheets	201
	Review of Chapter 10	210
CHAPTER 11	**Jesus and His Message in the Gospels According to Matthew, Mark and Luke**	**213**
	Introduction	213
	Notes and Guidelines for Student Activities	216
	Worksheets	219
	Review of Chapter 11	229
CHAPTER 12	**The Gospel According to John**	**233**
	Introduction	233
	Notes and Guidelines for Student Activities	236
	Worksheets	239
	Review of Chapter 12	249
CHAPTER 13	**Jesus' Death and Resurrection Heralds a New Hope**	**252**
	Introduction	252
	Notes and Guidelines for Student Activities	256
	Worksheets	261
	Review of Chapter 13	268

STUDENT ACTIVITY TOOL KIT — **271**

ANSWER KEY TO CHAPTER REVIEWS — **281**

ACKNOWLEDGMENTS — **287**

Introduction

The aim of any Catholic high school theology program must surely be to help participants to become better disciples of Jesus Christ, more open to the Holy Spirit, and to grow stronger in their faith in God, a faith that is lived out every day. This can only be achieved by enabling the young people to explore and discover the Truth contained within the Word of God as spoken through Scripture, Tradition and the teaching of the Church. Knowledge of the Truth, then, should lead the young people to action; that is, to Christian living in the world.

With this aim as our central focus, the *Credo* series presents the whole story and vision of Catholic faith in a manner appropriate to young people of high school age. It is a Christ-centered curriculum, in that all the books, in one way or another, are Christological, constantly referring to the Christ of Faith and the Jesus of History. The curriculum adheres precisely to the detailed prescriptions of the United States Conference of Catholic Bishops' *Doctrinal Elements of a Curriculum Framework for the Development of Catechetical Materials for Young People of High School Age* (2007), which champions Christology as an organizing theme for all texts and topics. The Introduction to the Framework states:

> The Christological centrality of this framework is designed to form the content of instruction as well as to be a vehicle for growth in one's relationship with the Lord so that each may come to know him and live according to the truth he has given to us. In this way, disciples not only participate more deeply in the life of the Church but are also better able to reach eternal life with God in Heaven.

Though the texts do not often use the language of spirituality, there is an intentional emphasis throughout the curriculum on spirituality. All of the books in the series emphasize and encourage the students' personal appropriation and deep individual engagement with the Catholic faith. The teaching dynamic seeks to engage the 'souls' of the young people, to delve into what they really think and feel, and how they will decide to live their faith in the light of what they have learned. The pedagogy or dynamic of the series may be summarized as 'bringing Life to Faith and Faith to Life'. And so the generative theme of each chapter is brought to the resources of Catholic faith for its spiritual wisdom—in order to bring it back to life again as owned Christian wisdom, as lived Christian faith in the world.

The program is 'apologetic' in approach, in line with the recommendation in the Framework that it should attempt 'to help those same young people develop the necessary skills to answer or address the real questions that they face in life and in their Catholic faith', offering them a reason 'for the hope that is within [them]' (1 Peter 3:15). Hence the *Credo* series presents the 'content' of the faith as a great and wise way to live one's life in the world; appeals to young people's best desires and hopes; offers coherent and persuasive rationale for faith convictions, and often points to the lived witness of people from both past and contemporary times who are faithful witnesses to Jesus Christ and the faith taught and lived by his Church.

Credo possesses a real commitment to active parental involvement in the catechetical instruction of young people, and so offers suggestions to encourage a 'Faith Connect' with the young people's family and parish.

Credo is strongly committed to justice and, therefore, the social and personal responsibilities of Christian faith are integrated into all the books and topics. While we present the Catholic faith as offering Good News and great hope for young people today, we also remind young people that living as a Christian presents a real challenge, that being a disciple of Jesus brings great personal and social responsibilities. This sense of both consolation and challenge, of hope and demand, can have particular appeal to adolescents. There is much 'therapeutic' religion—a consoling experience—around today, but little challenge, whereas young people need both.

The *Credo* series is also deeply and consistently committed to what the Church now calls a 'New Evangelization'. Moving beyond the 'old' evangelization which emphasized 'bringing them in' (converting into the Church anyone not yet Catholic), the 'New Evangelization' advocates 'bringing Christians out' into the world with a faith alive. Thus, evangelization means to live one's faith with enthusiasm in every arena of life, to be joyful and living witnesses to the Truth. The pedagogy that underpins the *Credo* series—from Life to Faith to Life—is essentially a mode of evangelization.

The material in the *Credo* series may easily be adapted to a parish youth catechesis program that meets once or twice a week or at intervals over a more extended period.

TITLES IN THE SERIES

The *Credo* series will cover the six core courses as outlined in the Curriculum Framework mandated by the United States Conference of Catholic Bishops.

The six core courses are:

I. God's Word Revealed in Sacred Scripture
II. Son of God and Son of Mary
III. The Promised One: Servant and Savior
IV. The Body of Christ: The Church
V. Encountering Christ in the Sacraments
VI. Living and Loving as Disciples of Christ

The framework also lists five electives, and the *Credo* series will offer texts on these. In all, the *Credo* series will constitute a four-year, eight-semester catechesis of the students. It is strongly recommended that the six core courses be taught in the order given in the Framework. Schools are asked to choose *two* from the five elective subject themes.

STRUCTURE AND PEDAGOGY

Most of the core texts have fourteen chapters, each chapter representing a week's schoolwork or five classes. Book 1, which has thirteen chapters, opens with an extra introductory piece entitled 'Before you begin. . . .', which presents an overview of the books of the Bible. It is strongly recommended that students have their own Bibles as they work through this course.

The teaching method used in the *Credo* series reflects the commitments and five 'movements' of the Shared Christian Praxis Approach as proposed by Thomas Groome. (For a comprehensive explanation of this approach, see Tom Groome, *Christian Religious Education*: *Sharing our story and vision;* San Francisco: Harper and Row (1980), now published by Jossey-Bass, San Francisco.)

The pedagogy or dynamic of the program may be summarized as 'bringing Life to Faith and Faith to Life'. The content of each chapter is presented under five major headings, used consistently within each chapter and reflected in the design. (See notes on design and layout below.) The primary intent is that the young people not simply *learn about* the content (though this is important) but that they *learn from* it and integrate it into their lives.

The first major heading, **Attend and Reflect**, establishes the generative theme of the chapter and engages the young people's interest. It encompasses **Movement One** of Groome's praxis approach (inviting the students to express their present praxis—thoughts, feelings, experiences and so on—around the theme), and **Movement Two** (inviting their deeper level of reflection on this praxis, personally or socially, using their reason, memory and/or imagination). The two movements are worked through under a variety of subheadings—such as 'Reflect and discuss', 'Let's probe deeper' and 'Over to you'—all fulfilling a function in the underlying dynamic of Life to Faith and Faith to Life.

Movement Three, encompassing three major headings—**Hear the Story**, **Embrace the Vision** and **Think It Through**, presents the Story and Vision of Christian faith through an exploration of Scripture and Tradition and theological reflection around the lesson theme. It highlights the spiritual wisdom of Catholic faith for young people today, what it offers and asks of their lives, and how it can be life-giving for both themselves and the world. Movement Three demands a certain amount of 'figuring out', as the philosophy and theology underpinning the Scripture and Tradition is 'unpacked' in a manner and at a level appropriate to young people and their world.

Each of the three sections involved in Movement Three also incorporates elements of Movements One and Two—mini attend-and-reflect moments—so that these mid-chapter sessions are not all teaching and instruction and presentation. Every session should see young people bringing Life to Faith! Also, every session will conclude with an opportunity for the young people to begin to bring Faith to Life. These middle weekdays offer features such as: 'Faith Word' (defining a term or phrase in religious language or theological discourse), 'Talk it over' (inviting reflective discussion) and 'What about you personally?' (challenging the young people to question themselves).

Movement Four and **Movement Five**, which are interlocked and explored mainly under the heading **Judge and Act**, move the dynamic back to life again.

We invite the young people first to *judge*; that is, to appropriate the content, make its spiritual wisdom their own, take it to heart, familiarize themselves with its implications for living, and affirm it as part of their worldview. This involves reflecting back on the material studied in the chapter and responding to it, both orally and in writing. Here we also offer the young people a 'Learn by example' (recounting the life of a saint or contemporary model of good living). The exercises offered at this point include *Journal Work* (personal reflection and writing in response to the chapter theme), *Research Projects* and more.

Then comes the final and perhaps the most important invitation, to *act*; that is, to take what they have learned into everyday practical living, apply it, implement its suggestions, and enlist the support of others, especially family and close friends, in carrying it through. Here we find headings such as *'Respond with your family and friends'*, *'What will you do now?'* and *'Learn by heart'* (usually a short quotation from Scripture summarizing the theme of the chapter), as well as various exercises and questions that encourage the young people to make decisions in relation to the challenge of living as disciples of Jesus. Throughout the *Credo* series there is a vast array of activities, ranging from research projects and journal work to debates and role-plays. In seeking to connect with young people where they are 'at', we also take seriously the intense encounter of adolescents with modern media and pop culture. And so we include activities that encourage media literacy and support religious and Catholic values.

Through all of these means, we seek to enable the young people to deepen their relationship with God the Father and with the Risen Jesus and with the Holy Spirit, the Advocate and Teacher. In each chapter, through different personal and group activities, we encourage the young people to ponder on the signs of God's loving presence in their lives.

There is a strong liturgical note running throughout the *Credo* series. In addition to a specific study of the Mass, the Sacraments and prayer in the appropriate texts, there are many opportunities for ritual prayer and meditation. We invite the young people to reflect on Scripture passages and to engage in quiet moments of personal prayer so that they may become more alert to God's presence and more open to his call. Each chapter ends with a closing prayer or ritual that 'captures' the central teaching of the chapter. The rituals, which are written specifically for young people, contain traditional prayers that are rooted in the Tradition of the Catholic Church and they also focus on the everyday issues and experiences young people encounter in living their faith. We encourage the young people to respond in prayer. Throughout the program we also encourage them to make prayer a part of their daily lives, not just in school.

In summary, in each book of the *Credo* series we invite young people to: *attend and reflect* on their lives; *hear* the story of God's love for them; *see* the vision of what God wants for them; *think* about what this means; and finally, having encountered the Word of God in Scripture, in the teaching of the Church and in the experience of Christians through the ages, *judge* how it might apply to their lives and make a decision to *act* according to God's will and as disciples of Jesus.

The confidence and support of the teacher is paramount where catechesis is concerned, for it is the faith and enthusiasm and spirit of the teacher that is communicated to the disciple now and always. The *Credo* series provides all the necessary tools to bring Jesus and the proclamation of the Kingdom into the classroom.

DESIGN AND LAYOUT OF STUDENTS' TEXT

In order to give the *Credo* series a distinct personality that is accessible and relevant to young readers, we have employed a hand-drawn motif in the margins of the students' text. Since the Middle Ages, embellishment by hand has formed a vibrant part of Christian visual tradition. Even now, over five hundred years after the invention of printing, calligraphic decoration is still to be found on blessings, cards, candles and so on.

The style of hand embellishment adopted for the margins of our text is inspired by the doodle—a ubiquitous feature of teenage life. Many teachers of high school theology and other areas of religious education have begun to employ the act of doodling as a technique to assist prayer. In much the same way that monastic scribes could focus their minds on God while copying and illuminating their codices, the act of doodling can provide a focus for the young person that acts as an aid to contemplation. The *Credo* series makes use of this by offering suggestions for the use of 'doodling' as a means of helping the young people to focus during their reflections on Scripture.

Each of the five chapter sections has its own color. Text and illustrations follow this color pattern throughout the series, making it very easy for both students and teachers to navigate the text.

The *Credo* series is illustrated with artwork that spans a variety of media and traditions. For centuries the Church has been one of the major patrons of artistic endeavor, and this relationship is reflected in the diversity of sacred imagery included in the *Credo* series.

TEACHER'S RESOURCE

The teacher's resource provides background theological notes and general advice for teachers. It also contains supplementary support and extend activities for each chapter. We offer these to help the young people (and you) to deepen their understanding of the concepts presented in the students' text, thus enabling them to connect and integrate the content with their own life experiences. Most of the activities are offered as photocopiable worksheets and they are also available on the *Credo* website.

JOSEPH F. MCCANN CM

Catechesis for Young People

A CATECHETICAL EDUCATION

Catholic religious formation (catechesis) and religious education in high schools in the United States is based on three documents: the *General Directory for Catechesis* (1998), the *National Directory for Catechesis* (2005) and the *Doctrinal Elements of a Curriculum Framework for the Development of Catechetical Materials for Young People of High School Age* (2007). These documents are the foundations for the high school texts that form the *Credo* series.

Catholic catechesis or Catholic religious education and formation must always focus on the Person of Jesus Christ. Its purpose is 'to put people . . . in communion and intimacy with Jesus Christ' (*General Directory for Catechesis* [GDC], no. 80). The *Directory* uses the word 'apprentice', suggesting that young people should learn to know Jesus, love Jesus and follow Jesus as a matter of personal decision and habitual action. Catechesis, it says, should promote 'full and sincere adherence to his person and the decision to walk in his footsteps' (GDC, no. 53). Like an apprentice, too, the student should learn the appropriate responses and practice the behaviors and skills that follow from this decision: 'an apprenticeship in the entire Christian life' (GDC, no. 30).

So, whether we use the word 'catechize' or the phrase 'religious education' or 'religious formation', what we do in a Catholic high school Theology class should present Jesus Christ to young people in a warm and appealing way, as well as make sure that they are knowledgeable and well informed about the Catholic faith. Perhaps the best description for that process would be 'catechetical education'.

All the books in the *Credo* series are, in one way or another, centered on Jesus Christ. Instead of a book on Jesus and a book on Sacred Scripture and one on the Sacraments and another on the Church and so on, the texts in this series focus on Jesus in relation to the individual topics.

The books offer a comprehensive study of the major themes of Catholic Christian faith in a manner and language appropriate to young people of high school age.

RELIGION AND LIFE

Often people confine their religion to their time in church on Sunday, and do not see it as relevant to the rest of their lives. When this happens, religion becomes more of a private matter than a communal one. It becomes more about personal relationships and individual devotions, with little to say about public life, social issues or world problems. Today, more and more people profess to be 'spiritual', meaning a kind of mental culture, but fail to recognize that a religious stance implies, or should imply, the deepest convictions about life, the most cherished commitments and the most crucial life decisions.

The Second Vatican Council recognized this 'dichotomy between the faith which many profess and their day-to-day conduct' as 'one of the gravest errors of our time' (*Constitution on the Church in the Modern World* [*Gaudium et Spes*], no. 43). Hence the *Directory* wants to see Christian faith and daily life integrated in religious teaching and learning and returns to this theme on a number of occasions. It refers to 'experience' as 'a necessary medium for exploring and assimilating the truths which constitute the objective content of Revelation' (GDC, no. 152). It describes 'catechetical pedagogy' (method of teaching) as 'interpreting and illuminating experience with the data of faith' (GDC, no. 153). It employs a striking verb to describe the task of the religious educator: 'Correlating life and faith' (GDC, no. 207). This involves bridging 'the gap between belief and life, between the Christian message and the cultural context' (GDC, no. 205). This is a striking idea because it points to a 'disconnect' between the teaching of Christian theology and the life of the contemporary world.

FROM LIFE TO FAITH TO LIFE

The *General Directory for Catechesis* wants the theology teacher to bring the human experiences of the students to the timeless truths of the Christian faith. This can be simply described as helping young people to 'bring their lives to the Christian faith' and, then, 'bring Christian faith to their lives'. The intended result—the teaching objective—is 'lived Christian faith'. In a nutshell, the movement is 'life to faith to life'. This is also the essential dynamic of the 'shared Christian praxis approach' to catechesis and religious education, as taught by Thomas Groome, the general editor of the *Credo* series. This approach is explained in detail in Groome's own article on page 10 of this resource.

The great twentieth-century Catholic thinker Bernard Lonergan SJ outlined how a person learns in four steps: first, turning one's attention to something; second, arriving at an understanding of something; third, coming to judgment about something; and finally, making a decision about something. The stages are often summarized in two simple commands: Be attentive; Be responsible.

Accordingly, a method of teaching that enables young people to 'know their faith' will:

- engage and promote their interests, in order that they pay attention to their own lives;
- help them to reflect critically on and learn from their lives in the world;
- encourage them to pay attention to and come to understand thoroughly the content of Christian faith;
- help them to make judgments correlating and integrating their 'lives' and 'faith';
- help them to reach decisions—about knowing, feeling and acting—regarding both life and faith.

These aims inform the structure for Groome's shared Christian praxis and the pedagogy in the *Credo* series.

WHAT CONTENT SHOULD WE TEACH?
The *General Directory for Catechesis* makes clear that the 'content' of catechesis is 'the Gospel message'. In this endeavor, the teaching of the Bible, Sacred Scripture, 'should have a pre-eminent position' (GDC, no. 127). The teacher should ensure, moreover, that interpretation of the Bible follows authentic Catholic teaching. The whole tradition of Catholic teaching should be faithfully taught; it does not do to 'cherry-pick'; that is, choose only the bits that suit our temperament and disposition or situation. The *Catechism of the Catholic Church* should be the guiding light for matters of doctrine, or, as the *Directory* says, 'the doctrinal point of reference for all catechesis' (GDC, nos. 93 and 121).

But teaching should not be purely factual and knowledge-based. The Christian faith has 'cognitive, experiential, and behavioral' aspects (GDC, no. 35). These three aspects are reflected in a very ancient phrase: '*lex credendi, lex orandi, lex vivendi*' or 'The law for believing is the law for praying and the law for living' (GDC, no. 122). Religious education is nothing if not 'holistic'. The theology teacher should engage people's heads, hearts and hands.

In response to the question of which topics to teach, the US bishops issued the document entitled *Doctrinal Elements of a Curriculum Framework for the Development of Catechetical Materials for Young People of High School Age* (2007). Its purpose is to provide a framework to help publishers and writers produce instructional material for catechesis. It takes up from the *Directory*, affirming its aim of centrality on Christ and involving Christian knowledge, personal relationship and responsible living. The *Credo* series adheres precisely to the detailed prescriptions outlined in this document.

Thorough knowledge and familiarity with Christian faith invites youth into the deep currents that have constituted the great river of Catholic thought and life for two thousand years. This includes Catholicism's *anthropology* (its positive understanding of the person and the covenant of nature and grace); its *cosmology* (a sacramental outlook on life and the universe); its *sociology* (that we 'are made for each other' and are our brothers' and sisters' keepers); its *epistemology* (merging our knowledge into spiritual wisdom), and so on. In this manner, catechetical education powerfully reinforces and, indeed, fulfills and completes education in secular subjects.

RELIGIOUS EDUCATION IS NOT CONFINED TO SCHOOL
The Christian community is needed to collaborate in the crucial task of Christian catechesis and Catholic religious education (GDC, no. 245).

Education cannot be successfully carried out if it is confined to the school alone. Young people must be aware of personal support and good example from friends, family, Church, from community groups and, indeed, from the wider society where appropriate. In the same way, religious formation takes place in the Christian faith community, including 'the family, parish, Catholic schools, Christian associations and movements, basic ecclesial communities' (GDC, no. 220).

What this means is that each Catholic is, at the same time, both catechized and catechist, learner and teacher in faith. One assists, as one can, in the formation of our youth, and, on occasion, is assisted in one's own growth in faith by the challenges and achievements of young Christians. The teacher who is not constantly learning in the classroom is hardly teaching at all. Galileo said in old age: '*Ancora imparo*.' (I am always learning.) There can be no better motto for a catechist.

THOMAS H. GROOME

A Shared Christian Praxis Approach

For many years I've been working to promote a 'shared Christian praxis approach' to catechesis and Religious Education. Originally much influenced by the conscientizing, emancipatory and praxis-based pedagogy of Paulo Freire, over the years, and from its employ across a great variety of contexts and cultures, age levels and time frames, this approach has developed and matured in its own right.

At core, a shared Christian praxis approach honors God's revealing presence and saving grace in the ordinary and everyday of people's lives and likewise the revelation and spiritual wisdom mediated by the Bible and Christian tradition. Its intent is to enable people to integrate their 'life' and 'Christian faith' into 'lived Christian faith', using a pedagogy that brings life to the Faith and brings the Faith to life.

That catechesis must teach Christian faith is patently obvious, but why attend to and actively engage people's lives as well? Clearly there is a whole underlying theology here of both Revelation and sacramentality, of how God continues to manifest his will and mediate his grace through the ordinary and everyday of life, as well as through Scripture/Tradition and the seven great Sacraments. However, the pedagogical rationale for engaging people's lives in order to teach for Christian discipleship is stated forcefully by the *General Directory for Catechesis*—placing a shared Christian praxis approach squarely within the present mind of the Church regarding catechetical methodology.

By way of pedagogy, the *General Directory* calls for 'a correct . . . correlation and interaction between profound human experiences and the revealed message' (no. 153). For it is by 'correlating faith and life' (no. 207) that 'catechesis . . . bridges the gap between belief and life, between the Christian message and the cultural context' (no. 205). Christian religious educators must not only teach the faith tradition but also engage people's lives in the world because 'experience is a necessary medium for exploring and assimilating the truths which constitute the objective content of Revelation' (no. 152). Thus, effective catechesis should present every aspect of the faith tradition 'to refer clearly to the fundamental experiences of people's lives' (no. 133). Catechists should engage participants' own lives in the world as integral to the catechetical curriculum because 'one must start with praxis to be able to arrive at praxis' (no. 245).[1]

Let me now review briefly what I have explained at length elsewhere[2]: the core components and the pedagogical movements of a shared Christian praxis approach.

An Approach: I deliberately refer to shared praxis as an approach to catechetical education rather than a method; in fact, many different methods can be used within its overarching commitments. 'Bringing life to faith and faith to life' suggests a heuristic framework for how a religious educator might craft an intentional teaching/learning event. As people embrace and practice its commitments and dynamics, however, it becomes their general style and can be effected in varied ways and circumstances.

Praxis: Since Paulo Freire resurrected 'praxis' in educational discourse, there has been debate about what precisely the term means. Indeed, much educational literature still favors the term 'experience' instead and I often refer simply to 'life'—as in 'learning from life'. However, praxis has a more agential meaning than experience. Praxis is reflective activity in which one is an initiator or agent, whereas experience connotes something that one undergoes. John Dewey struggled to transcend this passive connotation of 'experience' throughout his writings, never with complete success.

I understand and use praxis to mean purposeful human activity, what we do reflectively and imaginatively or how we reflect upon and intend what we are doing. As such, it attempts to hold theory and practice in a dialectical unity while imagining the outcome and consequences. So, praxis embraces reflective, active and creative activity. A praxis way of knowing is intentional reflection upon what one is doing or what is going on in order to imagine consequences and create new possibilities.

The active dimension of a praxis way of knowing engages any and all bodily, mental and volitional activities, and likewise pays attention to whatever is being done in people's 'life-world'. It can engage what people know, how they feel, what they do, or what is going on in the historical reality of their social/cultural context. The reflective aspect of praxis entails the whole human capacity for knowing, engaging reason, memory and imagination, to intentionally learn from and for life in the world. It entails critical reflection not as a negative exercise but as a positive act of discernment (from the Greek *krinein*) that looks inward through self-reflection and outward at the public world through social analysis. The creative aspect recognizes the likely consequences of present praxis, imagines what might be or should be, and acts to bring about the desired end.

Christian: Christian religious educators are under mandate to teach with integrity the fullness of Christian Revelation that is mediated through Scripture and Tradition. Not only must we teach the constitutive truths, values and practices of Christian faith but also make explicit its meaning and demands for the lives of disciples today. Favoring a narrative language pattern for good catechetical reasons,[3] I find it helpful to highlight both the 'Story' and 'Vision' of Christian faith. I use these terms as metaphors to symbolize the whole historical reality of Christian Revelation and the demands/promises that it makes upon the lives of its adherents and communities. Together this Story and Vision constitute the spiritual wisdom of Christian faith for lives today and how we are to live for God's Reign as disciples of Jesus—doing of God's will 'on earth as in heaven'.

Shared: A shared praxis approach entails creating a community of conversation among participants, encouraging them to engage actively in the teaching–learning dynamic. It calls them into partnership with each other, to learn together. The exchanges among participants should entail all the give and take, listening and sharing, agreement and disagreement, cherishing one's own truth while being open to the truth of others that is the mark of good conversation. 'Shared' in the title also reflects the intent to help people bring 'life' and 'faith' together, to integrate Christian faith into daily life as 'lived faith'. This amounts to people appropriating its spiritual wisdom as their own, coming to see for themselves and embrace its truth and meaning for their lives.

In summary, a shared Christian praxis approach to Religious Education/catechesis involves creating a community of conversation and active participation in which people reflect together critically on their own historical agency in time and place, and on their socio-cultural realities; have access together to the spiritual wisdom of the Christian Story and Vision; and are encouraged to appropriate this wisdom with the intent of renewed praxis of Christian faith toward the coming of God's Reign.

PEDAGOGICAL MOVEMENTS OF A SHARED CHRISTIAN PRAXIS APPROACH

The movements of a shared praxis approach should be much more symphonic than sequential; it should not be practiced as a lock-step process. This being said, the dynamic of 'bringing life to faith, and faith to life' suggests a pattern of pedagogical moves that fulfill the foundational commitments of this approach. I outline its dynamics as a focusing activity and five subsequent movements.

The Focusing Activity: Here the educator's intent is twofold:

- to engage people as active participants in the teaching–learning event;
- to focus a curriculum topic as something of real interest to the lives and/or faith of participants.

Thus, it should dispose people to participate actively by turning them to look at their own lives in the world, and begin to engage them with a generative theme, symbol or text—something of real import to their present praxis of life or faith or both.

Movement One (M1): Expressing the Theme as in Present Praxis: The educator's intent here is to encourage participants to express themselves around the generative theme, symbol or text from the perspective of their present praxis. They can express what they do themselves or what they see others doing, their own feelings or thoughts or life-centered interpretations, or their perception of what is going on around them in their socio-cultural context. The key is that people 'pay attention' to the focus and name what emerges as their own encounter with the theme, symbol or text—how they see it, engage it, interpret it, or whatever. Their expressions can be spoken, written, drawn, constructed or mediated by any means of human communication.

Movement Two (M2): Reflecting on the Theme of Life/Faith: The intent here is to encourage people to reflect critically on what they expressed in Movement One. As noted, critical reflection can engage reason, memory, imagination or a combination of them; such reflection can be both personal and social. Reason questions or questioning activities can ask why things are the way they are; what causes them to be this way; what their meaning might be; why participants' own perceptions or interpretations are as they are, and so on. Memory questions or questioning activities might ask participants about the origins of their present praxis, their own recall or past experiences regarding it, to uncover how the social history is shaping their expressions and to recognize how their own biography or social location influence how they respond to the theme, symbol or text, and so on. Imagination-type questions or activities invite people to imagine beyond present praxis for its likely consequences, its possibilities and its desired outcomes.

Movement Three (M3): Christian Story and Vision: Here the pedagogical task is to teach clearly the Christian Story and Vision around the particular theme, symbol or text, and to do so with integrity and persuasion. Though this will often entail a doctrinal review, it is more important that people have persuasive access to the spiritual wisdom of Christian faith around the particular life/faith focus. Likewise, it is important to intentionally raise up the Vision out of the Story, what Christian faith teaches and means for lives now around the topic and how best to respond.

Movement Four (M4): Appropriating the Wisdom of Christian Faith to Life: M4 begins the dynamic of moving back to life again with renewed Christian commitment (M5). The pedagogy here encourages people to come to see for themselves what the wisdom of Christian faith might mean for their everyday lives, to personally appropriate this wisdom and to 'take it to heart' in who they are and how they live. So the educator might inquire how participants are feeling, or what they are coming to recognize for themselves, what they agree with or disagree with or might add to what has been presented in M3, and so on.

Movement Five (M5): Making Decisions for Christian Faith: Here the intent is to give participants an opportunity to choose how to respond to the spiritual wisdom of Christian faith. Decisions can be cognitive, affective or behavioral—what people believe, how they might worship or relate with God in prayer, or the ethics and values by which to live their lives. The imperative is that all decisions be 'real', influencing how participants live their Christian faith and grow in identity as disciples of Jesus Christ.

Though I lay out these movements sequentially, let me reiterate that they have great flexibility and many possible combinations. I have often combined the focusing activity with M1, and M1 with M2; I've borrowed from M3—briefly—as a focusing activity to engage people's interests; I've often shared from M3 as the conversation of M1 and M2 unfold; I've done M3 and then some M4 to return to M3 again before going back to M4 and eventually on to M5; I've combined M4 and M5 only to return again to M3 for more access to the wisdom of the faith tradition. And many times the decisions made in M5 have constituted the focusing activity for the next gathering of an ongoing community of conversation.

More important than the movements are their underpinning commitments. The focusing act reflects commitment to engage participants in the teaching/learning dynamic and with something generative for their lives. M1 reflects commitment to have people pay attention to their own lives in the world and to express their present praxis. M2 reflects commitment to critical reflection, encouraging people to think for themselves, personally and socially, to question and probe, to reason, remember and imagine around the life/faith theme, symbol or text from the perspective of their present praxis. M3 reflects commitment to give people access to the Story and Vision of Christian faith, enabling participants to encounter its spiritual wisdom for their lives. M4 reflects commitment to appropriation, encouraging participants to integrate their lives and Christian faith, to make its spiritual wisdom their own. M5 reflects commitment to invite people to decision, choosing a lived faith response to the spiritual wisdom they have encountered.

These commitments to participation and conversation, to engaging and attending, to expressing and reflecting, to accessing and appropriating, and to decision-making should run throughout the process. In other words, engagement does not end with the focusing activity but must be maintained throughout; likewise expression is not limited to M1, nor reflection to M2, nor decision-making to M5, and so on. Rather, the religious educator should promote these activities throughout the whole event.

By way of 'educating faithful Christians in a dissenting world', I make explicit the following points. Overall, a shared Christian praxis approach is set within a community of conversation and shared faith, reflecting the broader community of the Church. The dialectics of conversation—the shared faith of the group—provides a buffer against unduly individualized discernment and whimsical decision-making; all is tested within a community of discourse. Then, its dynamics invite people to active participation, encouraging them to be agents of their faith rather than dependents; in this regard it seems more likely, by God's grace, to encourage faith development toward Christian maturity.

Then, its focusing act and opening movements honor people's own wisdom from life and God's presence in their lives. However, the pedagogy here also encourages critical reflection, personal and social, inviting people to 'think twice' about their actions and reflections rather than settling for personal bias or blithely accepting the influences of their social and cultural contexts.

Movement Three gives access to the 'whole Story' of Christian faith and its Vision for people's lives now, doing so with integrity; it should never compromise anything that is constitutive of Christian faith. However, the fact that Christian Story/Vision is mediated into the context of people's lives (their own stories and visions), highlighting its spiritual wisdom for life, enables the religious educator to present Christian faith in a persuasive way and yet without indoctrination—in a mode respectful of but also appealing to participants.

Movements Four and Five encourage people's own discernment and decision-making but assure that both are well informed by the constitutive truths of Christian faith. If people are intent on dissenting they will do so anyhow, regardless of the pedagogy. Shared praxis certainly does not encourage dissent but that people's honest thoughts and feelings be brought to explicit discourse in the teaching/learning community. There they can be addressed and tested in ways more likely to lead to lived faith as disciples of Jesus. No approach can promise more.

NOTES

1. Congregation for the Clergy, *General Directory for Catechesis*, USCCB: Washington, DC, 1998. It is fascinating that the Directory refers to this pedagogy which integrates 'life' and 'faith' as 'the pedagogy of God' (no. 139) and likewise of Christ (no. 140).
2. My most complete statement of a shared praxis approach is in *Sharing Faith: A Comprehensive Approach to Religious Education and Pastoral Ministry*, San Francisco, CA: HarperSanFrancisco, 1991; now published by Wipf and Stock Publishers, Eugene, Oregon, USA, 97401. See especially Chapters 4–10.
3. See ibid., pp. 138–142, for my rationale to favor a narrative paradigm for Christian Religious Education.

This article is an extract from *Exploring Religious Education: Catholic Religious Education in an Intercultural Europe*, Chapter 22, 'Educating Faithful Christians in a Dissenting World' by Thomas H. Groome (Dublin: Veritas, 2008).

HOSFFMAN OSPINO

Cultural Awareness in Religious Education

The education of Christians in their faith does not happen in a vacuum. It is a process that builds on and integrates with the cultural values and convictions that educators and students learn from family, friends, society and Church. We are cultural beings. The Second Vatican Council reminded Catholics that sharing the Good News happens in the context of the 'living exchange between the Church and the diverse cultures of people' (*Constitution on the Church in the Modern Word* [*Gaudium et Spes*], no. 44). Subsequent ecclesial documents introduced the term 'inculturation' to name such living exchange. For instance, the *General Directory for Catechesis* published in 1997 dedicates several sections to exploring the relationship between catechesis and culture through the lens of inculturation. According to the *Directory*, awareness about culture in catechesis is more than mere adaptation (no. 109) or translation (no. 112) of religious categories into any particular language. Cultural awareness is rather a process of discernment on the part of the faith community that affirms the elements of culture that give meaning to people in their everyday lives and have the potential to mediate the experience of God while preserving the integrity of the Gospel message (cf. nos. 109–113). Likewise, they must challenge the aspects of culture that are contrary to their faith. These affirmations and negations are a good starting point for our reflection as religious educators.

One of the most significant outcomes of contemporary globalization is the increased appreciation of the many cultures that shape the lives of women and men in our families, communities and schools. Not only are we able to know more about other cultures through the media, the internet and the myriads of literary resources that fill our libraries, but we can also engage in dialogue with people around us who see and interpret the world according to cultural criteria different from our own. Cultural diversity is inescapably present in our cities, our parishes, our schools and our classrooms. Some diversity has always been with us, but our awareness of it has been heightened by modern transportation and communication, by migration and globalization. Religious educators must develop a deepened sensibility about diversity and be more attentive to the impact of this reality on the way we educate in faith. This is a gift.

But every gift brings its own challenges. Some of us may feel more at ease with the idea of sharing different cultural perspectives on a particular issue or practice than others; some may prefer to focus on the common aspects of our human experience rather than on the differences. The truth is that it does not have to be either/or but should be both/and. Educating Christians in culturally diverse contexts like many of our schools and faith communities demands that we affirm our own cultural experiences *and* those of the people who walk with us on our life journeys; we must find that which we share in common *and* learn to appreciate that which makes us different. In some sense this is what makes our experience fully *catholic*.

Another challenge that the gift of cultural awareness poses for religious educators is how sincerely to embrace cultural diversity when we educate in faith and to affirm the cultural experiences of all the people we encounter (that is, teachers, students, administrators, parents). A quick look at the history of Christianity shows at least four attitudes: (1) Indifference before cultural diversity while focusing on the 'objectivity' and 'universality' of content; (2) Open rejection of cultural perspectives that are not similar or equal to those of a dominant group; (3) Adoption of some form of tolerance that expects progressive assimilation into a given culture, usually the culture of those who have the power to set the directions for the educational enterprise; (4) Openness to discovering elements of wisdom and truth in the various cultural contexts where Christian believers live, thereby enriching the experience of all participants in religious education. This last attitude is deeply ingrained in the nature and purpose of Catholic education, making it possible for Christianity to take root and become indigenous in every corner of the world. However, at various points in history the former attitudes, or some variations of these, have prevailed, contradicting the 'catholic' (that is, universal, inviting, inclusive, open) character of Christian religious education. Thus, it is imperative that we develop approaches to religious education that continue to affirm the wisdom of the Christian tradition in all possible forms *and* engage culture as a valid mediation of our encounter with God in history. In the culturally diverse contexts in which we educate Christians today, we must be attentive to and welcome the many cultural perspectives that people bring to the conversation.

Awareness of cultural diversity in religious education places before us a twofold invitation: (1) to understand better how God enters into relationship with us in history and (2) to acknowledge the experiences that we bring as human beings to that relationship. From this invitation then emerge two powerful insights that can significantly enrich the way we educate people in Catholic faith today:

1. God becomes present to us through history and culture
God comes to the encounter of women and men in the midst of our history and culture(s). God meets us in the here and now of our lives. One of the central convictions of our Judeo-Christian tradition is that God has a plan for us, that God has something to share with us, and we know about this because God has revealed it to us, especially through Jesus Christ.

Christians listen to, embrace and live God's message in different ways according to the historical and cultural conditions that shape our existences. From the first moments of historical Revelation, God has become present to women and men living in particular cultural contexts through words, actions, symbols and people; that is, ways that are unique to people's experiences and thus they can understand. Biblical language, for instance, is filled with rich Semitic imagery that affirms the relational character of human experience. Some Christians have used classical philosophical language to speak of God's divine presence and message, yet with the help of more abstract concepts and categories. Artists use their imagination to capture their experience of God and the Gospel message through a rich variety of expressions (for example, music, painting, architecture). Some cultures favor oral traditions to share their faith convictions with the younger generations. Others affirm the value of ritual and symbol to interpret their relationship with God.

Regardless of how we articulate our faith in the everyday of our lives, we do it with the resources that our culture provides. The greatness of the divine Revelation is manifested in that God freely and gratuitously chooses to enter into relationship with us according to the cultural experiences that shape our lives. Since we are much more aware of the diversity of cultural symbols, rituals and stories that mediate the experience of God in our diverse communities and schools, it is imperative that religious educators become aware of such cultural mediations and affirm their value for Christian education.

2. We see the world through the lenses of our particular culture
Culture is our human way of life; it is who we are, what we do and what we hope. In this sense, every human person simultaneously belongs to a culture and contributes as an architect of her or his own cultural reality. Culture is the matrix in which we are born and become human. At times the word 'culture' is understood as something merely external or artificial or something that some people have but we are not sure if we do too. This limited understanding is sometimes the consequence of our inability to name our own culture because we are seldom asked to do so. Is culture mainly defined by language or ethnicity or race or education or social location or religion or politics or history? The best answer that we can give to this question is: all of the above. Whenever we can identify the criteria and modes through which we interpret our immediate reality, then we are talking about culture.

This observation is very important when educating Christians in their faith. Most of the language, symbols, rituals and values that we use to talk about our faith are borrowed from the immediacy of our cultural experiences. It is easy to assume that when our young people hear the word 'church', each one of them has the same understanding, but we would be surprised. Let us think of a culturally diverse group of young people in a Catholic high school in the United States. For a young person raised in a Euro-American family, hearing the word 'church' may suggest a group of people to which one chooses to belong—or not. For a Hispanic student, 'church' may evoke images of family life. For an African-American student, to hear the word 'church' may lead her or him to think of Protestant Christianity, since these are the most common churches in neighborhoods that are predominantly Black.

The cultural circumstances that shape the lives of the women and men whom we encounter in religious education are the same circumstances that shape the language and categories that they use to express their faith. We must be attentive to such categories, intentionally integrating them into how we communicate Christian faith and how we encourage people to live it.

Furthermore, those whom we educate in faith are not the only ones who are shaped by particular cultural circumstances. Educators are as well. As religious educators we need to identify our own cultural assumptions and evaluate them on a continuous basis. How we teach, what we teach and why we teach (all curriculum questions) very much reflect our cultural values and convictions. The more aware we are about these values and convictions, the better we are able to foster authentic relationships with our young people and make responsible pedagogical decisions.

We enter the religious educational experience as human beings shaped by the richness of our own particular culture(s). Nonetheless, we are not exempt from biases and errors. For decades White Christian educators in the United States denied fellow Black Christians access to their schools on account of the color of their skin. In mission territories some Christian educators forced native populations to accept a faith that the latter did not understand. Sometimes religious educators may embrace inadequate or incomplete understandings of the Christian tradition and fail to present it with faithfulness. These educators do not necessarily mean harm or evil toward the people affected by their decisions, yet they operate according to unchecked cultural standards. It is crucial that we remain attentive about our cultural assumptions, affirm those that make us more human and authentic Christians, and question those that do not.

CONCLUSION

Cultural awareness is a pedagogical virtue. As such, we must learn it, cultivate it and perfect it on a continuous basis. We cannot lose sight that our contemporary societies, faith communities and schools are culturally diverse. We have the responsibility to learn what elements of culture mediate the experience of God for the people whom we encounter in our educational settings, and to challenge the aspects that counter God's presence. As Christian educators, then, we have the obligation to be culturally responsive and responsible when educating in faith. Our lives and the lives of those whom we encounter are deeply shaped by unique cultural experiences. Through these cultural values and convictions, we enter into relationship with one another and with God. May this be an invitation to grow in awareness about our own cultural being and that of the people we educate in faith.

CHAPTER 1

God's Desire for Us
Our Desire for God

INTRODUCTION

Chapter 1 explores the human search for meaning in life and asks where God fits into the grand scheme of things. The chapter is developed under five major headings:

- **ATTEND AND REFLECT**: Where do we find meaning in life?
- **HEAR THE STORY**: Human life is special!
- **EMBRACE THE VISION**: Human beings share in God's divine life
- **THINK IT THROUGH**: How do we recognize our desire for God?
- **JUDGE AND ACT** (*Activities and exercises that encourage the young people to integrate what they have learned in the chapter into their daily lives*)

Theological Background for the Teacher

HUMAN BEINGS AS SEARCHERS AND SEEKERS

All human beings are searchers: we all ask questions and search for meaning in life. These questions are of different types:

Foundational questions; for example: Why was I born? Why will I die? Why do people suffer?

Theoretical questions; for example: Why is there something rather than nothing? What is the nature of good and evil? How do we explain our feeling that we ought to be good?

Practical questions; for example: What type of person would I like to become? Where is the path to true happiness? What would make me happy?

Beneath all of the above are the *fundamental questions*; for example, How do we account for human desire? How do we explain the restlessness of the human heart? Why is that restlessness unique to human beings?

One of the best things we can do for young people is to encourage in them the facility to be questioners and seekers. In doing so, we enable them to stand in awe of the insight that gives rise to the question, and of the infinite horizons that the question exposes.

Young people will be at different stages in their recognition of themselves as questioners and seekers. Before you can help them embark on the journey of searching for meaning in life and of appreciating what it is that they are engaging in, you need to understand that:

- human beings are, by their nature, questioners and seekers. In the *Credo* series we encourage dialogue, whereby the young people express their present understanding, put words on their experience and hear others do the same;
- it is equally important to foster awe and wonder as it is to provide insights that may lead to answers;
- most importantly, foundational questions involve matters that are transcendent, and so the search for meaning in relation to these questions often has more to do with finding wisdom and insight than finding 'answers'.

HUMAN BEINGS AS INNATELY RELIGIOUS

The human person is 'by nature and vocation a religious person. Coming from God, going toward God, [the human person] lives a fully human life only if he freely lives by his bond with God' (*Catechism of the Catholic Church* [CCC], no. 44). The human person 'is made to live in communion with God in whom he finds happiness' (CCC, no. 45). It is God who has given us the priceless gifts of questioning and seeking. Ultimately, in the context of a Christian faith perspective, the only answer to the question of meaning revealed in Jesus Christ is God's presence with us and our relationship with God. God is the One whose very presence responds to our questions in ways that answers could never do. In chapter 1 we introduce the young people to the famous insight of St. Augustine: 'Our hearts are restless until they rest in you.'

Religion is a source of meaning because it provides a way of addressing such foundational questions as those raised by the facts of life and death. All religions provide a belief and value structure within which the value of human life and human progress can be measured. All religions acknowledge the validity of the quest for human happiness and all religions offer a map by which happiness can be pursued.

Jesus, the incarnate Son of God, is 'the true way' to happiness. In him the way to true happiness is most clearly and most fully revealed. We see this way to happiness in action in the life, Death, Resurrection and Ascension of Jesus, and continued in the daily lives of those who faithfully follow him. The Church, the sacrament of Christ in the world, proclaims and offers the fullest means to attain that happiness. For Catholics, the 'way of happiness', revealed by and in Jesus and shaped by Scripture and Tradition, is passed on by the teachings and life of the Church.

ADDITIONAL BACKGROUND READING
Catechism of the Catholic Church, nos. 26–43, 142–175, 356–379; *United States Catholic Catechism for Adults*, 1–9, 35–47, 67–68.

CHAPTER OUTCOMES
In all learning situations it is important to assess what the young people have learned and are striving to integrate into their lives. In each chapter of this text there are two overarching desired outcomes. They are: a) that the young people will come to a deeper understanding of the teaching of the Catholic Church and so be able to give an account of the Faith, and b) that they will choose to co-operate with the grace of the Holy Spirit and strive to grow in their own personal faith and in their relationship with God. The purpose of this text and the other texts of the *Credo* series is to help the young people to both grow in their understanding of the Faith and become articulate, faith-filled people, whose faith gives direction to their lives and influences how they live— the type of people they are and want to become. While it is reasonably easy to assess how well the young people remember and have understood the knowledge of the Faith (the information presented in a lesson), it is not quite so easy to assess their progress in terms of their faith formation. To facilitate the latter, we have incorporated the use of multiple strategies as identified by Bloom's taxonomy and its revision by Anderson and Krathwohl. We have also set out two sets of outcomes for each chapter: Learning Outcomes, which focus on the information presented in the chapter, and Faith-formation Outcomes, which focus on the opportunities provided for young people to integrate the knowledge of the faith of the Church into their lives—both of which help the young people to grow as people of faith.

All of the outcomes reflect the six tasks of catechesis as identified in the *General Directory for Catechesis* (1997) and the *National Directory of Catechesis* (2005). The tasks, which are integrated into all the texts in the *Credo* series, as stated in the National Directory, are:

- Promote knowledge of the Faith.
- Promote knowledge of the meaning of Liturgy and the Sacraments.
- Promote moral formation in Jesus Christ.
- Teach the Christian how to pray with Christ.
- Prepare the Christian to live in community and to participate actively in the life and mission of the Church.
- Promote a missionary spirit that prepares the faithful to be present as Christians within society.

CHAPTER OUTCOMES

Learning Outcomes
As a result of studying this chapter and exploring the issues raised, the young people should be able to:

- understand the difference between their wants, needs and desires;
- articulate their sense of themselves as searchers;
- understand that human beings are by nature searchers and seekers;
- understand that the human search for meaning is ultimately the search for God;
- recognize that the Book of Genesis is a faith account of Creation;
- explain how the Book of Genesis shows that human life is the high point of God's Creation;
- understand that human beings are created out of love and to love;
- recognize that man and woman are created equal in dignity;
- articulate how they recognize God's love in their lives;
- understand why there is restlessness at the heart of human existence;

- know the story of St. Augustine of Hippo, remember his statement 'Our hearts are restless until they rest in you' and explain its meaning.

Faith-formation Outcomes

As a result of studying this chapter and exploring the issues raised, the young people should also:

- recognize their own restlessness as part of what it means to be human;
- have a sense of God as Creator, and of human beings as the high point of God's Creation;
- value themselves as special in God's eyes;
- believe that they are loved by God;
- appreciate how their Catholic faith can help them in their search for true fulfillment;
- believe that their relationship with God will help them in their decisions about what is and is not important for them, now and in the future.

Teacher Reflection

As you prepare to begin this chapter, recognize that you too are a searcher. Take a moment to reflect on these quotations, relating them to your own search and your ministry as a theology teacher.

> The Meaning of Life. What is the meaning of human life, or, for that matter, of the life of any creature? To know an answer to this question means to be religious. You ask: Does it make any sense, then, to pose this question? I answer: The [person] who regards [their] own life and that of [their] fellow creatures as meaningless is not merely unhappy but hardly fit for life.
> — Albert Einstein

> The desire for God is written in the human heart because man is created by God and for God; and God never ceases to draw man to himself. Only in God will he find the truth and happiness he never stops searching for.
> — CCC, no. 27

> We plant the seeds that one day will grow.
> — Oscar Romero

> Human dignity rests above all on the fact that humanity is called to communion with God. This invitation to converse with God is addressed to men and women as soon as they are born. For if people exist it is because God has created them through love, and through love continues to keep them in existence. They cannot live fully in the truth unless they freely acknowledge that love and entrust themselves to their creator.
> — *Constitution on the Church in the Modern World* [*Gaudium et Spes*], no. 19

As you prepare to begin this chapter, become aware of:

- your own deepest desires;
- the fact the God is constantly reaching out to you.

Anticipate the seeds that you will sow as you prepare to work through this chapter with your students.

Notes and Guidelines for Student Activities

ATTEND AND REFLECT

Where do we find meaning in life?

Learning Outcomes
That the young people would:
- understand the difference between their wants, needs and desires;
- articulate their sense of themselves as searchers;
- understand that human beings are by nature searchers and seekers;
- understand that the human search for meaning is ultimately the search for God.

Faith-formation Outcome
That the young people would also:
- recognize their own restlessness as part of what it means to be human.

Overview
Chapter 1 begins by helping the young people to become more clearly aware of what it is that they are searching for. We move from there to help them acknowledge that, as human beings, unique among all the creatures created by God, they are by nature searchers. We encourage them to distinguish between their everyday wants and needs and their deepest desires. From here we lead them toward an awareness that at the center of humanity's searching is the desire for God, which is written on the human heart. (See CCC, nos. 27–30, 44–45, 1718.)

Supplementary Activities for 'Attend and Reflect'

Worksheet 1: 'Our Questions' *(page 25 of this resource)* encourages the young people to become aware of and name the kinds of questions that occupy their minds. It invites them to discuss these questions with their friends and to reflect together on their responses and on what this exercise teaches them about what is most important in their lives. Through this activity we encourage the young people to evaluate their priorities and to change them if necessary.

PROJECTS
Encourage the young people to choose *one* of the following projects. They will have an opportunity to discuss their findings at the end of the week.

Media Study
Working in groups, study a few popular TV or radio advertisements over the course of the week. Note the products being promoted and the reasons given for why people should buy them. Then work out the wants, needs or desires that are being targeted by the advertisements.

Or

Create an advertisement
Working in groups over the course of the week, create an advertisement for TV or radio directed at your own age-group. It could be for an event like a movie, a theatrical evening, a concert, a debate or lecture, a retreat or a social, or it could be for a Nativity set or other religious item. Discuss how you will depict or portray Christian motivation in the advertisement.

Or

Conduct a survey
Over the course of this week, carry out a survey among your family and friends to find out what they really desire in life. Be sure to ask your parents or guardians what they most desire for you in life; you may be surprised by the answers! Note the most popular answers that you get, but also try to distinguish the responses into wants, needs and desires. You might produce a bar chart to display the responses.

HEAR THE STORY

Human life is special

Learning Outcomes
That the young people would:
- recognize that the Book of Genesis is a faith account of Creation;
- be able to explain how the Book of Genesis shows that human life is the high point of God's Creation.

Faith-formation Outcomes
That the young people would also:
- have a sense of God as Creator, and of human beings as the high point of God's Creation;
- value themselves as special in God's eyes.

Overview
Section two, 'Hear the Story', introduces the young people to the first account of Creation in Genesis 1:1–2:4. We help them to begin to understand the Book of Genesis as a faith account of Creation rather than a scientific account. We introduce them to the fact that God saw all Creation and considered it good but that human beings are the high point of God's Creation. Created in the image of God, human beings alone have the capacity for self-reflection and to become aware of our own potential and of God's call to us to grow and develop into the best people we can be.

Supplementary Activity for 'Hear the Story'

Worksheet 2: 'Our Place in Creation' (*page 26 of this resource*) encourages the young people to read the first account of Creation in Genesis 1:1–2:4 and to reflect upon what it means to *live* in the image and likeness of God.

EMBRACE THE VISION

Human beings share in God's divine life

Learning Outcomes
That the young people would:
- understand that human beings are created out of love and to love;
- recognize that man and woman are created equal in dignity;
- articulate how they recognize God's love in their lives.

Faith-formation Outcome
That the young people would also:
- believe that they are loved by God.

Overview
Through reading and reflecting on the second account of Creation, we help the young people to understand that human beings are created out of love, that all human beings are created equal in dignity, and that the purpose of human life is love; love of God, of other people and of the created universe. We lead them to recognize signs of God's love in the people and the world around them. This section links back to the opening of the chapter and emphasizes that the universal human desire for God is satisfied by responding to God's love through reaching out to others in love.

Supplementary Activities for 'Embrace the Vision'

After studying the two Genesis accounts of Creation, the young people could be invited to read the story in **Worksheet 3: 'A Parable of Destruction'** (*page 29 of this resource*), which uses a similar framework to the Genesis accounts to describe the destruction of the earth. We give the young people the opportunity to imagine and write the ending for themselves. We then challenge them to decide if they want to be part of the destruction of the planet as described in this scenario.

Human beings are created out of love and are created to love. The need for self-actualization sometimes leads people to express that love for others in extraordinary ways.

Worksheet 4: 'Making a Difference' (*page 31 of this resource*) presents Blessed Mother Teresa of Calcutta and the Missionaries of Charity as an example of well-known people who have sought to 'give something back'. This worksheet invites the young people to 'imagine' how they might also 'make a difference' to the lives of others.

Worksheet 5: 'Nothing Really Worthwhile Comes Easily!' (*page 33 of this resource*) explores St. Basil the Great's commentary on Psalm 1:4, where he speaks of how, in part, he discovered for himself a key to finding the true meaning of life. We invite the young people to reflect first on what this man discovered and then to move on to think about their own search for meaning, and where God is part of that search. (See CCC, no. 45.)

Worksheet 6: 'Living in the Image of God' (*page 34 of this resource*) seeks to help the young people to deepen their awareness of themselves as being special in God's eyes. It also encourages their reflection on how they could actively become the 'image of God' in their own lives with others.

THINK IT THROUGH

How do we recognize our desire for God?

Learning Outcome
That the young people would:
- understand why there is restlessness at the heart of human existence.

Faith-formation Outcome
That the young people would also:
- appreciate how their Catholic faith can help them in their search for true fulfillment.

Overview
Section four, 'Think It Through', explores the fact that the desire for God is 'written on the human heart'. It emphasizes that human beings are created by God and for God, and that nothing other than God will fulfill our deepest longings and desires. We lead the young people to understand how their Catholic faith can help them to recognize God's love in their lives and enable them to respond to that love.

Supplementary Activity for 'Think It Through'

Worksheet 7: 'Fulfilling Our Deepest Longings' (*page 36 of this resource*) helps the young people to distinguish between their immediate wants and desires and those that are related to the deepest longings of the human heart which can only find fulfilment in God.

JUDGE AND ACT

Learning Outcome
That the young people would:
- know the story of St. Augustine of Hippo, remember his statement 'Our hearts are restless until they rest in you', and explain its meaning.

Faith-Formation Outcome
That the young people would also:
- believe that their relationship with God will help them in their decisions about what is and is not important for them, now and in the future.

Overview
In section five, 'Judge and Act', we introduce the young people to the story of St. Augustine, whose life journey finally led him to say, 'Our hearts are restless until they rest in you'. Through this section we seek to consolidate for the young people the reality of God's love in their lives and we encourage them to make specific decisions about how they can actively respond to that love. The meditation and Scripture reflection provided below seek to encourage that awareness.

Supplementary Activities for 'Judge and Act'

Discussion of Project
The following are suggestions for discussing the findings of the projects listed on page 20 of this resource.

If you conducted a study of TV or radio advertisements, discuss whether there was anything reflecting Christian values in any of the ads that you examined.

Or

If you created your own advertisement, talk about what you learned from the experience and what difficulties, if any, you encountered.

Or

If you conducted a survey of family and friends, did some of the responses surprise you? If so, explain why. What were the similarities and differences between your own desires and those of your family and friends?

Worksheet 8: 'Wisdom from St. Augustine' (*page 37 of this resource*) provides some well-known words of wisdom from the saint. We invite the young people to reflect on these and then relate their wisdom to their own lives.

Words of Wisdom Collection
Encourage the young people to create a personal collection of words of wisdom that inspire them. They could begin the collection with their favorite quotations from St. Augustine. Alternatively, they could share their ideas and create a class collection of inspirational quotations, which they could add to throughout the year.

Note: *The Prayer Reflections can always be adapted to suit the circumstances of the class or the preferences of the teacher.*

Directives for the Prayer Reflection at the end of the chapter
Encourage the young people to form a circle. Place a lighted candle in the center (if local fire regulations permit). (If you are using a lighted candle, you might open the Reflection with the words: 'A lighted candle is a symbol of the Risen Jesus.')

The prayer 'Conflicting Desires' should be read slowly and thoughtfully. You might allow the young people to read a line in turn, with a lengthy pause between the lines for silent reflection.

The group might like to add sentences, phrases or words to connect with their own ideas and thoughts.

Additional Prayer Suggestions

Guided Meditation: 'Allowing God to fulfill our longing'
(*See 'Student Activity Tool Kit', pages 274–6 of this resource, for further helpful suggestions in relation to conducting guided meditations.*)

First, recall with the young people that the prayer of meditation 'is above all a quest. The mind seeks to understand the why and how of the Christian life, in order to adhere and respond to what the Lord is asking' (CCC, no. 2705). Then read the following story aloud:

Once upon a time a beggar, really a holy dervish, came to the king with his begging bowl in hand, asking not just for alms, but whether the king was great enough to fill his bowl. The king laughed and said, 'Of course!' He summoned a servant and instructed him to fill the beggar's bowl with coins. He could be generous when he was in the mood and he intended to show this beggar what a great and wealthy king he was. The servant obeyed and filled the bowl with coins, more and more and more; hundreds, thousands—and still the bowl was nowhere near filled. The king became distressed, looking at the mouth of the bowl that was never full. He knew that if he kept trying, he'd end up poor himself: already he was feeling poor, helpless and foolish, caught out.

He looked at the beggar with searching eyes. 'Who are you? And what kind of bowl do you carry? You are making a beggar out of me. It is swallowing everything I own.'

The beggar looked back at the king and spoke: 'My bowl will never be filled, no matter how much you put in it, for my bowl is the want that is found in the heart of human beings.'

Now invite the young people to relax and close their eyes. . . . Invite them to become aware of Christ's presence with them. . . . (*Pause for a few moments.*)

Then, ask them to imagine a 'bowl-shaped space' deep inside them, in which resides all their questions, longings and desires. . . . Ask them to invite Christ to enter that space so that their desires are met with his presence. . . . Allow the young people to rest for a while in the awareness of Christ's presence deep within them.

Then, invite the young people to enter into a conversation with Christ, sharing their desire to come to know him more deeply, to grow in their love for him, and live as his disciple and friend.

Finally, invite them to open their eyes and to situate themselves once again in the room with their friends, knowing that Christ's presence will always remain deep inside them as he promised.

Teacher Tip: You could also use the above story to involve the young people in further reflection on the human search for meaning.

Scripture Reflection

(*See instructions for the use of doodling in prayer in the 'Student Activity Tool Kit', page 274 of this resource.*)

Use the following Psalm verse to engage the young people in prayer:

As a deer longs for flowing streams, so my soul longs for you, O God.

PSALM 42:1

You could introduce this prayer with the following or similar words:

> Lord, we thank you for creating us in your image and likeness. We know you are with us today as we gather to pray. We think of the words of the psalmist. . . .

CHAPTER 1 | WORKSHEET 1

NAME:

Our Questions

Any search begins with a question; for example: How do I get there? Why am I going there? Should I be taking a different course? Is there something better out there for me?

What kind of questions do you ask about your life? What questions do you think are linked to your search for the meaning of your life?

Read the list of questions below. When do you ask these questions: rarely, sometimes, all the time, or never? Quietly reflect on these questions and write your responses in your journal.

1. Why do people expect so much from me?
2. Will I go to college straight after school or will I take a year out?
3. If there was one thing I could change with my life, what would it be?
4. Why are the youngest in a family always spoiled, or so it seems?
5. Why can't I have more freedom at home?
6. Why are there so many rules in school?
7. Can I trust my friends to keep a secret?
8. Do my friends accept me for who I really am?
9. When I look in the mirror, am I happy with what I see?
10. Why do good people suffer?
11. What evidence is there that there really is a God?
12. What happens after we die?
13. Are there really such things as ghosts?
14. Will I ever get married?
15. How many children would I like when I get married?
16. Will I ever take drugs?
17. Am I in this place and this time for a purpose?
18. Do people like me?
19. Will my parents insure me on the insurance policy for their car?
20. Should I give some of my money to charity or volunteer to do charity work?
21. Why is there so much evil in the world?
22. Is there a meaning to coincidences or are they just … coincidences?
23. What would make me really happy?
24. What would I do if I won the lottery?

Now consider for yourself:

1. How many of the questions you often ask are concerned with yourself? With others? With God?
2. How many of the questions you seldom ask are concerned with yourself? With others? With God?
3. What do you think this exercise tells you about what is of most importance in your life?
4. What does it suggest in relation to how you might try to change?

With your friends, analyze and reflect upon what you have learned from this exercise.

CHAPTER 1 | WORKSHEET 2

NAME:

Our Place in Creation

Using the Book of Genesis, chapter 1: 1–31, complete the missing parts of the Creation story.

Day	God's work of Creation
1	God created light. God named the light 'day' and the darkness 'night'.
2	_____
3	_____
4	_____
5	_____
6	_____
7	God rested, looked at everything and saw that it was all very good.

How does the writer of the first account of Creation teach that the human person is the high point of God's Creation?

_____
_____
_____
_____
_____

Give examples of how you live in the image and likeness of God:

At home

_____
_____
_____

At school

_____
_____
_____

In your neighborhood

_____
_____
_____

Now write about something new and different you could do that would show the world that you are created in the image of God.

_____

_____

_____

_____

_____

_____

_____

_____

_____

_____

_____

_____

_____

_____

_____

_____

_____

_____

_____

CHAPTER 1 | WORKSHEET 3

NAME:

A Parable of Destruction

We live in a time when there is a keen awareness of 'pending ecological disaster', which is a consequence of individual and societal abuse of God's gift of creation. Read the following parable and then continue writing it, telling what happens both on the SECOND DAY before the end and on the LAST DAY.

And the smog and radioactive material fell on the seas and the dry land and contaminated every herb yielding seed and every fruit tree yielding fruit. And Man said, 'It is not very good, but we cannot put the clock back.' This was the FIFTH DAY before the end.

And by his work, Man created great deserts and changed climatic conditions so that winds swept dust off the earth skyward to mingle with the smog, which blotted out the sun by day and the moon by night, so that night and day became the same. And Man saw the work of his hands and said, 'Our conquest of Nature is almost complete.' And this was the FOURTH DAY before the end.

The THIRD DAY before the end, Man said, 'Let us dump our industrial effluents, raw sewage and garbage into the streams and waterways and seas.' And it was so. The waters upon the earth became foul so that all life in the waters died.

CHAPTER 1 | WORKSHEET 3 (CONTD.)

The SECOND DAY before the end

_____

_____

_____

_____

_____

_____

_____

_____

On the LAST DAY

_____

_____

_____

_____

_____

_____

_____

_____

REFLECT AND DISCUSS
- What is the difference between the attitudes of human beings as described in this account and the attitude of God as described in the accounts of Creation in Genesis?
- To what extent do you think the scenario described here reflects what is actually happening in our world?
- In your own life, how could you decide not to be part of the scenario described in this story?

NAME:

Making a Difference

Mother Teresa of Calcutta's vision of humanity and her dedicated service to the poorest of the poor inspired people to help others rise to the potential that God had given them. Blessed Mother Teresa, through the ministry of the Missionaries of Charity, continues to make a difference to the lives of countless people.

Mother Teresa and the Missionaries of Charity have something in common with you—like you they were created in the image of God, with many gifts and talents. They too spent many hours in classrooms, often daydreaming and wondering about their future. On the outside they looked just like any other young people, but on the inside a seed was being planted.

REFLECT AND SHARE

Join up with a partner to think of examples of people who are truly living the Gospel in the world today, whom you feel are 'making a difference'. These can be people you know or people you have heard about, from any walk of life. For example, you might mention a person in your parish or school or neighborhood who volunteers with a local agency that is serving people in need, or you might identify a person from the world of sport or entertainment who champions the rights and dignity of all people, or a politician who uses their position to influence the public debate on issues such as the right to life, and so on. Discuss briefly how each of these people 'make a difference' to the world in which we live.

WHAT 'DIFFERENCE' WILL *YOU* MAKE?

As you look around the classroom, see if you can make a list of each student's unique talent or gift or 'special' personality trait.

Then consider your list and think about the signs it holds of things that might come forth in the future of each of your classmates. For example: Is anyone particularly interested in music, or art, or sport, or writing? Is there anyone who is particularly kind and inclined to come to the aid of others? Anyone who gets concerned or angry about the plight of people who are suffering from poverty, neglect and so on—at home or in the world's poorer countries? Perhaps there are people in your group who are already making a real difference?

CHAPTER 1 | WORKSHEET 4 (CONTD.)

TALK IT OVER
Now rejoin your partner and discuss the following questions:

- Do you believe that you have a responsibility to give something back; for example, to your parents? To your Church? To society? To God?
- Do you have a sense that there is more to life than that which you see in the advertisements on TV? What could that 'more' be?
- How do you think all this is connected with the fact that you have been created in the image and likeness of God?

CLASS DISCUSSION
- Share your observations and insights in a class discussion on how each one of us can 'make a difference'.

CHAPTER 1 | WORKSHEET 5

NAME:

Nothing Really Worthwhile Comes Easily!

The following is from St. Basil the Great's commentary on Psalm 1:4. He speaks of how, in part, he discovered for himself a key to finding the true meaning of life.

Life's Journey

Life is called a 'way' because everything that has been created is on the way to its end.

When people are on a sea voyage, they can sleep while they are being transported without any effort of their own to their port of call. The ship brings them closer to their goal without their even knowing it. So we can be transported nearer to the end of life without our noticing it, as time flows by unceasingly. Time passes as you sleep. While you are awake time passes although you may not notice.

All of us have a race to run toward our appointed end. So we are all on our way.

This is how you should think of the 'way'.... The 'way' does not belong to you nor is the present under your control. But as each step succeeds step, enjoy each moment as it comes and then continue on your way.

TALK IT OVER
- What does St. Basil say is the key to life?
- Which lines suggest that St. Basil discovered for himself that the search for meaning is the search for God; that the answer is God?

WHAT ABOUT YOU PERSONALLY?
- Where does God fit in to your personal search? How might your desire for God and your confidence in his love guide your choices?
- Some people believe that chance events or coincidences in life are not chance at all, but really examples of Divine Providence, God's special caring love for each of us. Is there any reason for thinking the same about your own personal journey?

CHAPTER 1 | WORKSHEET 6

NAME:

Living in the Image of God

Imagine that the following advertisement appears in your local newspaper. Your friends tell you that you have all the qualifications and attributes necessary to get the job. You realize that it is God who has placed the advertisement.

Position Vacant

Energetic, enthusiastic young person to be the image of God in the world today. The successful applicant will be unique, capable of showing unconditional love to others and interested in finding new ways to use their gifts and talents for the benefit of others.

CHAPTER 1 | WORKSHEET 6 (CONTD.)

Now write out your application, showing how you meet the specified requirements and how you would go about fulfilling the task required.

_____

_____

_____

_____

_____

_____

_____

_____

_____

_____

_____

_____

_____

_____

_____

_____

_____

_____

_____

_____

_____

CHAPTER 1 | WORKSHEET 7

NAME:

Fulfilling Our Deepest Longings

List all your desires and longings that immediately come to mind.

_____

_____

_____

_____

_____

_____

Now list your deepest desires and longings, which only God can fulfill. These may include some of the things you have already listed above.

_____

_____

_____

_____

_____

_____

JOURNAL EXERCISE
Write a short reflection asking God to show you how you can find fulfillment of your deepest desires and longings.

CHAPTER 1 | WORKSHEET 8

NAME:

Wisdom from St. Augustine

REFLECTIVE ACTIVITY
Reflect on the following words of wisdom from St. Augustine:

Our hearts are restless until they rest in you.

God loves each of us, as if there was only one of us.

Faith is to believe what we do not see, and the reward of this faith is to see what we believe.

Find out how much God has given you and from it take what you need; the remainder is needed by others.

I have read in Cicero and Plato sayings that are wise and very beautiful; but I have never read in any of them: 'Come to me all ye that labor and are heavy burdened.'

Work with a partner or small group and choose *one* of these quotations from St. Augustine. Then reflect quietly for a few moments on what the quotation you chose means to you.

Discuss the following questions with your partner or group:

- What does this quotation tell you about St. Augustine's belief in God and how he related to God?
- How could believing the message and wisdom of this quotation make a difference to your life?

Review of Chapter 1

I. **Complete the statements.** Fill in the blanks so that each statement correctly states the faith of the Catholic Church.

1. The desire for _____ is inherent in human nature; it is written on the _____ of every person.
2. The Creation account in the Book of Genesis is not a _____ account of creation but a statement of _____ about the origins of the world.
3. In the first account of Creation God reveals to us that he has given human beings _____ over creation. This means that we are to be good _____ of all of creation.
4. Human life is an expression and image of _____ life.
5. Faith is both a _____ from God and a _____ act by which the believer gives adherence to God and freely assents to the whole truth that God has _____.

II. **Write a paragraph.** Explain whether you agree or disagree with the statement 'Human beings are the high point of God's creation'.

_____
_____
_____
_____
_____
_____
_____

III. Name key truths about human beings that are revealed in the second account of Creation. Choose one of those truths and describe its importance for daily living.

_____

_____

_____

_____

_____

_____

_____

IV. How would you respond? A friend says to you, 'I think it is just stupid to wait for heaven to be really happy.'

_____

_____

_____

_____

_____

_____

_____

CHAPTER 1 | CHAPTER REVIEW (CONTD.)

V. Make a 'disciple decision'.

1. What is the most important wisdom for life that you discovered in this chapter?

_____

_____

_____

_____

_____

_____

_____

_____

_____

2. Name several ways you can put that wisdom into practice. Choose one of the ways you identify and describe how you will make that wisdom part of your life right now.

_____

_____

_____

_____

_____

_____

_____

_____

_____

_____

_____

_____

CHAPTER 2

God Reaches Out to Us in Many Ways

INTRODUCTION

In chapter 1 we introduced the young people to the concept of the human search for meaning. At the heart of that search is the search for God and the longing deep within the human heart that cannot be satisfied except in God. Now in chapter 2 we examine the question of belief in God. The chapter is developed under five major headings:

- **ATTEND AND REFLECT**: Is it reasonable to believe in God?
- **HEAR THE STORY**: The heavens proclaim the glory of God
- **EMBRACE THE VISION**: We can begin to know God through human reasoning
- **THINK IT THROUGH**: Consider other arguments for God's existence
- **JUDGE AND ACT** (Activities and exercises that encourage the young people to integrate what they have learned in the chapter into their daily lives)

Theological Background for the Teacher

THE QUESTION OF GOD'S EXISTENCE

We begin chapter 2 by examining the question of belief. Is it possible to believe in a reality (someone or something) that is not material? Do we need scientific proof that something or someone exists before we can believe in it? Whether or not we can ever prove God's existence in a manner that is acceptable to science is open to debate; but even if we could, what purpose would it serve? And exactly what would it prove? Rather, 'the existence of God is not a problem to be solved, but a mystery to be lived' (Gabriel Marcel, 1889–1973).

PATHWAYS TO GOD

We seek to help the young people to come to know God more deeply and to develop their relationship with him, who has made himself known to us as a God of love, present to each one of us more intimately than even those with whom we have our closest relationships. In this and the following chapters we try to encourage the young people to respond to God's presence in their lives.

We introduce the young people to the three paths by which people can come to know God: creation, the human person and Divine Revelation. The *Catechism of the Catholic Church* states:

> Created in God's image and called to know and love him, the person who seeks God discovers certain ways of coming to know him. . . . These 'ways' of approaching God from creation have a twofold point of departure: the physical world and the human person.
>
> – CCC, no. 31

> By natural reason man can come to know God with certainty, on the basis of his works. But there is another order of knowledge, which man cannot possibly arrive at by his own powers: the order of divine Revelation. Through an utterly free decision, God has revealed himself and given himself to man. This he does by revealing the mystery, his plan of loving goodness, formed from all eternity in Christ, for the benefit of all men. God has fully revealed this plan by sending his beloved Son, our Lord Jesus Christ, and the Holy Spirit.
>
> – CCC, no. 50

We explore how we can come to know God in the beauty and grandeur of the created world, as well as through human reasoning.

Throughout their history, human beings have understood the beauty and grandeur of the universe, the order and purpose of all created things, from inanimate objects to human beings, as pointing toward the existence of a Creator who is wise and good. Everything has a beginning and an end. This points to an eternal Creator who has neither beginning nor end. Some students may raise a question about atheists. For the Church's response to atheism, see CCC, nos. 2123–2126, 2128, 2140.

Human beings, with all their potential for good, their thrust toward freedom and their longing for fulfillment and happiness, are in themselves signs of the immortality of the human soul. The restlessness of human beings and their constant search for 'more' point toward their origins in God, who alone can fulfill their deepest desires and yearnings.

> The world, and man, attest that they contain within themselves neither their first principle nor their final end, but rather that they participate in Being itself, which alone is without origin or end. Thus, in different ways, man can come to know that there is a reality which is the first cause and final end of all things, a reality 'that everyone calls God'.
> – CCC, no. 34, with quotation from St. Thomas Aquinas

In our discussion of this topic we introduce the young people to the five proofs of St. Thomas Aquinas and to the arguments of philosophers and thinkers who point to the very existence of evil, and human repugnance to evil, and the desire and effort to resolve it as itself pointing to the existence of God.

ADDITIONAL BACKGROUND READING
Catechism of the Catholic Church, nos. 31–43, 153–159, 302–314; *United States Catholic Catechism for Adults,* 1–9, 56–57.

CHAPTER OUTCOMES

See general note on page 18 of this resource.

Learning Outcomes
As a result of studying this chapter and exploring the issues raised, the young people should be able to:

- explain what it means to say that a person has 'faith';
- articulate why they believe in God and how their belief affects their lives;
- recognize images of God from the world of nature that are presented in the Old Testament;
- express in words and images their own images for God;
- know the story of St. Thomas Aquinas and explain his five proofs for the existence of God;
- understand the argument that the goodness of human beings reveals something of the goodness of God;
- understand the argument that we can recognize God in the depth of things;
- understand the concept of transcendence.

Faith-formation Outcomes
As a result of studying this chapter and exploring the issues raised, the young people should also:

- have reaffirmed their belief in God and his existence;
- be open to seeing the power and wonder of God in the created universe;
- through the use of their own intellect and reason, develop a deeper confidence in their belief in the existence of God;
- recognize the goodness they see in the lives of human beings as pointers toward the goodness of God;
- have an increased awareness of the presence of God in their own lives and of how they can respond to that presence.

Teacher Reflection

The Presence of God
I see his blood upon the rose,
And in the stars the glory of his eyes;
His body gleams amid eternal snows,
His tears fall from the skies.
I see his face in every flower;
The thunder and the singing of the birds
Are but his voice; and, carven by his power,
Rocks are his written words.

All pathways by his feet are worn;
His strong heart stirs the ever-beating sea;
His crown of thorns is twined with every thorn;
His Cross is every tree.

Notes and Guidelines for Student Activities

Note: In preparation for the Prayer Reflection at the end of the chapter you might encourage the young people to bring into the class some objects from the world of nature: stones, twigs, sand, seashells, leaves and so on.

ATTEND AND REFLECT

Is it reasonable to believe in God?

Learning Outcomes
That the young people would:
- explain what it means to say that a person has 'faith';
- articulate why they believe in God and how their belief affects their lives.

Faith-formation Outcome
That the young people would also:
- have reaffirmed their belief in God and his existence.

Overview
Chapter 2 beings by exploring the nature of faith, leading on to a discussion of what it means to have faith in God.

Supplementary Activity for 'Attend and Reflect'

Vox Pop
You might invite the young people to conduct a vox pop that asks the question: 'Do you believe in God? Why?/Why not?'

(See 'Student Activity Tool Kit', page 273 of this resource, for instructions on conducting vox pops.)

HEAR THE STORY

The heavens proclaim the glory of God

Learning Outcomes
That the young people would:
- recognize images of God from the world of nature that are presented in the Old Testament;
- express in words and images their own images for God.

Faith-formation Outcome
That the young people would also:
- be open to seeing the power and wonder of God in the created universe.

Overview
Section two, 'Hear the Story', focuses on the Revelation of God in the natural world. It explores particularly how the Old Testament authors used many elements of the natural world to describe some of the attributes of God.

Supplementary Activities for 'Hear the Story'

Having explored the various ways in which we can come to know and experience the presence of God in the world, it is important that the young people go a step further and actually come to know and experience more deeply for themselves God's presence in their lives. Sometimes we may not recognize that God is present in our experiences. The exercises in **Worksheet 1: 'God in Our World'** (*page 48 of this resource*) seek to enhance the students' awareness of God's presence in everyday life as well as in people's creativity.

The diary exercise in **Worksheet 2: 'A View from Apollo 8'** (*page 49 of this resource*) provides the young people with an opportunity to deepen further their awareness of the beauty of the earth. The deeper this awareness is, the more likely they will be to regard the earth with the awe that it deserves. This in turn will lead them to see more clearly God's presence in creation.

Teacher Tip: Students could use the Internet to search NASA for images of Earth from space or look at footage of the first moon-landing in 1969. They could also look at some of the photographs that Frank Borman took during his voyage in the *Apollo 8* spacecraft in 1968.

Worksheet 3: 'Images of God in the Bible' (*page 51 of this resource*) invites the young people to look carefully at some of the biblical references quoted in chapter 2 in order to identify images of God in the Bible.

Group Project
Invite the young people to make a collection of photographs and pictures that illustrate the wonders of creation. They could present the images as a poster collage or PowerPoint display and write a commentary to explain their meaning.

EMBRACE THE VISION

We can begin to know God through human reasoning

Learning Outcome
That the young people would:
- know the story of St. Thomas Aquinas and explain his five proofs for the existence of God.

Faith-formation Outcome
That the young people would also:
- through the use of their own intellect and reason, develop a deeper confidence in their belief in the existence of God.

Overview
Section three, 'Embrace the Vision', tells the story of St. Thomas Aquinas and explores his argument that through our human power of reasoning we can come to know of the existence of God.

Supplementary Activities for 'Embrace the Vision'

The exercise in **Worksheet 4: 'St. Thomas Aquinas'** (*page 53 of this resource*) provides the young people with an opportunity to revise what they have learned about Aquinas and his five proofs for the existence of God.

Worksheet 5: 'St. Thomas Aquinas in the Spotlight' (*page 55 of this resource*) provides role-cards to be photocopied and cut out for use in an 'In the Spotlight' activity. (*See the general instructions for 'In the Spotlight' activities in the 'Student Activity Tool Kit', page 273 of this resource.*)

Divide the class into five groups. Select five volunteers to play the role of Thomas Aquinas.
　Assign one 'Thomas' to each group and one of Thomas' arguments for the existence of God to each volunteer, who will argue his proofs before that group.
　Invite discussion and then, as time permits, have the volunteers playing the role of St. Thomas move from group to group.
　At the end of the activity, facilitate some further class discussion with questions such as:

- What argument do you find most convincing? Why?
- Could you think of other reasons or evidence to convince someone about the existence of God?

THINK IT THROUGH

Consider other arguments for God's existence

Learning Outcomes
That the young people would:
- understand the argument that the goodness of human beings reveals something of the goodness of God;
- understand the argument that we can recognize God in the depth of things;
- understand the concept of transcendence.

Faith-formation Outcome
That the young people would also:
- recognize the goodness they see in the lives of human beings as pointers toward the goodness of God.

Overview
In section four, 'Think It Through', the young people explore how we can come to meet God in the depth of created things, especially in human beings. In the gentleness of a parent's touch, in the generosity of a neighbor's helping hand, in the smile on a baby's face, we can see the presence of God.

Supplementary Activities for 'Think It Through'

The story in **Worksheet 6: 'Meeting God'** (*page 56 of this resource*) explores the presence of God in human beings.

Worksheet 7: 'The Human Response to Evil' (*page 57 of this resource*) invites the young people to consider their personal response to right and wrong, leading to an awareness of the human response to evil.

JUDGE AND ACT

Faith-formation Outcome
That the young people would:
- have an increased awareness of the presence of God in their own lives and of how they can respond to that presence.

Overview
In section five, 'Judge and Act', we introduce the young people to Katharine Drexel as an example of someone who paid attention to what God was saying to her in the ordinary events of her life. We encourage the young people to reflect on what God is saying to them now in their lives.

Supplementary Activities for 'Judge and Act'

Note: You might choose to read the story in Worksheet 8 as an alternative or in addition to that of St. Katharine Drexel (*page 37 of students' text*), especially if you wish to offer your students material reflecting the African-American/Black cultural family within the Church in the United States.

Worksheet 8: 'Divine Presence in Aztec Culture and Tradition' (*page 59 of this resource*) explains the concept of *flor y canto* (flower and song) and uses the account of Our Lady's apparition to St. Juan Diego, a Nahuatl (Aztec) Indian convert to Christianity, to illustrate how the Nahuatl people experience God's presence in their daily lives.

Directives for the Prayer Reflection at the end of the chapter
Begin the Reflection by encouraging the young people to form a circle around the items they have gathered. They should spend some time in silence looking at these items so as to feel a sense of wonder at the great things that God has created.

Then, those young people who would like to, might tell the others in the group what it is that most reminds them of God, for example:

'When I see a beautiful flower, it reminds me of the wonderful work of creation and the amazing beauty of God the Creator.'

'When I see a parent taking care of their infant, it reminds me of the unconditional love God has for all humanity.'

For the reading of Psalm 8, you might choose to allow the young people to read it, line by line, going around the circle in turn. If they wish, they could add in their own phrases or words to reflect their personal response to the sentiments being expressed.

Additional Prayer Suggestion

Scripture Reflection
(*See instructions for the use of doodling in prayer in the 'Student Activity Tool Kit', page 274 of this resource.*)
Use the following Psalm verse to engage the young people in prayer:

> **The LORD is my shepherd, I shall not want.**
>
> **PSALM 23:1**

You could introduce today's prayer with these or similar words: 'God our Creator, we know that you are always with us. We thank you for your constant, caring presence.'

After the young people have heard the prayer a number of times, and before they begin to doodle, ask them to imagine God caring for each one of them individually as a shepherd cares for his sheep.

CHAPTER 2 | WORKSHEET 1

NAME:

God in Our World

Choose **one** of the following activities.

1. Look through various newspapers and magazines for pictures or photographs or images that give you a sense of God present in our world. Then choose one of these and, on the lines below, explain your choice in a few sentences and say how it links with your experience of God present in your own life.

Or

2. Choose something that a poet or author or musician has produced which you think communicates a sense of God. Explain your choice.

_____

_____

_____

_____

_____

_____

_____

_____

_____

_____

CHAPTER 2 | WORKSHEET 2

NAME:

A View from Apollo 8

Imagine you were one of the three astronauts on board *Apollo 8* on Christmas Eve 1968. Complete your diary entry for that day, describing what happened and how you feel about it.

December 24, 1968

CHAPTER 2 | WORKSHEET 2 (CONTD.)

CHAPTER 2 | WORKSHEET 3

NAME:

Images of God in the Bible

With a partner, find these texts in chapter 2 and answer:
1. What does this text say about God?
2. Identify the image or images that most appeal to you and say why.

Romans 1:20
1.
2.

Psalm 23:1–3
1.
2.

Psalm 19:1–4
1.
2.

Psalm 18:2
1.
2.

Psalm 29:7–8
1.
2.

Deuteronomy 32:11
1.
2.

Give examples of other images of God from the Bible and explain what they say about God.

NAME:

St. Thomas Aquinas

Using the information provided in section three of this chapter, 'Embrace The Vision', complete the following fact-file on St. Thomas Aquinas and explain in your own words his five proofs for the existence of God.

Name	**Thomas Aquinas**
Year of birth:	
Place of birth:	
Religious order to which he belonged:	
His great text:	

Explanation of the Five Proofs

1. The existence of a 'Prime Mover'

_____
_____
_____

2. The existence of an 'Uncreated Creator'

_____
_____
_____

3. The existence of a 'Necessary Being'

_____
_____
_____

4. The existence of a 'Perfect Standard'

_____
_____
_____

5. The existence of an 'Intelligent Designer

_____
_____
_____

NAME:

St. Thomas Aquinas 'In the Spotlight'

Photocopy and cut out these role-cards for an 'In the Spotlight' class discussion on the existence of God.

ST. THOMAS AQUINAS

Your name is **St. Thomas Aquinas**. You were born in Italy in 1225 into a very wealthy family. As a teenager you were a bit of a rebel. You decided to join the newly founded Dominican order even though your family objected strongly, going so far as to imprison you in the family castle for more than a year. But you were determined and once you got your freedom you began studying Christian theology. In your biggest work, the *Summa Theologica*, you use human reasoning to explore the truths of the Bible. You believe that it is possible to provide rational arguments for God's existence. You are convinced that, without God, there can be no universe because to take away the cause is to take away the effect. You argue 'five proofs' for the existence of God. You believe they give sound and compelling reasons for God's existence.

ST. THOMAS AQUINAS' FIVE PROOFS FOR THE EXISTENCE OF GOD:

1. The existence of a **prime mover**—nothing can move itself; there must be a first mover. The first mover is called God.
2. Cause of existence—things that exist are created by other things; nothing can create itself. There must be, at the beginning, an **uncreated creator**, called God. God is the first cause of everything that is.
3. The existence of a **necessary Being**, which causes the existence of others. This necessary Being is called God.
4. Degrees of perfection—for any given quality (for example, beauty, goodness) there must be a **perfect standard** by which all such qualities are measured. This perfect standard is called God.
5. Intelligent design—we can see that the universe works and is ordered, thus we can conclude that it was designed by an **intelligent designer**. We call this intelligent designer God.

CHAPTER 2 | WORKSHEET 6

NAME:

Meeting God

Read the following story and then reflect on the questions below.

There once was a little boy who wanted to meet God. He knew it was a long trip to where God lived, so he packed his suitcase with Twinkies and a six-pack of root beer and he started his journey.

When he had gone about three blocks, he met an elderly woman. She was sitting in the park just staring at some pigeons. The boy sat down next to her and opened his suitcase. He was about to take a drink from his root beer when he noticed that the elderly lady looked hungry, so he offered her a Twinkie. She gratefully accepted it and smiled at him. Her smile was so pretty that the boy wanted to see it again, so he offered her a root beer. Once again she smiled at him. The boy was delighted! They sat there all afternoon eating and smiling, but they never said a word.

As it grew dark, the boy realized how tired he was and he got up to leave, but before he had gone more than a few steps, he turned around, ran back to the woman and gave her a hug. She gave him her biggest smile ever. When the boy opened the door to his own house a short time later, his mother was surprised by the look of joy on his face. She asked him, 'What did you do today that made you so happy?' He replied, 'I had lunch with God.' But before his mother could respond, he added, 'You know what? She's got the most beautiful smile I've ever seen!'

Meanwhile, the elderly woman, also radiant with joy, returned to her home. Her son was stunned by the look of peace on her face and he asked, 'Mother, what did you do today that made you so happy?' She replied, 'I ate Twinkies in the park with God.' But before her son responded, she added, 'You know, he's much younger than I expected.'

TALK IT OVER
- What do you think it was about the elderly woman that led the little boy to see God in her?
- What do you think it was about the little boy that led the woman to see God in him?

WHAT ABOUT YOU PERSONALLY?
- When and where do you search for God?
- How would you go about searching for God now?
- Did you ever believe that you had found God? Explain.

NAME:

The Human Response to Evil

In the boxes provided, make two separate lists: one of things that you believe most human beings would recognize as morally wrong; the other of things that most human beings would recognize as morally right.

Morally Wrong

Morally Right

Write your thoughts on the view of philosophers that humans have an in-built and God-given sense of right and wrong.

_____
_____
_____
_____
_____
_____
_____
_____

CHAPTER 2 | WORKSHEET 7 (CONTD.)

Theologians, philosophers, spiritual masters, poets—people of every place and time—speak to the reality of experiencing the presence of God in other people. Choose an example of a time when you recognized God's presence acting through someone you know. Write about this below. Alternatively, draw or paste in a picture to illustrate this and write a few sentences explaining your thoughts.

Divine Presence in Aztec Culture and Tradition

God manifests himself to us in many ways. One way to recognize the divine presence in our daily experience is through the contemplation of Creation, seeing the imprint of God in all its beauty (check out Romans 1:19–20). This is well illustrated by a powerful story from our Catholic tradition that recounts the apparition of Our Lady of Guadalupe in 1531 to Juan Diego, a Nahuatl (Aztec) Indian who had recently embraced Christianity.

During Juan Diego's time, the Nahuatl worldview rested on the conviction that many signs of nature were like divine speech. For the Nahuatl, human words are insufficient to express the greatness of the divine presence in our midst. Thus, we must be attentive to signs in nature that capture God's presence better than our best and most learned conversations. This is what the Aztecs call *flor y canto* (flower and song). For them, flower and song constitute the grammar that describes the harmony in nature; *flor y canto* make possible a deep communication between God and humanity.

In Juan Diego's world, the singing of birds pointed to the special presence of the divine; for the Nahuatl, birdsong indicated that something unique was about to happen. The beauty of flowers also reminded them of the divine presence. The presence of flower and song at the same time was a sign of divine truth and divine presence. And this is exactly what happened in the story of the encounter of Juan Diego with Our Lady of Guadalupe on a little hill at Tepeyac, outside of Mexico City.

One morning in December 1531, when dawn was about to break, the birds began to sing and a woman appeared to Juan Diego. She identified herself as 'Mary, the Mother of the true God . . . who is present in all places'. She explained that she wanted people to know God's great compassion and care for them, especially for the poor and downtrodden. Some days later, an image of Mary, as Juan Diego saw her, appeared on the front of his cloak; we know this image today as Our Lady of Guadalupe. The original is on display in the Basilica of Our Lady of Guadalupe in Mexico City.

Juan Diego's experience of Mary brought hope to a conquered people, gave voice to the poor, and reminded people that God is ever present in our lives. To confirm that what was happening was a true sign from God, Our Lady of Guadalupe instructed Juan Diego to go to the top of the hill, where he found beautiful flowers at a time of year when it would have been impossible for them to grow. The experience marked the beginning of a new hope sealed with *flor y canto*. God had spoken through Creation in the language of the Nahuatl, assuring them of his love for all and especially for the poor and downtrodden.

TALK IT OVER

Think for a few moments about the way the Nahuatl perceived God's presence in nature.

- Talk about the aspects of Creation that cause you to turn your mind and heart toward God and that reveal God's presence to you.

Review of Chapter 2

I. True or false. Mark the true statements 'T' and the false statements 'F'. Cross out the words that make the false statements false. Write the words that make the false statements true under each false statement.

_____ 1. The story of God is written in the natural world.

_____ 2. God is really present in our lives and in the world.

_____ 3. Our human mind can never comprehend God on its own.

_____ 4. The *Catechism* presents two paths though which every person can come to know God. These are creation and the human person.

_____ 5. St. Thomas Aquinas gave us proofs that use reason alone to prove that God exists.

_____ 6. Some philosophers say we can prove the existence of God from the fact that most human beings recognize a moral law.

_____ 7. Atheists cannot decide whether or not God exists.

_____ 8. Agnostics deny the existence of God.

_____ 9. Faith in God is reasonable.

_____ 10. 'Uncreated creator' refers to the idea that God is the absolute other.

CHAPTER 2 | CHAPTER REVIEW (CONTD.)

II. Name St. Thomas Aquinas' proofs for the existence of God. Choose and briefly explain one of Aquinas' proofs.

_____

_____

_____

_____

_____

_____

III. Explain the teaching of the Church. Write a brief paragraph on 1 or 2.
 1. The heavens proclaim the glory of God.
 2. We can know of God from the reaction of most humans to evil.

_____

_____

_____

_____

_____

_____

IV. How would you respond? A friend says to you, 'Sometimes it is very difficult to know and believe that God really exists. There is so much evil and suffering in the world.'

_____

_____

_____

_____

_____

_____

V. Make a 'disciple decision'.
   1. What is the most important wisdom for life that you discovered in this chapter?

   _____

   _____

   _____

   _____

   _____

   _____

   _____

   _____

   2. Name several ways you can put that wisdom into practice. Choose one of the ways you identify and describe how you will make that wisdom part of your life right now.

   _____

   _____

   _____

   _____

   _____

   _____

   _____

   _____

   _____

   _____

   _____

   _____

CHAPTER 3

God's Revelation through the Bible

INTRODUCTION

Throughout the *Credo* series we seek to lead the young people to an ever deeper understanding of the importance of the Bible as the book in which we encounter the Word of God, through which God reveals to us the wonder and majesty of himself and his plan for us and all creation. In chapter 2 we introduced the young people to the fact that we can come to know God because he is continually reaching out to us. God's self-Revelation takes place in many different ways. Chapter 3 concentrates on God's Revelation in the Bible. We lead the young people to an awareness of how they can come to know God and reach a deeper appreciation of his care for each of them, personally, through their own reading of the Bible.

Chapter 3 is developed under five major headings:

- **ATTEND AND REFLECT**: How does understanding the past help us to understand the present and shape our future?
- **HEAR THE STORY**: The Bible tells the story of God's action in human history
- **EMBRACE THE VISION**: The Bible reveals God's plan for humankind
- **THINK IT THROUGH**: Poetry, music and song as storehouses of meaning
- **JUDGE AND ACT** (*Activities and exercises that encourage the young people to integrate what they have learned in the chapter into their daily lives*)

Theological Background for the Teacher

THE NATURE OF DIVINE REVELATION

Divine Revelation is not the disclosure of abstract, timeless doctrines. Revelation is 'God's communication of himself and his loving plan to save us. This is a gift of self-communication, which is realized by deeds and words over time and most fully by his sending us his own divine Son, Jesus Christ' (*United States Catholic Catechism for Adults [USCCA]*, 526; see also *Catechism of the Catholic Church [CCC]*, no 50).

Revelation is about encountering a faithful, just and gracious God in the give and take of history. It is about concrete situations. It is about people living in community, experiencing loss as well as joy. It is about hope for a society in which the starving will be fed (Luke 1:53), in which the last will be first (Luke 13:30) and the downtrodden will be lifted up (Matthew 5:4). The Bible teaches that the possibilities of this vision are the task of every person. Through Sacred Scripture, God reveals himself and his ways in the reality of everyday events in people's lives.

The Word of God, the Revelation of God, through the Bible is a living engagement between God and ourselves. That Revelation and engagement involves not only information but also the self-communication of God's presence, loving kindness, promise and purpose, which calls forth and invites a loving faith response.

CONNECTING WITH THE PAST

Chapter 3 begins by focusing on the fact that knowing about God's self-Revelation in the past can help us to understand our lives today and why things are as they are. While the connection between the past and the present may seem more obvious to adults, young people tend to live very much in the present, with little valuing of the past, especially the past's contributions to the present. If we are to give the young people a sense of the importance of reading Scripture, we must first guide them to realize that learning about God's dealings with people in the past can help them to understand his relationship with us today. So, in this chapter, we talk about where we have come from, the people who have gone before us and the values and understandings they have handed down to us.

As the People of God, we go to the Bible to find and learn about the faith story of our ancestors in faith, to read about their understanding of themselves, their relationship with God, and his unending care and compassion for them. In this chapter we reintroduce the young people to the unfolding of God's plan for us in the stories of Abraham and Moses, stories that many of them have heard at home and learned about in the earlier years of their faith formation. These stories will deepen their understanding that a faith response to God's initiative, his self-Revelation, is called for; but that, even in the face of failure on the part of humankind, God always remains faithful. We introduce the young people to the fact that Jesus is the high point of God's Revelation, something they will return to many times throughout the text.

ADDITIONAL BACKGROUND READING
Catechism of the Catholic Church, nos. 50–67; *United States Catholic Catechism for Adults*, 11–19.

CHAPTER OUTCOMES

See general note on page 18 of this resource.

Learning Outcomes
As a result of studying this chapter and exploring the issues raised, the young people should be able to:

- articulate their understanding of how their past influences their present and shapes their future;
- give a brief overview and description of the books of the Bible;
- know the stories of Abraham and Moses;
- understand that the Bible reveals God's plan for humankind;
- understand the importance of the Old Testament in the life of Jesus;
- understand that Jesus, the Messiah, is the fulfillment of God's promise in the Old Testament;
- appreciate the Psalms as an expression of the prayers, hopes, joys and sorrows of the Israelite people;
- understand the concept of grace;
- know the story of St. Frances Xavier Cabrini.

Faith-formation Outcomes
As a result of studying this chapter and exploring the issues raised, the young people should also:

- be aware of the influence of the Bible in their lives;
- recognize God's call in their lives at this time and decide how they can respond to it;
- be able to indicate where they believe God has been active in their lives to date;
- consider how they might live the Great Commandment;
- recognize how their experiences are expressed in modern culture through music, films and so on;
- begin to experience the Psalms as sources for prayer in their lives;
- listen more attentively to the Bible readings proclaimed during the Liturgy and read the Bible more frequently on their own.

Teacher Reflection

Chapter 3 seeks to deepen the young people's understanding of the power of God's Word in the Bible. As you prepare to work through the chapter with the students, take some time to read and reflect upon the following meditation, which explores the possibilities and limitations of words.

Surprise Surprise!
Imagine that. . . .
When God had finished making the world
The very last thing that he did—
From under the Tree of Life he dug up
An old box and prized off the lid.
God had kept this surprise, had buried it deep;
Now, the lid had completely stuck fast.
God puffed and grunted and pulled and poked
Till his fingers were sore. But, at last
With one final, one *almighty* effort,
The lid flew off in God's hand.
The contents—grammar and words—spilled out
And ran riot all over the land
And over the seas and on every breeze,
Up mountains and down they ran,
A multitude of different languages
Calling to the woman and man:
'Run Adam, run Eve, you must try to catch us,
If you're ever to **speak** to each other
Or speak *for* yourselves, say *who* you are,
Relate to one another. . . .'

Words lit up silence, like fireworks,
Full-stops showered down like confetti,
Verbs hip-hopped, adjectives bip-bopped,
Sentences tangled-up like spaghetti.
Adam and Eve clapped their hands with delight
And leapt to their feet on the spot,
Chasing after the runaway words
To put language 'back in its box'.
And so began the hide-and-seek
That still continues today;
People searching and trying to find the right word
That will *mean* what they want it to *say*!
Sometimes they'll find the words they want
And everyone knows what they mean;
Sometimes they cannot—words escape them
Like a flimsy, elusive dream.
Mostly they just have to reach for whatever
Words are ready to hand;
Whatever words they can find at the time
And do the best that they can.
One thing people discovered was this:
Word and meaning stay close to each other
Like the beach stays close to the seaside,
Or the calf stays close by its mother.
But there was one word—no matter which language–
Whose meaning proved difficult to explain
Though everyone used it, confused it, abused it,
Time and time again.
God saw their difficulty, thought it was time
For his greatest surprise, so he sent
His Son, the second person of the Trinity,
To show the world what 'Love' meant.

66 | CREDO | GOD'S WORD REVEALED IN SACRED SCRIPTURE

Notes and Guidelines for Student Activities

ATTEND AND REFLECT

How does understanding the past help us to understand the present and shape our future?

Learning Outcome
That the young people would:
- articulate their understanding of how their past influences their present and shapes their future.

Overview
Chapter 3 opens with an exploration of how a person's identity is inextricably linked with their past and their family's history, shaping the person they are today. As the students read through pages 42–43 of their text, encourage them to discover more about how the history of their families has shaped the people they are today.

Supplementary Activities for 'Attend and Reflect'

Research Activity
Encourage the young people to discuss the following questions with close relatives, such as grandparents, uncles or aunts:
- How long ago did our family come to this country? This state?
- Where did they come from, and why did they choose to leave that place?
- What role did God or religion play in their lives?

Worksheet 1: 'Where Did Our Ancestors Come From?' (*page 71 of this resource*) is a fun activity that requires the young people to move around the classroom and ask one another about where their ancestors came from. It will help them both to reflect on where they themselves have come from and to learn more about the background of the other students in the class.

Worksheet 2: 'What Influences Me?' (*page 72 of this resource*) invites the young people to explore the things and people that have influenced who they are today. This activity will reinforce what they have already reflected upon in the pages of their text.

HEAR THE STORY

The Bible tells the story of God's action in human history

Learning Outcome
That the young people would:
- be able to give a brief overview and description of the books of the Bible.

Faith-formation Outcome
That the young people would also:
- be aware of the influence of the Bible in their lives.

Overview
Understanding the past can help us come to understand the present. We study our country's history in order to understand why things are as they are now. Through their reading of the Sacred Scriptures of ancient Israel, the Jewish people who lived at the time of Jesus came to understand him to be the Promised Messiah. We read the Bible today in order to understand the background and story that provides the context for our faith in Jesus Christ.

Supplementary Activity for 'Hear the Story'

The exercise in **Worksheet 3: 'The Books of the Bible'** (*page 73 of this resource*) will help the young people to familiarize themselves with the names and location of the various books in the Old and New Testaments.

EMBRACE THE VISION

The Bible reveals God's plan for humankind

Learning Outcomes
That the young people would:
- know the stories of Abraham and Moses;
- understand that the Bible reveals God's plan for humankind;
- understand the importance of the Old Testament in the life of Jesus;
- understand that Jesus, the Messiah, is the fulfillment of God's promise in the Old Testament.

Faith-formation Outcomes
That the young people would also:
- recognize God's call in their lives at this time and decide how they can respond to it;
- be able to indicate where they believe God has been active in their lives to date;
- consider how they might live the Great Commandment.

Overview
As they read through pages 46–48 of their text, the young people will begin to see that God's plan for humankind is revealed gradually through the stories of Abraham and Moses. Section three, 'Embrace the Vision', explores God's promise to remain faithful to his people and it introduces the young people to the Covenant. It presents Jesus the Messiah as the fulfillment of all God's promises and the climax of God's saving action and Revelation in history.

Supplementary Activities for 'Embrace the Vision'

Teacher Tip: You could ask the young people to read the full story of Abraham and Sarah, Genesis chapters 12 to 25, in pairs or threesomes. As they read through it, they could pick out and compile a list of the most dramatic events. Then, when they have finished the reading, they could choose one of these events and dramatize or present it using words, actions, mime, a freeze-frame (which is like a still photo) or a combination of two or more of these methods. When each group has performed their event, they could explain to the class why they chose that particular moment in Abraham's life. The same exercise could be repeated for reading the story of Moses in the Book of Exodus, chapters 2 to 20. Alternatively, depending on time and class size, you could divide the class into two groups and have one group work on Abraham and the other on Moses.

Worksheet 4: 'God's Plan for Humankind' (*page 74 of this resource*) offers the young people an opportunity to reinforce their understanding of the story of the Covenant, of Abraham and Moses and the Ten Commandments.

Through the story of Abraham the young people will have learned something of the importance of a name. God changed Abraham's name to indicate that Abraham had been given and accepted God's call to do a particular job. **Worksheet 5: 'My Name'** (*page 76 of this resource*) provides the young people with an opportunity to research and write about the origins of their own names.

THINK IT THROUGH

Poetry, music and song as storehouses of meaning

Learning Outcomes
That the young people would:
- appreciate the Psalms as an expression of the prayers, hopes, joys and sorrows of the Israelite people;
- understand the concept of grace.

Faith-formation Outcomes
That the young people would also:
- recognize how their experiences are expressed in modern culture through music, films and so on;
- begin to experience the Psalms as sources for prayer in their lives.

Overview

In section four, 'Think It Through', we introduce the young people to the context of the Psalms. We help them to see this art form as an expression of the hopes, fears and prayers of the people of the Old Testament.

Supplementary Activity for 'Think It Through'

Worksheet 6: 'Lines from My Favorite Psalms' *(page 78 of this resource)* invites the young people to choose some favorite psalms and say what it is they find meaningful in them.

The students' text explores the way music and song are vehicles of meaning. This will be easily recognized by young people, for whom music is very important. The text links this with the place of the Psalms in the lives of the Israelite people and how this art form is still used in the prayer of the Church today. We encourage the young people to make the Psalms part of their own prayer. The *Catechism of the Catholic Church* states:

> The Psalms both nourished and expressed the prayer of the People of God gathered during the great feasts at Jerusalem and each Sabbath in the synagogues. Their prayer is inseparably personal and communal; it concerns both those who are praying, and all men. . . . Their prayer recalls the saving events of the past, yet extends into the future, even to the end of history; it commemorates the promises God has already kept and awaits the Messiah who will fulfill them definitively. Prayed by Christ and fulfilled in him, the Psalms remain essential to the prayer of the Church.
>
> – CCC, no. 2586

JUDGE AND ACT

Learning Outcome

That the young people would:
- know the story of St. Frances Xavier Cabrini.

Faith-formation Outcome

That the young people would also:
- listen more attentively to the Bible readings in church and read the Bible more frequently on their own.

Overview

In section five, 'Judge and Act', we help the young people to revise some of the truths from God's Revelation that they have studied in this chapter. We challenge them to apply one of these truths to their lives. We also tell the story of St. Frances Xavier Cabrini, the patron saint of immigrants.

Supplementary Activities for 'Judge and Act'

The story in **Worksheet 7: 'Understanding the Past'** *(page 79 of this resource)* illustrates how an understanding of the past not alone enhances but is essential to our understanding of the present. From this we help the young people to appreciate the importance of understanding the context within which the inspired human authors of Sacred Scripture wrote, in order to come to know the meaning of what God is communicating through their words.

Research Project

You might encourage the young people to research the work of the Cabrini Mission Foundation, which is an organization committed to advancing St. Frances Xavier Cabrini's mission and legacy of healing, teaching and caring around the world. Alternatively, they could research the work of the St. Cabrini Home in New York, which is still run by the Missionary Sisters of the Sacred Heart with the help of lay collaboration and support.

Directives for the Prayer Reflection at the end of the chapter
To begin the Reflection, play the music the young people have chosen, while a representative of the group speaks the prayer from Philippians 2:6-11 (or the words of a poem or song the class has selected) in a way that conveys the deep feelings in it to others.

Additional Prayer Suggestion

Scripture Reflection
(*See instructions for the use of doodling in prayer in the 'Student Activity Tool Kit', page 274 of this resource.*)

Use the following Psalm verse to engage the young people in prayer:

> O LORD, you have searched me and known me.
>
> **PSALM 139:1**

CHAPTER 3 | WORKSHEET 1

NAME:

Where Did Our Ancestors Come From?

With this worksheet and a pen, move around the classroom asking everyone to sign his or her name in the box that states where their ancestors came from. Remember, some people may have to fill in more than one box!

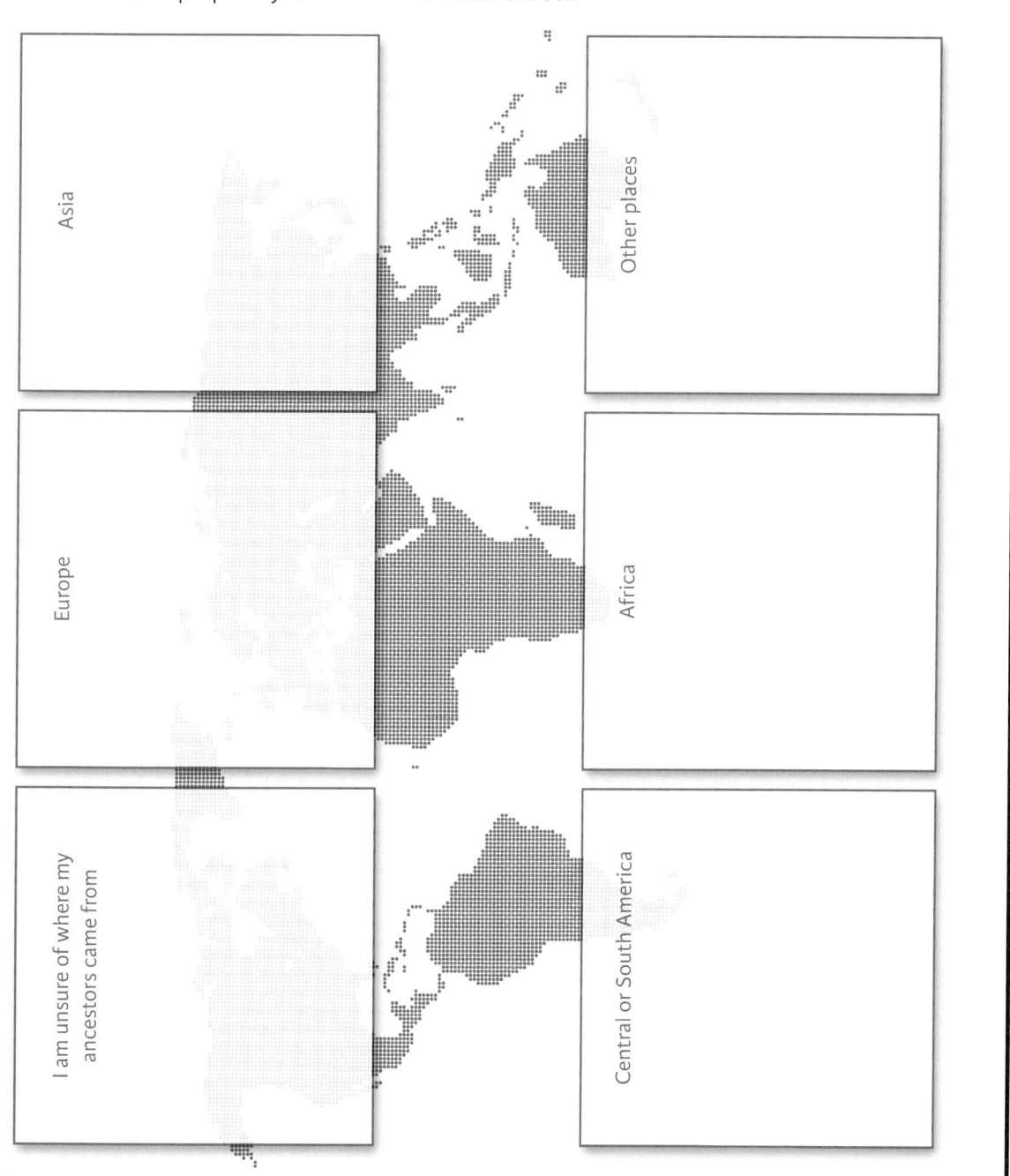

CHAPTER 3: GOD'S REVELATION THROUGH THE BIBLE | WORKSHEET 1 | 71

CHAPTER 3 | WORKSHEET 2

NAME:

What Influences Me?

Complete the following diagram, identifying the main influences on you as a person. Then color each circle red, yellow or blue depending on the level of influence. *Red* would indicate a major influence; *yellow* a medium influence; *blue* a minor influence. In the spaces outside the diagram, write words that explain where or who these influences have come from.

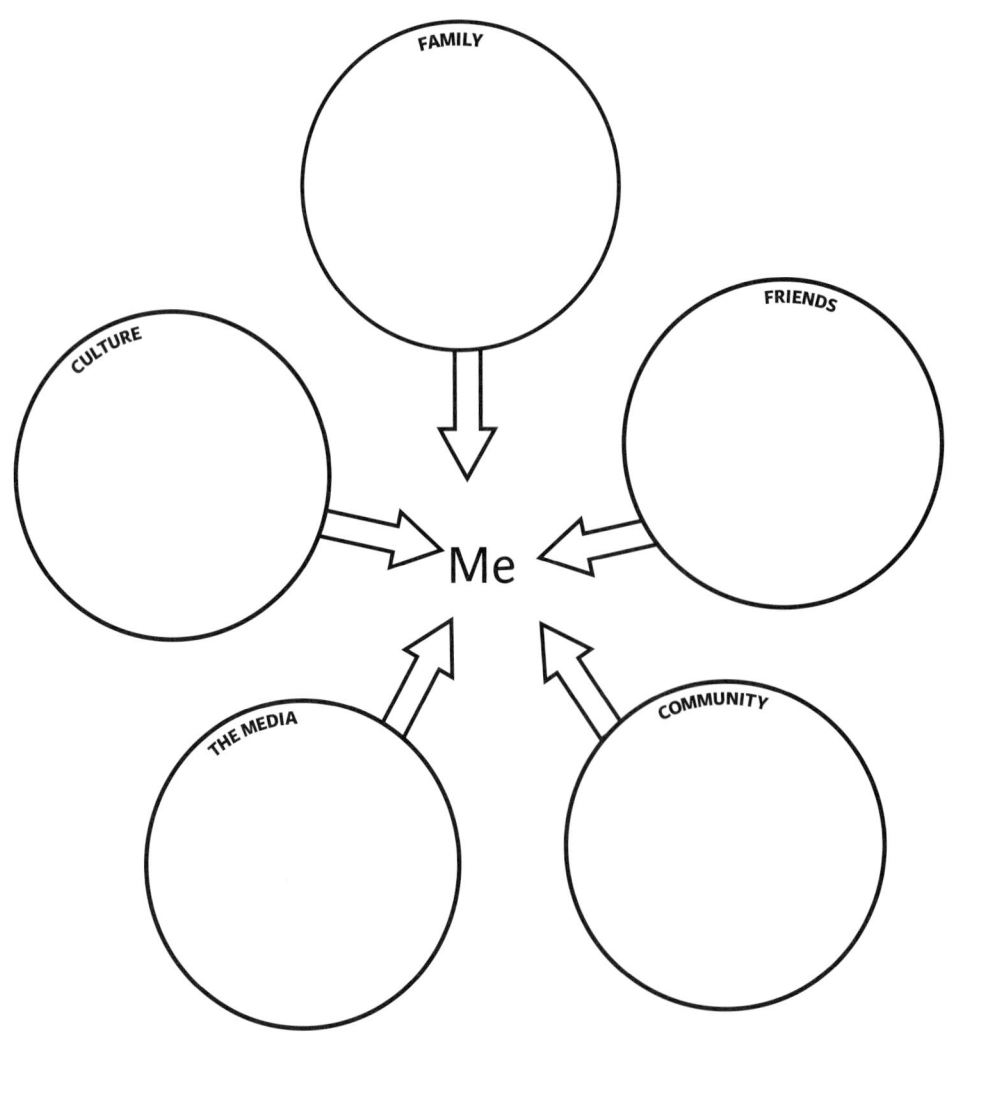

72 | CREDO | GOD'S WORD REVEALED IN SACRED SCRIPTURE

CHAPTER 3 | WORKSHEET 3

NAME:

The Books of the Bible

Use your Bible to help you fill in the missing names.

OLD TESTAMENT

Historical Books
- _____
- 1 MACCABEES
- ESTHER
- _____
- TOBIT
- NEHEMIAH
- EZRA
- 2 CHRONICLES
- _____
- 1 KINGS
- 2 SAMUEL
- 1 SAMUEL
- _____
- JUDGES
- JOSHUA

Torah
- DEUTERONOMY
- NUMBERS
- LEVITICUS
- EXODUS
- GENESIS

Prophetic Books
- MALACHI
- _____
- HAGGAI
- ZEPHANIAH
- _____
- NAHUM
- MICAH
- _____
- OBADIAH
- AMOS
- JOEL
- _____
- DANIEL
- _____
- BARUCH
- LAMENTATIONS
- _____
- ISAIAH

Wisdom Books
- SIRACH (ECCLESIASTICUS)
- _____
- SONG OF SOLOMON
- _____
- PROVERBS
- _____
- JOB

NEW TESTAMENT

Epistles
- REVELATION
- _____
- 3 JOHN
- 2 JOHN
- _____
- 2 PETER
- _____
- JAMES
- HEBREWS
- _____
- TITUS
- 2 TIMOTHY
- _____
- 2 THESSALONIANS
- _____
- COLOSSIANS
- PHILIPPIANS
- _____
- GALATIANS
- 2 CORINTHIANS
- _____
- ROMANS

Gospels
- ACTS OF THE APOSTLES
- _____
- LUKE
- _____
- MATTHEW

CHAPTER 3 | WORKSHEET 4

NAME:

God's Plan for Humankind

> Moses · Revelation · Jesus · prophets · messiah · desert · Palestine
> love · Ten Commandments · Abraham · Covenant · Egyptians · Sinai
> Canaan · Chosen People · Sarah · freedom

Fill in the blanks using the words in the box.

The Old Testament tells of the agreement that God and the Israelites entered into, which was known as the _____. There were two sides to this agreement. The Israelite people promised to obey God's Law, and God agreed that they would have a special and unique relationship with him. This was how they came to be known as the _____ _____. God called a man named _____ to leave his country and his home and travel with his wife, _____, to a land that God would show them. That land was _____ (later known as _____, which today is in Israel). God promised to make Abraham and his descendants into a great nation.

Eventually, Abraham's descendants had to flee from Canaan and were forced into slavery by the _____. God called a man named _____ to lead the people out of slavery and on to _____ once again. God called the scattered tribes of Israelites under Moses' leadership and entered into the Covenant with them. While the Israelites were on their journey through the _____ God appeared to Moses on Mount _____

CHAPTER 3 | WORKSHEET 4 (CONTD.)

and revealed to him the oral Torah (Law) as well as the _____ _____, which were written on two tablets of stone. Later, the Israelites forgot their Covenant with God and they neglected the Ten Commandments. The _____ reminded them that God loved them and wanted them to _____ others. God promised through the prophets that he would send a savior or _____ who would establish a New Covenant between human beings and God. So, when the time was right, God the Father sent _____, his own Son, the climax of God's action and _____ in history.

NAME:

My Name

On the lines provided, write the story behind your name. The following questions may help to get you started.

> Your **Christian name**: Who chose it? Why did they choose that name? Is it connected to someone in your family or is it connected to your family's faith story?
>
> Your **surname**: Where did it originate? What nationality does it belong to? When did your ancestors first settle in the United States?

My Christian name:

_____

_____

_____

_____

_____

_____

_____

_____

_____

My surname: _____

CHAPTER 3 | WORKSHEET 6

NAME:

Lines from My favorite Psalms

In the space below, write out some verses from your favorite psalms. Then, at the bottom of the page, write a few sentences explaining your choices and what they mean for you.

CHAPTER 3 | WORKSHEET 7

NAME:

Understanding the Past

God's Word—Revelation—has been passed on to us through Sacred Scripture and Sacred Tradition. This activity will help you to understand the teaching of the Catholic Church that it is vital for us to know the context within which the inspired human authors of Sacred Scripture wrote; namely, the literary genre, the culture and events of their time, and so on. The Church pays careful attention to these details in authentically interpreting the meaning of Scripture. In order to help you understand the importance of this teaching of the Church, let's read and examine the following story. It highlights the importance of our using this principle in coming to know the meaning of what God is communicating through the written words of the human authors he inspired to write Sacred Scripture.

Ritual Cat

When a spiritual teacher and his disciples began their evening meditation, the cat that lived in the monastery made such noise that it distracted them. So the teacher ordered that the cat be tied up during the evening practice. Years later, when the teacher died, the cat continued to be tied up during the meditation session. And when the cat eventually died, another cat was brought to the monastery and tied up. Centuries later, learned descendants of the spiritual teacher wrote scholarly treatises about the religious significance of tying up a cat for meditation practice.

REFLECT AND DISCUSS
- What do you think is the main message in this story?
- What was the error that led to such confusion?
- How does this relate to our reading of Sacred Scripture?

REFLECT ON YOUR OWN
- Think of some ritual or celebration that takes place regularly in your family; for example, Thanksgiving, Christmas, birthdays. Now imagine someone new coming to live with your family, who doesn't know the story of how your family has always carried out such celebrations. What would need to happen before the 'newcomer' would be able to begin to understand what was taking place, and why would this be important?

NAME:

Review of Chapter 3

I. Fill in the blanks. Use the terms in the box to state correctly the faith of the Catholic Church. Not all of the words provided will be used.

> prophets · Jesus · Abraham · Word of God · Messiah · Mount Sinai
> Kingdom of God · covenant · Great Commandment
> Moses · Psalms · Jewish people

1. The Bible is the _____ written in human language.
2. The word 'testament' means '_____'.
3. The _____ are songs of prayer.
4. God chose _____ to be the founder of God's chosen people.
5. Through the _____, God promised to send a Savior, who would establish a New Covenant between God and all human beings.
6. God chose _____ to lead the Israelites out of slavery to freedom in the Promised Land.
7. God revealed the Ten Commandments on _____.
8. Jesus is the _____, the Anointed One, whom God promised to send to his people.
9. The central theme of Jesus' teaching was the _____.
10. The _____, or law of love, was first revealed in the Old Testament.

II. Name the two main parts of the Bible and briefly describe what each part passes on to us.

___

III. Write a paragraph. Explain the faith of the Catholic Church in its teaching that 'Jesus is the climax of God's action and Revelation in history'.

___

IV. How would you respond? A friend says to you, 'Why do you read the Bible so much? Don't you get enough history in school?'

___

V. Make a 'disciple decision'.
   1. What is the most important wisdom for life that you discovered in this chapter?

   _____

   _____

   _____

   _____

   _____

   _____

   _____

   _____

   2. Name several ways you can put that wisdom into practice. Choose one of the ways you identify and describe how you will make that wisdom part of your life right now.

   _____

   _____

   _____

   _____

   _____

   _____

   _____

   _____

   _____

   _____

   _____

   _____

CHAPTER 4

The Bible: The Inspired Word of God

INTRODUCTION

Chapter 4 explores what biblical inspiration means and the implications for us today of the fact that the Bible is the divinely inspired Word of God. This chapter seeks to help the young people to become more aware of how the Bible can inspire them in their own lives. The chapter is developed under five major headings:

- **ATTEND AND REFLECT**: What does it mean to be inspired?
- **HEAR THE STORY**: The Bible is the inspired Word of God
- **EMBRACE THE VISION**: The Bible speaks to us today just as it spoke to the generations of old
- **THINK IT THROUGH**: How should we honor our Sacred Scripture?
- **JUDGE AND ACT** (Activities and exercises that encourage the young people to integrate what they have learned in the chapter into their daily lives)

Theological Background for the Teacher

We begin chapter 4 by focusing on the notion of inspiration as we use it in ordinary, everyday discourse. What do we mean when we say, for example, 'That was an inspired decision'? We invite the young people to reflect upon their own experience of feeling inspired and where it might come from.

BIBLICAL INSPIRATION

In this chapter we examine what it means to say that the Bible is the divinely inspired Word of God. Here we are referring to the divine assistance given to the human authors. Guided by the Holy Spirit, they made full use of their talents and abilities in writing the sacred texts, while at the same time remaining faithful to the truth that God intended them to teach. (See *United States Catholic Catechism for Adults*, 516.) This explanation of this teaching of the Church is summarized in the *Constitution on Divine Revelation* [*Dei Verbum*] of the Second Vatican Council, in which we read:

> Those things revealed by God which are contained and presented in the text of [S]acred [S]cripture have been written down under the inspiration of the [H]oly Spirit. For [H]oly [M]other [C]hurch, relying on the faith of the apostolic age, accepts as sacred and canonical the books of the Old and New Testaments, whole and entire, with all their parts, on the grounds that, written under the inspiration of the [H]oly Spirit (see Jn 20:31; Tim 3:16; 2 Pet 1:19–21; 3:15–16), they have God as their author, and have been handed on as such to the Church itself. To compose the sacred books, God chose certain men who, all the while he employed them in this task, made full use of their powers and faculties so that, though he acted in them and by them, it was as true authors that they consigned to writing whatever he wanted written, and no more.
>
> – *Dei Verbum*, no. 11

The Holy Spirit worked deep within the psyche of the biblical authors, building them up, inspiring them, calling them, challenging them. At the same time the sacred authors would have brought their own ideas and the influence of their time and culture into what they wrote, working away as best they could using their own powers and energies. All the while the Holy Spirit was with them, illuminating their judgment as to what themes, details or events they should record. In other words, the Holy Spirit was at work in the whole process that led to the composition of the Bible, the formation of the Tradition, all the drafts and redrafts, until the final texts that were accepted by the Church were written. Those final inspired texts, which have been gathered into our Bible, provide a written account of God's Revelation and call to life. 'Still, the Christian faith is not a "religion of the book". Christianity is the religion of the "Word" of God, "not a written and mute word, but incarnate and living"' (*Catechism of the Catholic Church* [CCC], no. 108, quoting St. Bernard).

In this chapter, as well as helping the young people to deepen their understanding of what it means to say that the Bible is the inspired Word of God, we also help them to become more aware of how the Bible can be inspirational for their lives. Our hope is that the Bible will be a significant influence in their lives in the future.

ADDITIONAL BACKGROUND READING
Catechism of the Catholic Church, nos. 101–133; *United States Catholic Catechism for Adults*, 21–33; Vatican II, *Constitution on Divine Revelation* [*Dei Verbum*], nos. 7–10.

Teacher Reflection

Researching the Riddle

Lost sheep is rescued; the shepherd rejoices.
The woman stops looking when her coin is found.
The prodigal bemoans heeding wrong voices;
regret finds a penitent son homeward bound.
Ask—Seek—Knock. These are powerful choices
as writers Matthew and Luke clearly re-sound.
I propose you a riddle, hear and explore.
What when it's found is still hunted the more?

When searching for anything worth searching for,
ask the right questions as a plan you unfold.

How do I seek? Which paths can I ignore?
Who can I trust? What is fraud? What is gold?
Where should I look? Dare I knock on heaven's door?
Seek with your heart, you will find but never hold
evidence that compels your life-long pursuit.
Knock often, discover true wisdom en route.

CHAPTER OUTCOMES

See general note on page 18 of this resource.

Learning Outcomes
As a result of studying this chapter and exploring the issues raised, the young people should be able to:

- discuss what inspiration means and how they have been inspired in their own lives;
- understand that the Bible is the inspired Word of God;
- articulate what it means to say that the biblical authors were divinely inspired;
- understand why the Bible is the Word of God;
- explain how we can understand what the Bible is saying to us today;
- understand the role of the Magisterium in interpreting the Word of God in the Bible;
- demonstrate that they are aware of the widespread influence of the Bible in the world;
- explain how Jews, Muslims and Christians honor their sacred scriptures;
- give examples of how people today are influenced by the Bible;
- link what they have learned in this chapter with an awareness of God's dream for each one of them.

Faith-formation Outcomes
As a result of studying this chapter and exploring the issues raised, the young people should also:

- recognize moments of inspiration in their own lives;
- come to a deeper sense of the Bible as the Word of God;
- develop a deeper confidence in their ability to find meaning in the Bible;
- read the Bible with an awareness of its power to be inspirational in their lives.

Notes and Guidelines for Student Activities

ATTEND AND REFLECT

What does it mean to be inspired?

Learning Outcomes
That the young people would:
- discuss what inspiration means and how they have been inspired in their own lives;
- understand that the Bible is the inspired Word of God.

Faith-formation Outcome
That the young people would also:
- recognize moments of inspiration in their own lives.

Overview
In this chapter we help the young people to understand what it means to say that the Holy Spirit assisted the writers of Sacred Scripture so that 'they have God as their author' and 'they consigned to writing whatever he wanted written, and no more' (*Dei Verbum*, no. 11). We encourage them to become aware of the influence of the Holy Spirit in their own lives.

We begin by helping the young people to understand the meaning of inspiration and to become aware of times when they were inspired. We then introduce them to the teaching of the Church that the Bible is the inspired Word of God.

Supplementary Activity for 'Attend and Reflect'

Group Work/Discussion
Invite the young people to work in small groups and think of examples of the influence of the Bible on political, social, artistic, literary or cultural life today. They could recall references to biblical stories or ideas in books or poems they have read, in plays or movies they have seen or in music they have listened to. They could then share their best examples with the class.

HEAR THE STORY

The Bible is the inspired Word of God

Learning Outcomes
That the young people would:
- articulate what it means to say that the biblical authors were divinely inspired;
- understand why the Bible is the Word of God.
-

Faith-formation Outcome
That the young people would also:
- come to a deeper sense of the Bible as the Word of God.

Overview
Chapter 4 seeks to bring the young people to an awareness of the influence of the Bible on the world. Worksheets 1 and 2 begin to explore this.

For young people, the events and teachings recorded in the Bible can seem 'a thing of the past', something remote from their lives and irrelevant to what is happening to them on a daily basis. We seek to help them realize and come to value deeply that the Bible is God's Word to each of them right now. In this sacred text, God's very own Word, they will find the inspiration and guidance to live their lives, day in and day out, as God intended and as Jesus showed us how.

Supplementary Activities for 'Hear the Story'

Worksheet 1: 'God Speaks to Us through the Bible' (*page 88 of this resource*) aims to help the young people to deepen their awareness of God speaking to them through Sacred Scripture by reflecting on words from Pope Benedict XVI and the prophet Jeremiah. These extracts are easy to understand and have the potential to be influential in deepening the young people's relationship with God and helping them to be aware of how the Word of God in the Bible can make a difference to their lives.

Worksheet 2: 'Phrases from the Bible' (*page 90 of this resource*) invites the young people to look up a number of biblical references to find phrases that have come into common use in the English language. This leads into a class discussion on other well-known phrases that have their origins in the Bible.

Worksheet 3: 'The Inspiration of the Holy Spirit' (*page 92 of this resource*) reminds the young people that while the biblical authors were inspired by the Holy Spirit, they too have received the gift of the Holy Spirit, which can make a difference in their lives.

EMBRACE THE VISION

The Bible speaks to us today just as it spoke to the generations of old

Learning Outcomes
That the young people would:
- be able to explain how we can understand what the Bible is saying to us today;
- understand the role of the Magisterium in interpreting the Word of God in the Bible.

Faith-formation Outcome
That the young people would also:
- develop a deeper confidence in their ability to find meaning in the Bible.

Overview
In section three, 'Embrace the Vision', we help the young people to understand that today the Bible is interpreted for us by the Church's Magisterium. We explore the different factors that biblical scholars take into account and we introduce the concept of literary genre. This will be dealt with more explicitly in a later chapter.

Supplementary Activity for 'Embrace the Vision'

Group Project
Encourage the young people to work in groups and find accounts of a public event that has been reported in the world or national or their local media in the recent past. For example, a sports event, or an accident in which people lost their lives, or a crisis situation in the developing world, or a political development. They should gather together a number of different accounts of the same incident or event. Remember, most newspapers can be accessed on line.

In their groups, they could discuss:
- How do the accounts differ in their portrayal of the event?
- How are they the same?
- What different literary styles are used in the presentation of stories?
- How does the way the event is described affect the reader's perception of what happened?

The young people could then report their findings to the whole class.

You could conclude this activity with a general discussion on how the young people might apply what they have learned from it to their own reading of the Bible.

THINK IT THROUGH

How should we honor our Sacred Scripture?

Learning Outcomes
That the young people would:
- demonstrate that they are aware of the widespread influence of the Bible in the world;
- be able to explain how Jews, Muslims and Christians honor their sacred scriptures;
- give examples of how people today are influenced by the Bible.

Overview
In section four, 'Think It Through', the young people learn about how Jews, Muslims and Christians honor their sacred texts. From this they explore how the Bible has influenced some of the values and aspects of the life of Christians in the United States.

Supplementary Activities for 'Think It Through'

Teacher Tip: The students' text encourages 'peer teaching' when reading the information on the ways in which Christians, Jews and Muslims honor their scriptures. There are instructions for peer teaching in the 'Student Activity Tool Kit', pages 271–2 of this resource.

Worksheet 4: 'Values from the Bible' *(page 93 of this resource)* invites the young people to identify values of society that are rooted in the Bible.

JUDGE AND ACT

Learning Outcome
That the young people would:
- link what they have learned in this chapter with an awareness of God's dream for each one of them.

Faith-formation Outcome
That the young people would also:
- read the Bible with an awareness of its power to be inspirational in their lives.

Overview
Section five, 'Judge and Act', further explores the influence of the Bible on the world, with particular reference to the United States. By drawing on Dr. Martin Luther King Jr.'s 'I Have a Dream' speech, we encourage the young people to imagine God's dream for the world and for each of them.

Supplementary Activities for 'Judge and Act'

Worksheet 5: 'The Bible's Influence on Speeches and Declarations' *(page 95 of this resource)* seeks to deepen the young people's awareness of the influence of the Bible on the world. It includes quotations from the 'Universal Declaration of Human Rights' and the famous 'I Have a Dream' speech of Dr. Martin Luther King, Jr.

Teacher Tip in relation to Worksheet 5: Following the young people's feedback on the influence of the Bible on the speeches and declarations given in Worksheet 5, be sure to confirm that:
- the first article from the Universal Declaration of Human Rights reflects Jesus' preaching on justice; for example the Golden Rule (Luke 6:31) and the parable of the Good Samaritan (Luke 10:30–37);
- the influence of Genesis 1:26 may be seen in the Declaration of Independence;
- in his famous 'I have a dream' speech, Dr. Martin Luther King, Jr. made Isaiah's dream of a new exodus (Isaiah 40) his own as he spoke in prophetic tones.

Worksheet 6: 'God's Dream for the World' *(page 96 of this resource)* invites the young people to write what they believe is God's dream for humanity based on what they have learned from the Bible and Church teachings. It also encourages them to consider how they can play a part in making this dream a reality.

Worksheet 7: 'About the Bible' *(page 97 of this resource)* will help the young people to revise some of the information that they have learned in this chapter.

Directives for the Prayer Reflection at the end of the chapter
You will need a lectern or a stand for the Bible, as well as two candles to be placed on either side.
Ask the young people to stand while the Bible is brought, in procession, to the lectern. Light the candles (if local fire regulations permit).

Additional Prayer Suggestion

Scripture Reflection
(See instructions for the use of doodling in prayer in the 'Student Activity Tool Kit', page 274 of this resource.)

Use the following verse from the Book of Jeremiah to engage the young people in prayer:

> **Before I formed you in the womb, I knew you.**
>
> **JEREMIAH 1:5**

CHAPTER 4 | WORKSHEET 1

NAME:

God Speaks to Us through the Bible

Read and reflect on these words of Pope Benedict XVI:

> We need to devote ourselves constantly anew to the spiritual reading of Sacred Scripture; not only to be able to decipher and explain words from the distant past, but to discover the word that the Lord is speaking to me, personally, here and now.

Now read the following passage from the Book of Jeremiah in the Old Testament:

> Now the word of the LORD came to me saying,
> 'Before I formed you in the womb I knew you,
> and before you were born I consecrated you;
> I appointed you a prophet to the nations.'
> Then I said, 'Ah, Lord GOD! Truly I do not know how to speak, for I am only a boy.' But the LORD said to me,
> 'Do not say, "I am only a boy";
> for you shall go to all to whom I send you,
> and you shall speak whatever I command you.
> Do not be afraid of them
> for I am with you to deliver you.'
>
> – Jeremiah 1:4–8

Pope Benedict XVI invites us to discover what God is saying to each one of us, personally, here and now. From the Book of Jeremiah we discover that we are never too young to be all that God wants us to be. Today God says to you '*Do not be afraid for I am with you*'.

On the lines provided, write a response to this message. Tell God how these words make you feel. You might describe a time when you felt too young or too afraid or too shy to do what you believed God was calling you to do. Tell God about the difference believing this message will make to the way you live and act from here on.

_____

_____

_____

_____

_____

_____

_____

_____

_____

_____

_____

_____

_____

_____

_____

_____

_____

CHAPTER 4 | WORKSHEET 2

NAME:

Phrases from the Bible

Look up the following biblical references and find in them phrases or words that are often used today in common speech. Write the phrases on the noticeboard. Then, on the lines provided below, give examples of how these phrases are used today.

For example, in Galatians 5:4 we find the phrase 'fallen away from grace'. In everyday speech this phrase is used to describe situations where someone has done something that annoys others or causes others to regard them negatively. The phrase is often used to describe such a situation between an individual and their superior. A person might say: 'He [or she] has fallen from grace.'

**Genesis 25:31 · Galatians 5:4 · Daniel 2:33 · Exodus 21:24 · James 5:11
John 20:25 · Matthew 16:3 · Matthew 5:13**

_____

_____

_____

_____

_____

_____

_____

BRAINSTORM
Think of other commonly used English phrases that have their roots in the Bible.

_____

_____

_____

_____

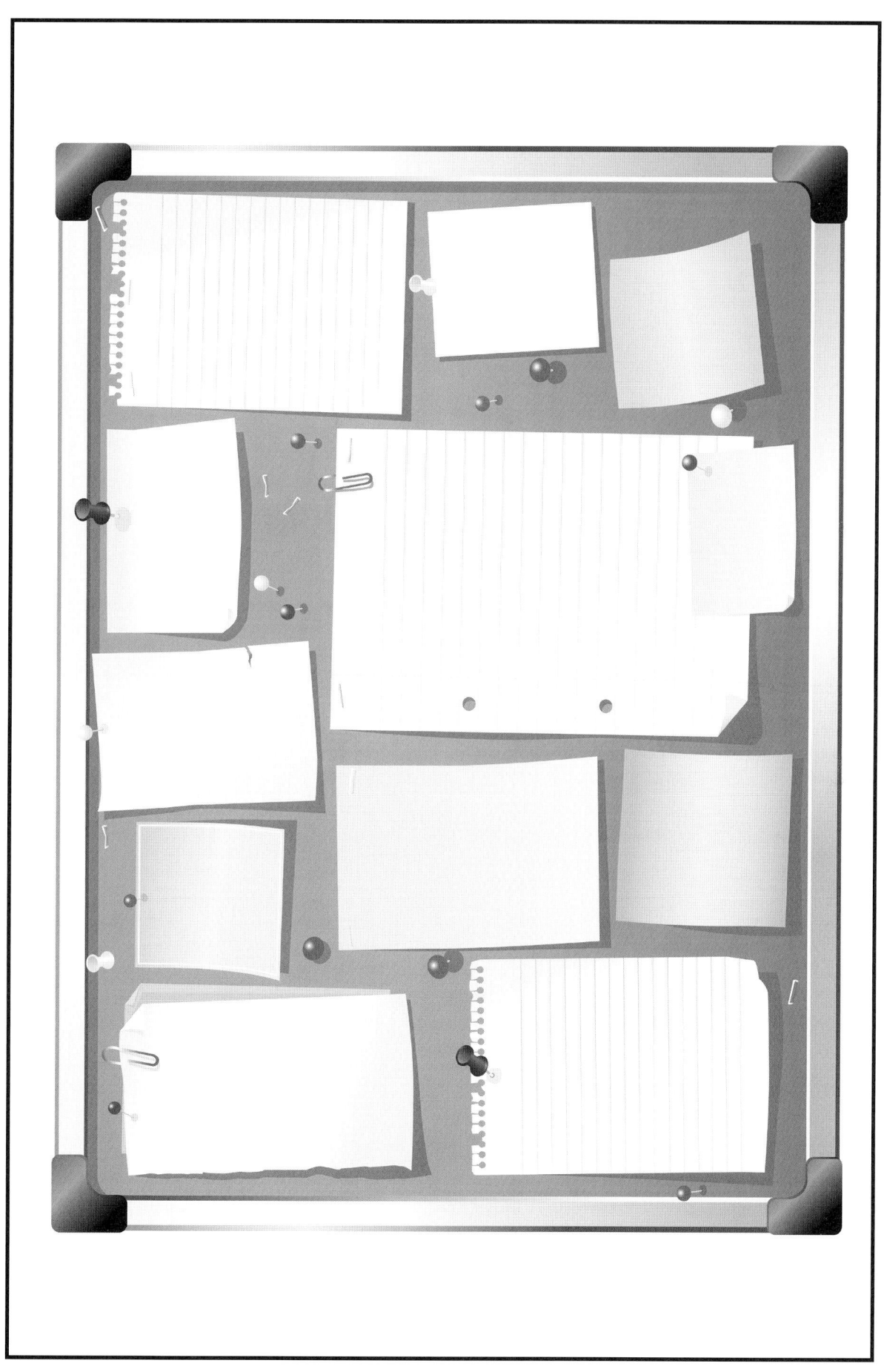

CHAPTER 4 | WORKSHEET 3

NAME:

The Inspiration of the Holy Spirit

The human authors of Sacred Scripture were inspired by the Holy Spirit. Remember you received the gift of the Holy Spirit when you were baptized and you were strengthened by the gift of the Holy Spirit when you were confirmed.

Choose one of the Seven Gifts of the Holy Spirit listed below. Then, on the lines provided, describe a time when you felt inspired by the Holy Spirit to use this gift. Try to explain how it influenced you.

**Knowledge · Understanding · Courage · Right judgment
Wisdom · Reverence · Wonder and Awe**

_____
_____
_____
_____
_____
_____
_____
_____

Now, share with the group or with the person next to you a story about a time when someone was inspired to use one of the Gifts of the Holy Spirit to help or encourage you.

CHAPTER 4 | WORKSHEET 4

NAME:

Values from the Bible

The following are some of the values of our society that are rooted in the Bible.

- Our respect for peace
- Our search for justice
- Our hope for universal neighborliness
- Our energy for human rights
- Our concern for the poor
- Our love of family

Find a biblical passage that would support each of these values in our society today. On the lines provided below, write out a quotation for each one from the passage you have chosen.

Our respect for peace

_____

_____

_____

_____

Our search for justice

_____

_____

_____

_____

CHAPTER 4 | WORKSHEET 4 (CONTD.)

Our hope for universal neighborliness

_____

_____

_____

Our energy for human rights

_____

_____

_____

Our concern for the poor

_____

_____

_____

Our love of family

_____

_____

_____

CHAPTER 4 | WORKSHEET 5

NAME:

The Bible's Influence on Speeches and Declarations

The Bible has had a great influence on documents and speeches that speak of the inherent dignity and the equal and inalienable rights of every human being, and of the vision of a society and world built upon the biblical message of justice.

The First Article of the Universal Declaration of Human Rights of the United Nations (1948) states:

> All human beings are born free and equal in
> dignity and rights. They are endowed with
> reason and conscience and should act towards
> one another in a spirit of brotherhood.

The Declaration of Independence (1776) states:

> . . . that all men are created equal, that they are endowed by their
> Creator with certain unalienable Rights, that among these
> are Life, Liberty and the pursuit of Happiness.

Dr. Martin Luther King Jr. in his well-known and often-repeated 'I have a dream' speech of 1963 proclaimed:

> I have a dream that one day every valley shall
> be exalted, every hill and mountain shall be
> made low, the rough places will be made plain,
> and the crooked places will be made straight,
> and the glory of the Lord shall be revealed, and
> all flesh shall see it together.

GROUP WORK/DISCUSSION
- Each of the core ideas expressed in the above quotations are rooted in passages from the Bible. Find and read the passages in your Bible that serve as the foundation of each of the quotations.
- See if you can find any other extracts from famous speeches or declarations that were influenced by the Bible.
- Imagine that you have been asked to write a speech for the President, a member of Congress, or another public figure, that addresses an important issue facing the country, your state, or town or city. Name the issue you will address and find a passage in the Bible that you would use for the inspiration and foundation of your speech.

CHAPTER 4 | WORKSHEET 6

NAME:

God's Dream for the World

What is God's vision for the world? In your own words describe God's dream for the world based on what you have learned from the Bible and Church teachings.

_____
_____
_____
_____
_____
_____
_____
_____

Now consider and write down your ideas on how you could help make this dream a reality.

_____
_____
_____
_____
_____
_____
_____
_____

NAME:

About the Bible

Match the words in the left column that fit best with the words in the right column. Then write out the full sentences on the lines provided.

1. The Church teaches that the Bible is. . . .
2. The Church teaches that the Bible can. . . .
3. The Church teaches that the human authors of the Bible. . . .
4. The Bible is sometimes called. . . .
5. The Bible was written. . . .
6. The Bible is divided into two main parts. . . .
7. The Church teaches that the Bible is a. . . .
8. The Church teaches that. . . .

were inspired by the Holy Spirit to write what God wanted to reveal.

Sacred Scripture.

the Word of God.

the Old Testament and the New Testament.

sacred and unique text.

the Bible is without error in teaching the truths of God's Revelation for our salvation.

inspire people in a positive way.

over many centuries by many different authors.

CHAPTER 4 | WORKSHEET 7 (CONTD.)

1. _____
   _____

2. _____
   _____

3. _____
   _____

4. _____
   _____

5. _____
   _____

6. _____
   _____

7. _____
   _____

8. _____
   _____

NAME:

Review of Chapter 4

I. Fill in the blanks. Complete the following paragraph so that it correctly states the teaching of the Catholic Church.

The task of giving an authentic **(1)** _____ of the Word of God, whether it is in **(2)** _____ form or in the form of **(3)** _____, has been entrusted to the **(4)** _____, the living teaching office of the Church, alone. Its authority in this matter is exercised in the name of **(5)** _____ **(6)** _____. This means that the task of interpretation has been entrusted to the **(7)** _____, the Bishop of Rome, and to the **(8)** _____ in communion with him. Sacred **(9)** _____ and Sacred **(10)** _____ make up a single deposit of the Word of God.

II. Choose either 1 or 2.
   1. Define each term.

a. Biblical inspiration: _____

_____

_____

_____

_____

_____

b. Inerrancy: _____

c. Literary genre: _____

d. Biblical translation: _____

CHAPTER 4 | CHAPTER REVIEW (CONTD.)

2. Write a paragraph. Explain the statement 'The Bible is the Word of God in human language'.

_____
_____
_____
_____
_____
_____

III. Write a paragraph answering the question 'What makes the Bible the Word of God?' In your response, include in your own words the faith concepts of 'biblical inspiration' and 'inerrancy'.

_____
_____
_____
_____
_____
_____

IV. How would you respond? A Muslim friend says to you, 'I only read the Qur'an in Arabic. There are so many translations of your Bible, you can never really come to know the truth of what your God has revealed.'

_____
_____
_____
_____
_____
_____

V. Make a 'disciple decision'.
1. What is the most important wisdom for life that you discovered in this chapter?

_____

_____

_____

_____

_____

_____

_____

_____

2. Name several ways you can put that wisdom into practice. Choose one of the ways you identify and describe how you will make that wisdom part of your life right now.

_____

_____

_____

_____

_____

_____

_____

_____

_____

_____

_____

_____

_____

CHAPTER 5

The Bible: God's Living Word for Our Lives

INTRODUCTION

Chapter 5 explores the Bible as the living Word of God for our lives. The chapter is developed under five major headings:

- **ATTEND AND REFLECT**: How are major events communicated to us today?—a clue to how to read the Bible
- **HEAR THE STORY**: The Bible's journey from oral tradition to the written word
- **EMBRACE THE VISION**: The living Word of God through the ages
- **THINK IT THROUGH**: The challenge of remaining faithful to the Word of God
- **JUDGE AND ACT** *(Activities and exercises that encourage the young people to integrate what they have learned in the chapter into their daily lives)*

Theological Background for the Teacher

FROM ORAL TO WRITTEN TRADITION

Chapter 5 begins by identifying the ways that news is communicated in today's world. Young people today take for granted communication through internet, blogging, mobile phones and so on—not to mention twenty-four-hour news bulletins on radio and TV covering events from all corners of the globe. Today's world is very different from the world in which the Scriptures were written. It is important that the young people are aware of this difference in their study of the Bible.

When the Sacred Scriptures were first being formed, the primary means of passing on a story was through oral communication. People did not rely on the written word, which we take for granted today. Communities passed on their traditions, epics and laws orally, often while gathered around a fire at night or when they came together for worship or celebrations. The sayings of the wise were memorized and passed on orally from generation to generation even as written communication became more prevalent. And so we try to help the young people to imagine what it was like to live and communicate in that very different environment.

Israelite literature started around the time of King David (d. c.970 BC). This literature was based on the stories, epics and myths that were passed on orally for centuries. For example, much of the prophetic literature in the Bible was initially prepared for oral delivery and transmission. In this context the role of the community was crucial. The words of the spokesperson would only be accepted if in some way they reflected what the community regarded as true and gave voice to its values and self-understanding. This was the case even when one of the speakers, such as one of the prophets, was critical of the community. In the telling of the stories, the community reclaimed its memories and, in the process, strengthened its sense of cohesion. Thus, the community had a huge influence on the messages and stories that were communicated, in a way that would never happen with the written word.

Some of the Israelite traditions would have belonged to individual tribes. Others would have been part of the liturgy of specific sanctuaries. The great prophets had schools of followers who memorized their sayings. The elders and judges of the Israelite towns and villages preserved and developed the legal traditions that stemmed from the Covenant.

The political unity that David achieved led to the gathering and collection of the various traditions into a normative piece of literature for all the tribes. Once this process started, the literature expanded, until eventually the final texts of the Old Testament were written down. Even then, the oral antecedents of the text were never forgotten. When the law was written by the priests and scribes, it still had to be proclaimed aloud to the People of God. In 622 BC King Josiah 'read in their hearing all the words of the book of the covenant' (2 Kings 23:2). Other sections of the biblical texts were first intended to be sung. That was the way with most of the Psalms, the songs of Miriam and Deborah, Exodus 15:21 and Judges 5. In Revelation 1:3 we read: 'Blessed is the one who reads aloud the words of the prophecy, and blessed are those who hear and who keep what is written in it.'

In the first century AD the rabbis continued to entrust their teachings to living minds, to be memorized and transmitted by word of mouth, even though ample written resources were available to them. The written text was mediated, expounded and developed by word of mouth. All this rests on this fundamental insight: the Word of God is not the dead letter of the text but a living communication, communicated by God's Spirit, human prayer, struggle and experience. This means that the Word is alive for each generation.

THE CANON OF SCRIPTURE

In this chapter we introduce the young people to the canon of Scripture. The *Catechism of the Catholic Church* states:

> It was by the apostolic Tradition that the Church discerned which writings are to be included in the list of the sacred books. This complete list is called the canon of Scripture. It includes 46 books for the Old Testament and 27 for the New.
> – CCC, no. 120

The official decision by the Roman Catholic Church establishing the canon did not take place until the Council of Trent (1545–63), though the books of the canon had been widely agreed upon for centuries. While all Christians accept the twenty-seven books of the New Testament to be part of the canon, the Protestant Reformers included in the Old Testament only the thirty-nine books in the Hebrew canon. The canon established by the Catholic Church also includes the seven books, written in Greek, found in the Septuagint, the Greek version of the Bible. 'The canon, in short, was only finally determined on the basis of long experience of the Church with a large variety of writings, some of which, in that collective experience, were to be included in the canon, and hence to be regarded as authoritatively inspired, while others were to be excluded, and hence to be regarded as lacking in such inspiration'. (See Benedict Hegarty, *The Bible: Literature and Sacred text*. Dublin, Ireland: Veritas, page 30.)

In short, it was through the discernment of the Church, guided by the Holy Spirit who had guided the sacred authors in the first place, that it was determined which books faithfully and accurately passed on the faith of the Apostolic Tradition and, thus, were to be included in the list of sacred books. There were other books in circulation in the early Church—for example, the Gospel of Thomas and the Acts of Paul and Thecla—that were judged not to have accurately passed on the faith of the apostolic Church and, therefore, these were not included on the list.

ADDITIONAL BACKGROUND READING
Catechism of the Catholic Church, nos. 65–67, 73, 120–127, 134–141, 324; Vatican II, *Constitution on Divine Revelation* [*Dei Verbum*], nos. 2–6, 11–20.

CHAPTER OUTCOMES

See general note on page 18 of this resource.

Learning Outcomes
As a result of studying this chapter and exploring the issues raised, the young people should be able to:

- understand the difference between how information is communicated today in comparison to biblical times;
- understand the importance and nature of oral tradition;
- demonstrate that they are aware of the place of oral tradition in today's world and in the world of people in biblical times;
- articulate why the Bible came to be written;
- understand what is meant by the canon of Scripture;
- understand how the canon of Scripture came to be agreed;
- reflect on the importance of words in life, leading toward an understanding of the Bible as the Word of God and, finally, of Jesus as the Living Word of God;
- understand the difficulties faced by translators of the Bible;
- understand the importance of biblical scholarship;
- know about the life of St. Jerome.

Faith-formation Outcomes
As a result of studying this chapter and exploring the issues raised, the young people should also:

- have an increased awareness of God's presence in particular times or events in their lives;
- be able to articulate what is the Good News for them at this time;
- recognize what the teaching of Jesus says to them for their lives right now;
- value more deeply the spiritual wisdom that is available to them in the Bible;
- select a passage of Scripture as a motto for their lives.

Teacher Reflection

Remember words are life;
Child, husband, mother, wife:
Remember, and I'm done:
Words taken one by one
Are poems as they stand—
Shore, beacon, harbor, land,
Brook, river, mountain, vale,
Crow, rabbit, otter, quail:
Faith, freedom, water, snow.
Wind, weather, floor, and floe.
Like light across the lawn
Are morning, seas, and dawn:
Words of the green earth growing—
Seed, soil, and farmer sowing.
Like wind upon the south.
Amen. Put not asunder
Man's first word: 'wonder . . . wonder . . .'

Notes and Guidelines for Student Activities

ATTEND AND REFLECT

How are major events communicated to us today?—a clue to how to read the Bible

Learning Outcome
That the young people would:
- understand the difference between how information is communicated today in comparison to biblical times.

Faith-formation Outcome
That the young people would also:
- have an increased awareness of God's presence in particular times or events in their lives.

Overview
Chapter 5 begins by exploring how the mass media communicate news of events simultaneously throughout the world today. We examine the possibility of bias in the stories. We then compare the way news is communicated today with how it was done in Old Testament times. In this way we introduce the young people to the concept of oral tradition.

Supplementary Activity for 'Attend and Reflect'

Worksheet 1: 'When God Is Present in My Life'
(*page 109 of this resource*) invites the young people to reflect on times when they have felt that God was really present in their lives. We hope that the experience of doing this exercise will make them more alert in the future to the presence of God with them.

HEAR THE STORY

The Bible's journey from oral tradition to the written word

Learning Outcomes
That the young people would:
- understand the importance and nature of oral tradition;
- demonstrate that they are aware of the place of oral tradition in today's world and in the world of people in biblical times;
- articulate why the Bible came to be written;
- understand what is meant by the canon of Scripture;
- understand how the canon of Scripture came to be agreed.

Faith-formation Outcome
That the young people would also:
- articulate what is the Good News for them at this time.

Overview
Section two, 'Hear the Story', begins by exploring the meaning of oral tradition. It then explains how the oral tradition of the Israelites was committed to writing, eventually leading to the development of the Old Testament and New Testament canons.

Supplementary Activities for 'Hear the Story'

Christian Whispers
We want the young people to appreciate that it is important to listen to stories and also to be aware that all stories are an interpretation of events by one or more persons. But messages communicated orally can change considerably as they pass from person to person. To explore this, and as an introductory activity to this part of the chapter, you might invite the young people to engage in a game of 'Christian Whispers', which works as follows:

- Choose a quotation from the Bible that the young people are not familiar with and give it to one student to read.
- That student then whispers the quotation to the person beside them.
- The second student then whispers the quotation to the next person, and this continues until every student in the class has heard it.
- The last person who hears it has to tell the others in the class what he or she heard.
- The young people then compare the original quotation with the final version.

Follow-up discussion: What does this exercise teach us about the nature and reliability of oral communication? How might this relate to why the Scriptures, for many years passed on as oral tradition, eventually came to be written down?

Worksheet 2: 'My Family's Oral Tradition' (*page 110 of this resource*) offers the young people an opportunity to tell a story from their own family's oral tradition and to think about the significance of having and sharing such stories. As they become more aware of how oral tradition functions in their own family situations, they will have a greater sense of how important it must have been for people in biblical times.

Worksheet 3: 'The Development of the Old Testament Canon of Scripture' (*page 111 of this resource*) and **Worksheet 4: 'The Development of the New Testament Canon of Scripture'** (*page 113 of this resource*) offer revision exercises based on the information given in section two.

EMBRACE THE VISION

The living Word of God through the ages

Learning Outcome
That the young people would:
- reflect on the importance of words in life, leading toward an understanding of the Bible as the Word of God and, finally, of Jesus as the Living Word of God.

Faith-formation Outcome
That the young people would also:
- recognize what the teaching of Jesus says to them for their lives right now.

Overview
Section three, 'Embrace the Vision', examines the phrase 'The Word of God': as spoken at the dawn of creation; as committed to writing in the Sacred Scriptures; and finally as revealed in the Person of Jesus Christ.

Supplementary Activities for 'Embrace the Vision'

The early followers of Jesus wanted everyone to hear the Good News that Jesus had given them. **Worksheet 5: 'Words of Jesus'** (*page 115 of this resource*) invites the young people to choose one statement of Jesus that they think is Good News for them and to say how believing in its wisdom could change their lives. This activity will encourage them to make the words of Jesus a source of wisdom for their lives.

Group Activity
Encourage the young people to work in groups to discuss and then agree on words of Jesus that they would really like to remember. Using their chosen words, they could make posters to hang on the classroom or school walls.

THINK IT THROUGH

The challenge of remaining faithful to the Word of God

Learning Outcomes
That the young people would:
- understand the difficulties faced by translators of the Bible;
- understand the importance of biblical scholarship;
- know about the life of St. Jerome.

Overview
Section four, 'Think It Through', examines the difficulties faced by translators of Scripture and the

importance of biblical scholarship. We highlight the importance of making the Word of God in the Bible a living word for our lives. In this context we introduce the young people to the life and work of St. Jerome.

Supplementary Activity for 'Think It Through'

Worksheet 6: 'Fact-file on St. Jerome' (*page 116 of this resource*) will help the young people to recall what they have learned about this Father of the Church and great biblical scholar.

JUDGE AND ACT

Faith-formation Outcomes
That the young people would:
- value more deeply the spiritual wisdom that is available to them in the Bible;
- select a passage of Scripture as a motto for their lives.

Overview
In section five, 'Judge and Act', we introduce the young people to Archbishop Desmond Tutu as someone who always tries to live the spiritual wisdom he has learned from the Bible.

Supplementary Activities for 'Judge and Act'

Worksheet 7: 'Quotations from Archbishop Desmond Tutu' (*page 117 of this resource*) presents some quotations from the archbishop that reflect his spiritual wisdom. We invite the young people to read the quotations and choose one that they find inspirational for their own lives.

Research Project
Encourage the young people to research the life and work of Archbishop Desmond Tutu. They could begin by reading or listening to some of his speeches, especially his acceptance speech when he was awarded the Nobel Peace Prize in 1984. There are numerous internet sites where they can listen to Archbishop Tutu telling his own story.

Or

Ask the young people to use the internet to find some quotations from Archbishop Tutu that they hear as living words for their life today. Encourage them to decide how they will put these words into practice. They could add their favorite quotation(s) to their Words of Wisdom collection.

Additional Prayer Suggestion

Meditative Exercise
(*See 'Student Activity Tool Kit', pages 274–6 of this resource, for helpful suggestions in relation to conducting guided meditations.*)

LEADER
Today we are going to reflect on Mary's response to the angel: 'Let it be with me according to your word' (Luke 1:38), and what God might be saying to us for our lives, right here and right now.

Sit comfortably in your seat. Become aware of your breathing. Feel your breath going in and out of your lungs . . . bringing life to every part of your body.

Become aware of God, who dwells within you and is present with us now. Remember that he loves each one of us with an everlasting love that nothing can change. It was he who called us into being and it is he who sustains us each day.

Ask God: What are you asking me to do in my life right now? Listen to see if you can hear what is being asked of you. . . . Perhaps it is something that involves your family, or a friend. . . . Or maybe God is asking you to spend more time in prayer, or to change the way you think about something or someone. (*Pause for a few moments.*)

Can you give the same response as Mary did? 'Let it be with me according to your word.' (*Pause*)

What would it mean if you really agreed to do whatever God is asking of you? (*Pause*)

In your heart, say to God, 'Let it be with me according to your word.' (*Pause*)

Imagine what God says to you. (*Pause*)

When you are ready, open your eyes. Decide when you will do whatever God is asking of you right now.

NAME:

When God Is Present in My Life

Recall and name three times when you really believed God was present in your life. In each case, say why you believed God was present at that time.

I believed God was really present in my life when

_____

_____

_____

_____

I believed God was really present in my life when

_____

_____

_____

_____

I believed God was really present in my life when

_____

_____

_____

_____

NAME: _____

My Family's Oral Tradition

Write a brief version of your favorite story from your family's oral tradition.

_____
_____
_____
_____
_____
_____
_____
_____

Now explain why you think it is important that the people in your family know this story.

_____
_____
_____
_____
_____
_____
_____

CHAPTER 5 | WORKSHEET 3

NAME:

The development of the Old Testament Canon of Scripture

> forty-six · Greek · Trent · inspiration · deuterocanonical
> canon · New Testament · Septuagint · Israelites
> King David · Revelation · canonical

Fill in the blanks using the words in the box.

The sacred writings that have been gathered in our Old Testament evolved over many hundreds of years. They are the written expression of the faith of the _____, which was first passed on in their oral traditions or stories. During the reign of _____ _____ (1000–926 BC), which was a time of great peace and prosperity for the Israelites, a collection was made of the written texts that existed. This was how the _____, or official collection of the books of Sacred Scripture, began to be formed; but it was not completed until centuries later. As the community tried to live as God's own people, in response to God's _____, they gradually discerned which books bore the character of divine _____ and, therefore, could be called the Word of God.

While the members of the early Church were beginning to write and compile their own Scriptures, which would become the _____ _____, they continued also to cherish and revere the Jewish Scriptures as the revealed Word of God.

During the first centuries of the Church, there were two listings of _____ writings accepted by the Jewish people, one shorter and one longer, before the official Old Testament

CHAPTER 5 | WORKSHEET 3 (CONTD.)

canon was established. The longer list was based on a _____ translation of the Hebrew Scriptures, called the _____. The early Church debated which Jewish 'canon' to accept. Eventually, at the Council of _____ in 1546, the Catholic Church officially embraced the longer listing of Old Testament canonical books, while the Protestant Reformers favored the shorter listing. We now count _____ Old Testament books in the Catholic Bible. However, most Protestant Bibles now include the disputed books, calling them _____ (literally 'second canon').

The development of the New Testament Canon of Scripture

> Revelation · Epistles · Good News · letters · Gospel writers
> earliest · Apostles · way · official · Gospels
> twenty-seven · canon · God · 70 · Ascension · eyewitness

Fill in the blanks using the words in the box.

After Jesus' Resurrection and _____, his disciples remembered and continued to preach what he had proclaimed through his words and actions. They first spread the _____ _____ of the Kingdom of God throughout the Mediterranean countries, preaching in the same way as they had seen Jesus preach. It was only when the Church was established in far-off places that the leaders began to write _____ in which they continued to instruct and encourage Christians to live as disciples of Jesus. The letters of St. Paul and the other Apostles were the _____ writings of the New Testament.

As the Apostles and the other disciples who were eyewitnesses to the life and mission and Death and Resurrection of Jesus began to grow old and die, the members of the early Church feared that the message of his life and teaching would be lost if it were not written down. Thus, beginning around the year AD _____, the Apostles and Evangelists (meaning _____ _____) and their disciples began to write down what the Apostles and the other disciples of Jesus had been preaching. They gathered the oral traditions, memoirs and other writings that had been circulating within the early Church, and the formation of the four _____ in the New Testament began.

Over three decades, four different accounts of the Gospel were written, as well as the Acts of the _____, the _____ and the Book of _____ (also known as Apocalypse). Eventually, after a century of teaching, preaching, editing and writing, the New Testament books were completed.

Along with the writings that eventually formed the New Testament, other writings, even several gospels, were written. The leaders of the early Church had a number of rules for deciding whether a book was 'inspired' and to be accepted as part of the _____, or canonical, writings of the Church. Was it written by or closely connected to an Apostle or _____ of the life and mission of Jesus? Did it ring true to the person and teaching of Jesus, as we know him from other New Testament books? Did it help people to follow the _____ of life modeled by Jesus and now expected of his disciples? Was the book accepted generally among Christians? Finally, the present list of _____ New Testament books was agreed as canonical and eventually became part of the _____ of Sacred Scripture. The canon of Scripture refers to the list of Old and New Testament books that are accepted by the Catholic Church as the inspired Word of _____.

NAME:

Words of Jesus

Read the following words of Jesus and choose the statement that you think is really good news for you. On the lines provided, describe how you think your life would be affected if you truly believed in the wisdom of this statement.

> Blessed are the peacemakers, for they will be called children of God.
> – Matthew 5:9

> Do not worry about your life, what you will eat or what you will drink, or about your body, what you will wear. Is not life more than food, and the body more than clothing? Look at the birds of the air; they neither sow nor reap nor gather into barns, and yet your heavenly Father feeds them. Are you not of more value than they?. . . . Therefore do not worry, saying, 'What will we eat?' or 'What will we drink?' or 'What will we wear?' For it is the Gentiles who strive for all these things; and indeed your heavenly Father knows that you need all these things.
> – Matthew 6:25–32

> Let the little children come to me, and do not stop them; for it is to such as these that the kingdom of God belongs.
> – Luke 18:16

> The Son of Man came to seek out and to save the lost.
> – Luke 19:10

> If you ask anything of the Father in my name, he will give it to you.
> – John 16:23

_____
_____
_____
_____

CHAPTER 5 | WORKSHEET 6

NAME:

Fact-file on St. Jerome

Using the information in chapter 5 of your theology text, complete the following fact-file on St. Jerome, one of the Fathers of the Church and a great biblical scholar.

Name: _____

Year of birth: _____

Place of birth: _____

Circumstances of baptism: _____
_____

At age thirty-three: _____
_____

Best known for: _____
_____

Famous advice: _____
_____

Patron saint of: _____
_____

Feast day: _____

CHAPTER 5 | WORKSHEET 7

NAME:

Quotations from Archbishop Desmond Tutu

Each of these quotations from Archbishop Tutu, the Anglican Archbishop of Cape Town, South Africa and winner of the 1984 Nobel Prize for Peace, is rooted in the wisdom of Sacred Scripture. Read them and choose one that you think would be inspirational for your own life. Write or draw how you imagine these words of Archbishop Tutu might inspire you.

'If you are neutral in situations of injustice, you have chosen the side of the oppressor.'

'I think we shouldn't be dismissive of anybody. I always reckon that each one of us has the capacity to become a saint, anyone and everyone.'

'So people actually, if they want to know "What is God like?", they would have to look at you and me and see us as being compassionate, because God is compassionate, as being loving, because God is loving.'

CHAPTER 5 | CHAPTER REVIEW

NAME:

Review of Chapter 5

I. Multiple choice. Circle the letter next to the word that best completes each statement so that it accurately states the teaching of the Catholic Church.

1. The Bible is the _____ Word of God.

   A. revised · B. spoken · C. inspired · D. Latin · E. printed

2. The canon of Scripture is the _____ list of sacred writings accepted by the Catholic Church as the inspired Word of God.

   A. official · B. earliest · C. largest · D. oldest · E. canonical

3. The Roman Catholic canon lists _____ books in the Old Testament.

   A. twenty-four · B. thirty-two · C. forty-six · D. seventy-three · E. none of the above

4. The Roman Catholic canon lists _____ books in the New Testament.

   A. twenty-seven · B. thirty-two · C. forty-six · D. seventy-three · E. none of the above

5. The Old Testament is also known as the _____.

   A. Old Bible · B. First Scriptures · C. Jewish Scriptures · D. Scriptures of ancient Israel · E. Torah

6. The writings in the Old Testament began to be collected during the time of _____.

   A. Abraham · B. Moses · C. King David · D. Jesus · E. The early Church

7. The New Testament was originally written in _____.

   A. Hebrew · B. Aramaic · C. Greek · D. Latin · E. English

118 | CREDO | GOD'S WORD REVEALED IN SACRED SCRIPTURE

CHAPTER 5 | CHAPTER REVIEW (CONTD.)

8. The writers of the four accounts of the Gospel in the New Testament are called the four _____.

   A. Prophets · B. Apostles · C. Disciples · D. Evangelists · E. Gospel writers

9. The _____ contain early versions of some of the Old Testament texts.

   A. Torah · B. Pentateuch · C. Prophets · D. Dead Sea Scrolls · E. Septuagint

10. _____ first translated the Bible into a modern language.

    A. The Catholic Church · B. Desmond Tutu · C. St. Jerome · D. Martin Luther · E. St. Augustine

II. Write a paragraph. Choose either 1 or 2.
   1. Explain the term 'oral tradition' and its relationship to Sacred Scripture.
   2. Name and explain the steps in the writing of the four accounts of the Gospel.

_____
_____
_____
_____
_____
_____
_____
_____
_____
_____
_____
_____
_____
_____

CHAPTER 5 | CHAPTER REVIEW (CONTD.)

III. Write a paragraph. Explain the meaning of the statement, 'Jesus is the living Word of God. Through his life and teaching he spoke the final Word of God's Revelation.'

_____
_____
_____
_____
_____
_____
_____
_____
_____

IV. How would you respond? An eighth grader asks you, 'Since the Bible says "an eye for an eye and a tooth for a tooth", is it okay to get even with someone who is spreading rumors about me? Why can't I tell lies about them?'

_____
_____
_____
_____
_____
_____
_____
_____
_____
_____

V. Make a 'disciple decision'.
   1. What is the most important wisdom for life that you discovered in this chapter?

   _____
   _____
   _____
   _____
   _____
   _____
   _____
   _____

   2. Name several ways you can put that wisdom into practice. Choose one of the ways you identify and describe how you will make that wisdom part of your life right now.

   _____
   _____
   _____
   _____
   _____
   _____
   _____
   _____
   _____
   _____
   _____
   _____
   _____

CHAPTER 6

The Bible: A Blueprint for Living

INTRODUCTION

Chapter 6 sets out to help the young people to recognize and value the Bible as *the* source of inspiration and direction for living and for prayer and worship. The chapter is developed under five major headings:

- **ATTEND AND REFLECT**: How can words make a difference to our lives?
- **HEAR THE STORY**: The Bible can be a powerful influence
- **EMBRACE THE VISION**: The place of the Bible in Church life, teaching, Liturgy and worship
- **THINK IT THROUGH**: Applying the Word of God in Scripture to daily prayer and daily life
- **JUDGE AND ACT** (*Activities and exercises that encourage the young people to integrate what they have learned in the chapter into their daily lives*)

Theological Background for the Teacher

THE BIBLE AS A SOURCE OF WISDOM AND GUIDANCE

The Bible has for generations spoken to us through letter, sermon, analysis, proverb, myth and story. The Bible is recommended reading for all who wish to be spiritually refreshed and renewed. People read the Bible for a wide variety of reasons. Many people read the Bible in search of guidance for daily living. Some people may wish to deepen their knowledge and appreciation of Scripture. Others may read the Bible because they recognize it as a source of insight into the mystery of God and the meaning of human existence.

The biblical message of care for one's neighbor has reverberated down through the centuries. According to the Law in the Pentateuch, there can be no legislation on the basis of class or status in society, religious or civil. Aristocrat and peasant are one. Throughout Sacred Scripture there is a prevailing concern for the oppressed, the disinherited, the weak, the poor and the afflicted that voices a deep respect for human life and bodily integrity. The vulnerable in society merit special attention. For example, when a woman is widowed, her husband's brother must marry her to prevent her losing her home and security (Deuteronomy 25:5–10); the alien should be treated with hospitality and protected (Deuteronomy 16:12).

In vivid language the prophets raged against the evils of their day. Amos, an eighth-century-BC prophet who proclaimed his message during a time of great prosperity in Israel, condemns social injustice with ruthless severity. He describes the wealthy merchants as they trample on the heads of the poor and defenseless: 'They sell the righteous for silver, and the needy for a pair of sandals—they who trample the head of the poor into the dust of the earth, and push the afflicted out of the way' (Amos 2:6–7). He attacks hypocritical religious practice: 'I hate, I despise your festivals, and I take no delight in your solemn assemblies. . . . Take away from me the noise of your songs: I will not listen to the melody of your harps. But let justice roll down the waters, and righteousness like an ever-flowing stream' (Amos 5:21–23).

The Bible is a source of wisdom and advice. In the Book of Ecclesiasticus, or Sirach, which is one of the Wisdom writings, the writer Sirach teaches: 'Stand firm for what you know, and let your speech be consistent. Be quick to hear, but deliberate in answering. If you know what to say, answer your neighbor; but if not, put your hand over your mouth' (Ecclesiasticus [Sirach] 5:10–12). In the Psalms the Word of God offers us peace and the assurance of God's abiding, saving presence: 'The Lord is my shepherd, I shall not want' (Psalm 23).

The story of Jesus in the accounts of the Gospel, with its sharply crafted sayings and its challenging vision and triumphant love, has captivated people through the ages and influenced not only their philosophy of life but, ultimately, the way they live their life. In the coldness of pagan society the early Church communities were places of warmth and support. Throughout the writings of St. Paul there is a personal touch and sense of involvement: 'Timothy, my co-worker, greets you. . . . I Tertius, the writer of this letter, greet you in the Lord' (Romans 16:21–22); 'The churches of Asia send greetings' (1 Corinthians 16:19); 'See what large letters I make when I am writing in my own hand!' (Galatians 6:11). Following the teachings of Christ in the New Testament, the great monasteries of the Middle Ages were places of spiritual and physical care for all who visited.

The Bible is also a source of prayer and reflection. Catholics read and are helped to reflect upon passages from Scripture during the Liturgy of the Word at every Mass and at the celebration of the Sacraments. The Word of God, Sacred Scripture, is the basis of many forms of prayer: the Divine Office draws heavily on the Bible. *Lectio divina* is a form of prayer that seeks to help people to pay attention to God's Word in Sacred Scripture and to take it to heart in their daily lives.

One of the goals of this chapter is to alert young people to the fact that there are and will be many times in their lives when the Bible can be a source of help or inspiration. The worksheets provided for this chapter will focus upon achieving this goal.

ADDITIONAL BACKGROUND READING
Catechism of the Catholic Church, nos. 131–132, 1093, 1096, 1100, 1153–1158, 1163–1178, 1177, 2205, 2566–2589, 2653–2655; *United States Catholic Catechism for Adults*, 464, 473–474, 477–478.

Teacher Reflection

It Is Not Enough
It is not enough to know.
It is not enough to follow
the inward road conversing in secret.

It is not enough to see straight ahead,
to gaze at the unborn
thinking the silence belongs to you.

It is not enough to hear
even the tiniest edge of rain.

You must go to the place
where everything waits,
there, when you finally rest,
even one word will do,
one word or the palm of your hand
turning outward
in the gesture of gift.

And now we are truly afraid
to find the great silence
asking so little.

One word, one word only.

CHAPTER OUTCOMES

See general note on page 18 of this resource.

Learning Outcomes
As a result of studying this chapter and exploring the issues raised, the young people should be able to:

- identify times when words had an influence on their lives, leading to an appreciation of the power of words;
- understand the place of the Bible in Church teaching and worship;
- understand the concept of *lectio divina*;
- pray with biblical texts, especially through *lectio divina*;
- become familiar with the Church's liturgical year;
- appreciate the importance of the Psalms in the prayer and music of the Church;
- understand the concept of Liturgy;
- know the Our Father as the prayer of Jesus and become aware of how it links with their life experience today;
- find passages from the Bible that link with situations in their world.

Faith-formation Outcomes
As a result of studying this chapter and exploring the issues raised, the young people should also:

- be more conscious of how they use words and realize how their words can affect others;
- be able to identify times when they have heard a 'Word of God' for them from the Bible;
- make a greater effort to hear the Word of God in the readings at Mass;
- value the Our Father more deeply;
- be open to receiving wisdom for their lives from the Bible.

Notes and Guidelines for Student Activities

ATTEND AND REFLECT

How can words make a difference to our lives?

Learning Outcome
That the young people would:
- identify times when words had an influence on their lives, leading to an appreciation of the power of words.

Faith-formation Outcome
That the young people would also:
- be more conscious of how they use words and realize how their words can affect others.

Overview
Chapter 6 begins by exploring the power of words, leading the young people to become aware that the words we use can have an impact, positive or negative, on other people.

Supplementary Activities for 'Attend and Reflect'

Teacher Tip: You could develop the brainstorm activity on words of healing/words of hurt into a game. Have the class work in two teams—'Team Heals' and 'Team Hurts'. Write the team names on the board and list the names of the members under each. One at a time, a student from each team goes up to the board and writes a word in their category, 'Heals' or 'Hurts'. The team that finishes first with the most relevant words wins!

You might like to extend the activity by showing a clip from the film *Tuesdays with Morrie*.

The young people might also like to read the book *Tuesdays with Morrie*.

HEAR THE STORY

The Bible can be a powerful influence

Learning Outcomes
That the young people would:
- understand the place of the Bible in Church teaching and worship;
- understand the concept of *lectio divina*;
- pray with biblical texts, especially through *lectio divina*.

Faith-formation Outcome
That the young people would also:
- be able to identify times when they have heard a 'Word of God' for them from the Bible.

Overview
In section two, 'Hear the Story', we examine the way in which the Bible is used in different traditions; for example, in the Pentecostal or Evangelical traditions as well as in the Catholic Church. We look at the effect of the Protestant Reformation on how Catholics used the Bible in the past and we explore the place of the Bible today in the lives of Catholics and in the Liturgy and worship of the Church. Finally, we introduce the young people to *lectio divina* as a way of praying with the Scriptures.

Supplementary Activities for 'Hear the Story'

The story in **Worksheet 1: 'Living God's Word'** (*page 127 of this resource*) further emphasizes the need to find ways of linking the Word of God in Sacred Scripture with our daily lives.

We are trying to encourage the young people to see the benefits of reading the Bible as a source of direction for their lives and for deepening their relationship with God. **Worksheet 2: 'The Bible Offers Advice for Life'** (*page 129 of this resource*) presents the students with examples of situations in life where someone might turn to the Bible for help and guidance. We invite them to look up several biblical references to discover where a person might find help in a variety of situations.

Worksheet 3: 'The Bible: Words of Wisdom' (*page 130 of this resource*) gives the young people some words of wisdom from the Bible to add to their own Words of Wisdom collection.

EMBRACE THE VISION

The place of the Bible in Church life, teaching, Liturgy and worship

Learning Outcomes
That the young people would:
- become familiar with the Church's liturgical year;
- appreciate the importance of the Psalms in the prayer and music of the Church;
- understand the concept of Liturgy.

Faith-formation Outcome
That the young people would also:
- make a greater effort to hear the Word of God in the readings at Mass.

Overview
Section three, 'Embrace the Vision', examines the place of the Bible in the Liturgy of the Word at Mass and introduces the young people to the Liturgical Year. They have already looked at the importance of the Psalms in the lives of people in Old Testament times; here we explore the importance of the Psalms in the music and prayer of the Church today.

Supplementary Activities for 'Embrace the Vision'

Class Activity
If possible, arrange for the young people to visit a monastery or a convent where the monks or the sisters pray the Divine Office each day. Arrange for them to attend one of these prayer times. Afterward, they could reflect together on the experience.

Research Projects
Encourage the young people to choose one or more of the following projects.

Talk to someone who is a reader at Mass in your parish. Ask that person about the preparation she or he does to read the Scriptures well. Ask, 'How do you feel when you are proclaiming the Word of God at Mass?' Share your findings with the rest of the group.

Or

Research the impact of the Gregorian Chant music of the Cistercian monks of the Heiligenkreuz Monastery in Vienna, Austria. In 2008 they were signed by Universal Music (which boasts such performers as Amy Winehouse and Eminem). Why do you think Universal Music was interested in promoting a group such as this? Who does this type of music most appeal to and why might this be so? Does it appeal to young people? Why or why not? (If you like what you hear, you might consider buying a copy of their CD and using it for some of your meditations at home and/or in school.)

Or

Find out more about the Taizé community. Listen to some of the music and prayers. Why do you think it has such appeal for young people? Does it appeal to you? Why or why not?

THINK IT THROUGH

Applying the Word of God in Scripture to daily prayer and daily life

Learning Outcomes
That the young people would:
- know the Our Father as the prayer of Jesus and become aware of how it links with their life experience today;
- find passages from the Bible that link with situations in their world.

Faith-formation Outcome
That the young people would also:
⊙ value the Our Father more deeply.

Overview
In this and the preceding chapters we have been helping the young people to learn more about the Bible. Section four, 'Think it Through', seeks to help them to be more aware of how the Bible can be influential in their own lives. It focuses particularly on the Lord's Prayer.

Supplementary Activity for 'Think It Through'

Worksheet 4: 'Reflection on the Our Father' (*page 132 of this resource*) explores the meaning of the Lord's Prayer. This could be read in conjunction with the section entitled 'The Lord's Prayer' on pages 107–108 of the students' text.

JUDGE AND ACT

Faith-formation Outcome
That the young people would:
⊙ be open to receiving wisdom for their lives from the Bible.

Overview
The chapter concludes with the story of Jean Donovan. The young people reflect on this story as an example of how one person took the Word of God to heart and allowed it to transform her life. This reflective exercise should challenge the young people to take the Word of God to heart in their own lives.

Supplementary Activities for 'Judge and Act'

Design a Poster/Flier
Encourage the young people to use some of the ideas they have found in chapter 6 to design a poster or flier inviting young people of their age to be part of a Youth Bible Study Group in their neighborhood. They should try to convey that the Bible—the Word of God—is the most powerful and life-giving reading of all; that reading the Bible can change lives and bring true and lasting happiness; that it can support and sustain us if we read it regularly and really try to live what it teaches. They should be as creative as possible and use phrases from the text and a variety of colors and images.

Group Project
Invite the young people to create a poster of images or a Powerpoint presentation to illustrate one issue or situation in the world that concerns them; for example, the destruction of the environment; the extent of unemployment; the problems of poverty and homelessness; the daily struggle of people just to survive, and so on.

When they have collected their images, they should try to find a passage or words from Scripture that they think addresses the situation they have chosen.

Teacher Tip: Show the documentary *Roses in December*, which is based on the life of Jean Donovan (1953–80), a lay volunteer missionary in El Salvador who was killed by death squads while ministering with the poor.

Encourage the young people to pray each day during a single week using *lectio divina*, as outlined in their theology text. Then invite them to fill in **Worksheet 5: 'Lectio Divina Diary'** (*page 134 of this resource*).

Additional Prayer Suggestion

Scripture Reflection
(*See instructions for the use of doodling in prayer in the 'Student Activity Tool Kit', page 274 of this resource.*)

Use the following Psalm verse to engage the young people in prayer:

> **The Lord is my light and my salvation, whom shall I fear?**
>
> **PSALM 27:1**

CHAPTER 6 | WORKSHEET 1

NAME:

Living God's Word

Read this story before moving on to the activity below.

There was a priest who came to a new parish. He gave his first sermon and it was great and everybody was talking about it all week. So, the next Sunday he got up and, guess what, he gave the very same sermon! And well, OK, that didn't faze anybody, that's understandable; there were people who weren't there last Sunday; so it was good that he gave the same sermon.

But on the third, fourth and fifth Sundays, he gave the very same sermon. That was a little too much, so two little elderly ladies in tennis shoes were delegated to go around the back and speak to him in the sacristy—and they were very diplomatic about it. One of them said, 'Father, that's a very good sermon.' And he said, 'Thank you very much, I'm delighted.' 'It's very good, I must say. We like it very much.' 'That's good. Thank you, thanks for telling me.' 'We were just wondering though Father. . . .' 'Yes?' 'We were just wondering if you knew that you were giving the same sermon each. . . .' 'Oh, yes, I know that.' 'Well, we were just wondering—I hope you don't mind us asking you—do you have other sermons?' 'Oh I have surely. I have a whole lot more.' 'We were asked to ask you, you know, I hope you won't be offended, but will you be going on to the other sermons some time?' 'Oh, I will, and I'm looking forward to that.' 'We want to be able to tell our friends, Father, when will you be doing that?' And he said, 'Oh, I'll be going on to the next sermon as soon as I see you doing something about the first one.'

CHAPTER 6 | WORKSHEET 1 (CONTD.)

REFLECTIVE EXERCISE

Write about a time when you heard something in the Word of God proclaimed at Mass or in the homily that made a difference in your life. If this has never happened, write about why you think this is so.

CHAPTER 6 | WORKSHEET 2

NAME:

The Bible Offers Advice for Life

There are times in our life when we might turn to the Bible for advice. Some of these occasions are listed in the left column on the chart below. Look up the Bible references provided and match each situation listed with the phrase from Scripture that you think might help a person at such a time.

The situation	A phrase from Scripture that might help
Trying to make a difficult decision	
Experiencing anxiety	
Falling in love/getting married	
Feeling your faith is being put to the test	
Thanking God	
Baptism	
When someone is ill	
When a loved one has died	

1 Corinthians 13:4–13 • Proverbs 3:5–6 • James 1:2–4 • Psalm 57:18–19
Wisdom 3:1–3 • Psalm 34:1 • Matthew 6:25–30 • Romans 6:3–5

CHAPTER 6 | WORKSHEET 3

NAME:

The Bible: Words of Wisdom

Select your favorite Bible quotations from the list below to add to your Words of Wisdom collection.

Do not boast about tomorrow,
   for you do not know what a day may bring.
                        – Proverbs 27:1

For thus says the Lord:
As a mother comforts her child,
   so I will comfort you.
                        – Isaiah 66:12,13

One who is wise among his people
   will inherit honor,
and his name will live forever.
                        – Ecclesiasticus [Sirach] 37:26

Listen to advice and accept instruction,
   that you may gain wisdom for the future.
                        – Proverbs 19:20

You shall be my people
   and I will be your God. – Jeremiah 30:22

The ways of the Lord are right,
   and the upright walk in them,
   but transgressors stumble in them.
                        – Hosea 14:9

Do not seek your own advantage, but that of the other. – 1 Corinthians 10:24

No one can serve two masters. You cannot serve both God and wealth.
                        – Matthew 6:24

Some pretend to be rich, yet have nothing;
   others pretend to be poor, yet have great wealth. – Proverbs 13:7

Blessed are the pure in heart, for they will see God. – Matthew 5:8

Bread gained by deceit is sweet,
   but afterward the mouth will be full of gravel. – Proverbs 20:17

REFLECTIVE EXERCISE
Write about how you think living according to the wisdom in one of the quotations you chose could make a difference to your life.

CHAPTER 6 | WORKSHEET 4

NAME:

Reflection on the Our Father

Read the following reflection on the Our Father, also known as the Lord's Prayer, section by section. Pause after you read each section to think for a moment about what you have just read. In the first two sections we address God the Father and place ourselves in his presence. In the last seven sections we petition God. The first three petitions 'carry us toward God'—'the sanctification of his name, the coming of the Kingdom and the fulfilment of his will'. In the last four we 'present our wants to him: they ask that our lives be nourished, healed of sin, and made victorious in the struggle of good over evil' (*Catechism of the Catholic Church*, no. 2857).

We begin the Lord's Prayer by placing ourselves in God's presence.

OUR FATHER
It was Jesus who taught his disciples the Our Father; they in turn taught it to us. We can call God 'Father' because, through our Baptism, we share in Jesus' relationship with God the Father. We are daughters and sons of God, and so we can turn to God as easily as we would turn to a good parent. We can trust in God as truly as we would in a good parent. Just as Jesus trusted God the Father, we too should trust him as 'little children' would trust their own parents. The adjective 'our' when we say the Our Father means that we believe we are God's people and that he alone is our God. Despite their many divisions, all Christians pray the Our Father.

WHO ART IN HEAVEN
God is unlike any earthly parent. God surpasses anything we could ever imagine in holiness, in love, in truth. Heaven is God's dwelling place. By 'heaven' we don't mean a space in the concrete sense. So God is not 'elsewhere'. God is with us, dwelling in our hearts.

Now we bring before God seven petitions. The first three are to do with God's own honor and glory, while the next four ask for God's mercy for ourselves.

HALLOWED BE THY NAME
We pray that God's name be acknowledged as holy and treated by all people in a holy way. God has shown his holiness to us in the many times he sought to save humanity, through Moses, Abraham and, finally, through Jesus, the incarnate Son of God. God continues to manifest his holiness to us today. We are called to be holy in our own lives.

THY KINGDOM COME
We pray that, while we wait for the final coming of Christ, the values of love, peace and justice proclaimed by Jesus Christ and passed on to us in Scripture will shape the world in which we live. In other words, we pray that our world will be a place in which people live according to the values of the Kingdom of God. While we make this petition to God, we know that the Kingdom will only come about with the help of the Holy Spirit working in and through us.

THY WILL BE DONE ON EARTH AS IT IS IN HEAVEN

God's Kingdom will come only when his will is done on earth as it is in heaven. It is both difficult and takes courage to do God's will. Jesus is our model and source of strength as we strive to do so. The Gospels reveal to us that Jesus found it difficult to do the will of his Father. In Mark's Gospel we hear Jesus during the Agony in the Garden sharing with his Father how difficult it was: 'Father, for you all things are possible; remove this cup from me.' However, this difficulty did not get in the way of Jesus following the will of his Father and fulfilling the work the Father sent him to do. So he concluded, 'Yet, not what I want, but what you want' (Mark 14:63). In the Our Father we pray that we will recognize God's will and have the courage to live in accordance with it.

GIVE US THIS DAY OUR DAILY BREAD

When we pray this petition we are expressing our trust that God who has given us life will give us all we require to live as his children, now and for ever. However, we cannot say 'Give us this day our daily bread' without showing concern for those in our world who are in need. We must live the virtue of solidarity and must share the responsibility to care for one another and for all the members of the human family. We are called to work to set up just structures in our world. We are called to share both our material and our spiritual goods with those in need.

AND FORGIVE US OUR TRESPASSES AS WE FORGIVE THOSE WHO TRESPASS AGAINST US

We trust in God's mercy and forgiveness. Jesus' whole earthly life, especially his suffering, Death and Resurrection, revealed the love and forgiveness of God. Jesus' parable of the Prodigal Son helps us understand the depth of that love. In this petition, we truly show our commitment to live the Gospel. We acknowledge that God's mercy and forgiveness can touch our hearts only to the extent that we forgive those who have hurt us. We know that there are no limits to the love and forgiveness of God. So we pray that we will have the courage to forgive our enemies and those who hurt us.

AND LEAD US NOT INTO TEMPTATION

We ask God to help us to resist temptation—everything that tries to move us to turn away from God and his love—and sin. At the beginning of his public life Jesus was tempted. He overcame the temptation by prayer and by reasserting the priority of his relationship with his Father to be the center of his life. We know that we need to pray in order to have the strength to overcome temptation in our own lives.

BUT DELIVER US FROM EVIL

We pray to be freed from all evil—past, present and future. This includes evil that others visit upon us, as well as evil that we could do to ourselves. We ask for the gift of peace.

NAME:

Lectio Divina Diary

Complete the diary below after each occasion that you have prayed using *lectio divina* this week. Beside the name of the day, write the title of the biblical passage or story (or the Bible reference) that you used. Then answer the five questions in the spaces provided.

1. What stood out for you in the passage?
2. What did you say to or ask God?
3. What did you hear God saying to you?
4. Who or what did you pray for or about?
5. What are you going to do or change in your life now?

Sunday

1.
2.
3.
4.
5.

Monday

1.
2.
3.
4.
5.

Tuesday

1.
2.
3.
4.
5.

Wednesday

1.
2.
3.
4.
5.

CHAPTER 6 | WORKSHEET 5 (CONTD.)

Thursday

1.
2.
3.
4.
5.

Friday

1.
2.
3.
4.
5.

Saturday

1.
2.
3.
4.
5.

NAME:

Review of Chapter 6

I. Fill in the blanks. Use the terms in the box to state correctly the faith of the Catholic Church. Not all of the words provided will be used.

> Acts of the Apostles · Liturgy of the Word · Plainchant
> Lectionary · Breviary · Sacred Tradition – Liturgy · liturgical
> Book of Revelation · sacramental · two · three

1. The Catholic Church teaches that every Catholic should read the Bible in the context of _____.
2. The _____ describes life in the early Church.
3. The _____ is the Church's official public worship.
4. The _____ is an integral part of the celebration of the Mass and the other Sacraments.
5. The _____ contains the Scripture readings that are proclaimed at Mass.
6. The Scripture readings are read at Sunday Mass over a _____ year cycle.
7. The Church's year of worship is called the _____ Year.
8. The Liturgy of the Hours is also known as the _____.
9. The prayers and readings that are part of the Liturgy of the Hours are gathered in a book known as the _____.
10. _____ is an example of how the Church uses music in prayer.

CHAPTER 6 | CHAPTER REVIEW (CONTD.)

II. Name and describe three examples that point to the importance of the Bible in the Liturgy and prayer life of the Church.

_____

_____

_____

_____

_____

III. The Liturgical Year celebrates the central mysteries of our faith revealed in Sacred Scripture. Name the seasons of the Liturgical Year. Choose one of the seasons and explain its meaning using a passage from the Bible.

_____

_____

_____

_____

_____

IV. How would you respond? A Protestant friend says to you, 'The Bible is far more important in my life than in your life and the life of Catholics.'

_____

_____

_____

_____

_____

V. Make a 'disciple decision'.
   1. What is the most important wisdom for life that you discovered in this chapter?

   _____
   _____
   _____
   _____
   _____
   _____
   _____
   _____

   2. Name several ways you can put that wisdom into practice. Choose one of the ways you identify and describe how you will make that wisdom part of your life right now.

   _____
   _____
   _____
   _____
   _____
   _____
   _____
   _____
   _____
   _____
   _____
   _____

CHAPTER 7

The Bible Is the Book of the Church

INTRODUCTION

One of our principal aims in the *Credo* series is to motivate the young people to read the Bible more frequently and to grow in their understanding of what the Word of God is saying to them for their own lives. The Church encourages us to read the Bible *for ourselves*, but not to do so *by ourselves*. The Bible is not a book whose meaning is immediately obvious, sometimes even to biblical scholars. We need help and guidance to understand its message. So, in this chapter we introduce the young people to the various sources of help that are available to assist us in reading the biblical texts. With such help and guidance, the Bible can help us to understand the meaning of our lives and to make meaning out of our lives from day to day.

Chapter 7 is developed under five major headings:

- **ATTEND AND REFLECT**: How can we know what the Bible means?
- **HEAR THE STORY**: The contexts in which each of the books of the Bible was written
- **EMBRACE THE VISION**: The teaching authority of the Catholic Church
- **THINK IT THROUGH**: We must approach the Bible with an open mind and heart
- **JUDGE AND ACT** (*Activities and exercises that encourage the young people to integrate what they have learned in the chapter into their daily lives*)

Theological Background for the Teacher

THE BIBLE TELLS A SINGLE STORY

We help the young people to appreciate that the Bible is not a carefully produced piece of literature by a single human author in which each book harmonizes with the previous or the next. Rather, the Bible, which is a collection of many writings, has many interlocking elements that are often in tension with one another; but all come together to form a single, wonderful story: the story of God's unconditional love for humankind since the beginning of time, a story fully revealed in Jesus Christ. 'All Sacred Scripture is but one book, and that one book is Christ, "because all divine Scripture is fulfilled in Christ" ' (*Catechism of the Catholic Church* [CCC], no. 134, quoting Hugh of St. Victor).

THE IMPORTANCE OF BIBLICAL CONTEXT

In chapter 8 we will explore the different kinds of writing in the Bible. In this chapter we introduce the young people to the importance of being aware of the context in which the sacred books were written. The authors, while they were inspired by the Holy Spirit to commit to writing what God wanted them to write, were people of their time and place. They came from very different cultures to ours, and so their worldview was very different from ours. They wrote out of an understanding that was shaped by the knowledge available at the time. They did not have the advantage, for example, of the insights and discoveries that became available through the journeys of the great explorers. Neither did they have the insights of modern science, archaeology or medicine that we take for granted today. Therefore, when we read any text from the Bible we need to take into account what the authors knew or believed about the world and how it functioned.

Biblical scholars down the centuries have sought to reconstruct the world from which this great book came so as to help us all understand it better, not alone as the Word of God to us but also as a social document and a multifaceted collection of literature. Thus, the Bible must be read in its environment, and its environment reveals a gradual evolution of insight over a thousand years, coupled with a variety of approaches and attitudes. (See CCC, no. 110.)

In this chapter we take one well-known piece of biblical text, the parable of the Good Samaritan, and we help the young people to read it in a new light—armed with a new knowledge of the political, religious, social and historical understandings of the time in which the parable was first told by Jesus. We help them to see that without this background knowledge they could never fully understand the depth of meaning within such a parable or what Jesus wanted his listeners to do as a result of hearing it.

Most importantly, we must keep in mind that the authors of the Bible were people of faith. They believed in God. They believed that God was with them, watching over them, leading them toward the promise of eternal life. They wrote in the context of a resounding belief in the presence of an ever-loving God. Their overarching aim was to lead others to believe in the same God and that he loved them too.

THE ROLE OF THE MAGISTERIUM

In this chapter we also teach the young people about the role of the Church's Magisterium as the guardian of the truth that has been handed down to the successors of the Apostles in every age.

> The teaching office of the Church, the Magisterium—that is, the pope and the bishops in communion with him—has the task of authoritatively interpreting the Word of God.
> – *United States Catholic Catechism for Adults* [USCCA], 32

As Catholics, we accept the interpretation of the Bible offered by the Magisterium. Because the meaning of the text is not always obvious, there is the possibility of misinterpretation. So, while we must read the Bible for ourselves and find there the inspiration it offers for the particular circumstances of our own daily lives, we must do so in the context of the believing community of the Church.

> 'The Church, through its magisterium, has been entrusted with the task of authoritatively interpreting what is contained in revelation, so that "all that is proposed for belief, as being divinely revealed, is drawn from one deposit of faith" (*Dei Verbum*, no. 10). In some cases, these doctrines have been explicitly defined; in others, they are universally considered to be an essential and irreformable element of the one Catholic faith.'
> – *United States Catholic Catechism for Adults*, 133, quoting from USCCB, *The Teaching Ministry of the Diocesan Bishop (1992)*

ADDITIONAL BACKGROUND READING
Catechism of the Catholic Church, nos. 85–87, 100, 109–114, 137; *United States Catholic Catechism for Adults*, 27–31; Pontifical Biblical Commission, *Interpretation of the Bible in the Church* (1993), nos. 5–19.

CHAPTER OUTCOMES

See general note on page 18 of this resource.

Learning Outcomes

As a result of studying this chapter and exploring the issues raised, the young people should be able to:

- appreciate that different people will interpret the same event differently;
- give examples of circumstances that could lead to misinterpretation of a situation or message;
- articulate the importance of context in arriving at the correct interpretation of a situation or message;
- understand the importance of knowing the context when interpreting the Bible's message for our lives;
- understand the historical, political and faith contexts of the biblical writings;
- apply this to specific passages from the Bible;
- give reasons why we need the Church to help us interpret what the Bible means for our lives;
- understand the role of Sacred Tradition and of the Magisterium in interpreting the Bible;
- identify a number of guiding principles for reading the Bible;
- write a modern version of the parable of the Good Samaritan;
- choose a passage from the Sermon on the Mount and understand and apply it to their lives.

Faith-formation Outcomes

As a result of studying this chapter and exploring the issues raised, the young people should also:

- have a greater awareness of how they interpret and at times misinterpret information and situations;
- realize that they need the help of the Church to interpret what the Bible means for their lives;
- value the role of Sacred Tradition and of the Magisterium in helping them to interpret the Bible for their lives;
- understand the meaning of the parable of the Good Samaritan for their lives;
- be more likely to see the Bible as a source for motivation and inspiration in their lives.

Teacher Reflection

I want to be remembered for having wove the Word subtly through every fabric and design, hiding it and then uncovering detail, color, thread and line. Wrapping all of earth and all its creatures in a cloth fair, delicate and fine, that held a people's hopes and bread and fragments and pieces of heart to raise the dead. I want to be remembered for having shorn the sheep and gathered wool and spun and carded and made garments against the cold. And then to have weathered all the storms and dwelled in the high mountain passes and found the deep and greenest grasses for their hungers. And stayed, keeping watch over them, singing and humming them home, with the Word. Amen.

Notes and Guidelines for Student Activities

ATTEND AND REFLECT

How can we know what the Bible means?

Learning Outcomes
That the young people would:
- appreciate that different people will interpret the same event differently;
- give examples of circumstances that could lead to misinterpretation of a situation or message;
- articulate the importance of context in arriving at the correct interpretation of a situation or message;
- understand the importance of knowing the context when interpreting the Bible's message for our lives.

Faith-formation Outcome
That the young people would also:
- have a greater awareness of how they interpret and at times misinterpret information and situations.

Overview
Chapter 7 opens by reflecting on the way in which situations and words can be misinterpreted. This is followed by a discussion of context and meaning, as a lead up to an exploration of what is necessary in order to interpret the Bible correctly.

Supplementary Activities for 'Attend and Reflect'

Photographic Project
This activity will help to demonstrate the truism, 'Your standpoint is your viewpoint'. The young people use a digital camera or their mobile phone to take pictures of a number of predetermined sites or objects in their local area. With their photographs they create a Powerpoint slide show or collage and caption it. They then take turns at presenting their images to the class (or they make presentations in small groups).

Discussion questions:
- How are the images the same or different?
- When a number of people took a picture of the same thing, what made the images different?
- How does this activity make us aware of how we should look at images in the media?

We want the young people to appreciate that it is important to know the context in which the Sacred Scriptures were written. The story in **Worksheet 1: 'Things Are Not Always As They Appear'** (*page 146 of this resource*) explores how, without knowing all the facts of a situation, a person can have a very limited view of what is really going on.

HEAR THE STORY

The contexts in which each of the books of the Bible was written

Learning Outcomes
That the young people would:
- understand the historical, political and faith contexts of the biblical writings;
- apply this to specific passages from the Bible;
- give reasons why we need the Church to help us interpret what the Bible means for our lives.

Faith-formation Outcome
That the young people would also:
- realize that they need the help of the Church to interpret what the Bible means for their lives.

Overview
Section two, 'Hear the Story', discusses the importance of understanding the historical, political and faith contexts of the biblical writings. It also explores some of the reasons why we need the guidance of the Church to help us interpret the Bible's message for our lives.

Supplementary Activity for 'Hear the Story'

Worksheet 2: 'Our World/The World of the New Testament' (*page 147 of this resource*) invites the young people to think about the different contexts in which the New Testament was written. In doing so, they will come to a better understanding of the influences that shaped the presentation and content of the New Testament.

EMBRACE THE VISION

The teaching authority of the Catholic Church

Learning Outcome
That the young people would:
- understand the role of Sacred Tradition and of the Magisterium in interpreting the Bible.

Faith-formation Outcome
That the young people would also:
- value the role of Sacred Tradition and of the Magisterium in helping them to interpret the Bible for their lives.

Overview
Section three, 'Embrace the Vision', explores the role of the teaching authority of the Church in interpreting the Bible for today. Specifically, it introduces the young people to the place of Sacred Tradition and of the Magisterium in the life of the Church. This material will most likely be new to the students.

Supplementary Activities for 'Embrace the Vision'

In **Worksheet 3: 'Who Can Help Us to Read and Understand the Bible?'** (*page 148 of this resource*) the young people revise what they have learned about the help and guidance that is available to them as they try to read and understand the meaning of the Word of God in the Bible for their lives.

Research Project
Find and read a recent statement or teaching from the Catholic bishops in the United States. What does the statement mean for your life right now?

THINK IT THROUGH

We must approach the Bible with an open mind and heart

Learning Outcomes
That the young people would:
- identify a number of guiding principles for reading the Bible;
- write a modern version of the parable of the Good Samaritan.

Faith-formation Outcome
That the young people would also:
- understand the meaning of the parable of the Good Samaritan for their lives.

Overview
Section four, 'Think It Through', provides the young people with a number of guidelines or principles to help them interpret the Bible for their lives. They are then given the opportunity in class to apply these guidelines to specific passages from the Bible.

Supplementary Activities for 'Think It Through'

Role-play
Encourage the young people to role-play a modern version of the parable of the Good Samaritan—perhaps one that they have written themselves.

Chapter 7 contains a lot of information, some of which will be new to the students. The crossword in **Worksheet 4: 'The Bible Is the Book of the Church'** (*page 149 of this resource*) should help them recall what they have studied.

Answers to the crossword:
Across: 1. Bishop; 5. Interpret; 6. Tradition; 9. Scripture; 10. Theologian; 11. Magisterium.
Down: 2. Spirit; 3. Pope; 4. Irenaeus; 7. Doctrine; 8. Oral.

JUDGE AND ACT

Learning Outcome
That the young people would:
- choose a passage from the Sermon on the Mount and understand and apply it to their lives.

Faith-formation Outcome
That the young people would also:
- be more likely to see the Bible as a source for motivation and inspiration in their lives.

Overview
In section five, 'Judge and Act', we introduce the young people to the story of St. Francis of Assisi and how he found direction and meaning for his life from the Bible.

Supplementary Activities for 'Judge and Act'

In this chapter the young people read the parable of the Good Samaritan and discuss its meaning. In **Worksheet 5: 'Understanding the Parables of Jesus'** (*page 150 of this resource*) we invite them to read the parable of the Lost Sheep and to reflect on how believing in its message could impact upon their lives.

Additional Prayer Suggestion

Scripture Reflection
(*See instructions for the use of doodling in prayer in the 'Student Activity Tool Kit', page 274 of this resource.*)

Use the following Scripture verse to engage the young people in prayer:

Blessed are the peacemakers.

MATTHEW 5:9

CHAPTER 7 | WORKSHEET 1

NAME:

Things Are Not Always As They Appear

Read the following story, where things are not quite as they appear on the surface.

A guy was pulled over by a State Trooper. 'Sir,' the trooper said, 'you are the five thousandth person to cross this traffic counter wearing a seat belt. You have just won $5,000! What are you going to do with all that money?' 'Well,' the driver said slowly, 'I don't rightly know for sure but I suppose the first thing I oughta do is buy a driver's license…'. So the lady sitting next to him said, 'Oh, don't pay any attention to him, Officer. He's always a smart aleck when he's drunk.' Then the guy in the back seat said, 'I told you we wouldn't get very far in a stolen car.' And finally a muffled little voice from the trunk yelled, 'Hey, buddy, are we over the border yet?'

TALK IT OVER
- Talk about the lessons that might be learned from this story.
- Share stories of situations in which you discovered that things were not as you had first thought they were.

CHAPTER 7 | WORKSHEET 2

NAME:

Our World/The World of the New Testament

Using the information in 'Hear the Story' on pages 117–18 of your theology text, identify some of the ways in which our world today is different from Palestine and the world at the time of Jesus.

My World Today	The world/Palestine at the time of Jesus
Historical	Historical
Political	Political
Faith	Faith

CHAPTER 7 | WORKSHEET 3

NAME:

Who Can Help Us to Read and Understand the Bible?

Using the information in sections two and three of chapter 7, 'Hear the Story' and 'Embrace the Vision', write a few lines explaining the role the following might play in guiding us as we try to read and understand the Bible.

Biblical scholars

Tradition/Church teaching

The Magisterium

Bible Study Group

The Holy Spirit

The Bible Is the Book of the Church

ACROSS
1. A successor to the Apostles.
5. Attempt to understand something for one's own life.
6. The body of teaching of the Church that has been handed down through the ages.
9. Name given to the text of the Bible, often prefixed by the word 'Sacred'.
10. An expert in Sacred Scripture/religious issues.
11. The teaching office or teaching authority of the Catholic Church.

DOWN
2. Divine and holy, Third Person of the Blessed Trinity.
3. The head of the Roman Catholic Church.
4. Church Father; first Christian theologian.
7. Another word for official teaching of the Church.
8. Passed on by word of mouth.

CHAPTER 7 | WORKSHEET 5

NAME:

Understanding the Parables of Jesus

In chapter 7 of your theology text you read the parable of the Good Samaritan and discussed its meaning for our lives today. Now read another parable that Jesus told his followers – the parable of the Lost Sheep.

> 'Which one of you, having a hundred sheep and losing one of them, does not leave the ninety-nine in the wilderness and go after the one that is lost until he finds it? When he has found it, he lays it on his shoulders and rejoices. And when he comes home, he calls together his friends and neighbours, saying to them, "Rejoice with me, for I have found my sheep that was lost." Just so, I tell you, there will be more joy in heaven over one sinner who repents than over ninety-nine righteous people who need no repentance.' (Luke 15:4–7)

REFLECT AND DISCUSS

We have all been in the position of the Lost Sheep. In all likelihood you will find yourself in this position again and again. Now write a few sentences about the difference it will make to your life if you really believe what Jesus was saying in the parable of the Lost Sheep.

_____
_____
_____
_____
_____
_____

NAME:

Review of Chapter 7

I. **Define these terms.**

1. Magisterium _____
_____
_____
_____

2. Sacred Tradition _____
_____
_____
_____

3. Apostolic Tradition _____
_____
_____
_____

4. Historical context of a biblical passage _____
_____
_____
_____

5. Faith context of a biblical passage _____
_____
_____
_____

CHAPTER 7 | CHAPTER REVIEW (CONTD.)

II. Compare and contrast. Choose either 1 or 2.
1. Write about some of the differences between the world in which we live and the world in which the Bible was written.
2. Explain the link between Sacred Scripture and Sacred Tradition.

_____

_____

_____

_____

_____

_____

III. Write a paragraph. Summarize the elements we need to examine in order to understand the meaning of a biblical text. Mention the parable of the Good Samaritan in your response.

_____

_____

_____

_____

_____

_____

IV. How would you respond? A friend who is not Catholic asks you, 'Why do Catholics believe in things that are not in the Bible?'

_____

_____

_____

_____

_____

_____

V. Make a 'disciple decision'.
1. What is the most important wisdom for life that you discovered in this chapter?

_____
_____
_____
_____
_____
_____
_____
_____

2. Name several ways you can put that wisdom into practice. Choose one of the ways you identify and describe how you will make that wisdom part of your life right now.

_____
_____
_____
_____
_____
_____
_____
_____
_____
_____
_____
_____

CHAPTER 8

Interpreting the Word of God in the Bible

INTRODUCTION

We have looked at how important it is to understand the context in which the books of the Bible were written. In this chapter we explore the different literary genres used by the writers of the Bible and how we should approach them in reading and interpreting the sacred texts.

Chapter 8 is developed under five major headings:

- **ATTEND AND REFLECT**: How does the Bible offer wisdom for life?
- **HEAR THE STORY**: Approaching the different literary genres and writing styles in the Bible
- **EMBRACE THE VISION**: The literal meaning is a basis for the broader interpretation of Scripture
- **THINK IT THROUGH**: How, then, should we read the Bible?
- **JUDGE AND ACT** (Activities and exercises that encourage the young people to integrate what they have learned in the chapter into their daily lives)

Theological Background for the Teacher

LITERARY GENRES IN THE BIBLE

The young people are well aware of literary genres from their study of English literature. This chapter introduces them to the different literary genres found in the Bible. We help them to understand that an awareness of the particular genre of any piece of biblical text is critical to understanding the meaning the inspired author wished to communicate. (See *Catechism of the Catholic Church*, nos. 109 and 110 and *United States Catholic Catechism for Adults*, 'Interpretation of Scripture', 27.)

History, hymns, wisdom sayings, poetry, parable and other forms of figurative language all have their own truth, but in order to discover what that truth is it is important not to confuse them with one another. A parable cannot be read as if it were history, or poetry understood to be scientific fact. In reading the Bible we must first of all find out if the piece we are reading is history, poetry, a collection of proverbs and so on. A classic example, and one that is referred to in the students' text, is the opening chapters of the Book of Genesis. What is on the agenda in these chapters? Are they about science? If so, they are in serious conflict with contemporary theories on the origin of the universe and the evolution of the species. Or are they largely mythological? Here again we run into problems. The mythological is often unfavorably contrasted with the historical or the scientific. Biblical scholars have analyzed the role of the Genesis Creation accounts and concluded that they are dealing with truth, but in their own way. Genesis is about issues such as the roots of evil in human choice, the equality of the sexes and the blessings of creation.

This chapter provides the young people with many opportunities to be involved with Scripture passages written in a variety of literary genres. It is hoped that this practical work will help them to be more adept at recognizing the literary genre of any particular Scripture passage or text and, therefore, enable them to understand better the meaning the sacred author intended to convey.

ADDITIONAL BACKGROUND READING

Catechism of the Catholic Church, nos. 106, 108–114, 315–320; *United States Catholic Catechism for Adults*, 27–31; Pius XII, *Divina Afflante Spiritu* (1943); Vatican II, *Constitution on Divine Revelation* [*Dei Verbum*], nos. 11–13; Pontifical Biblical Commission, *Interpretation of the Bible in the Church* (1993); Benedict XVI, Apostolic Exhortation, *Verbum Domini*, September 30, 2010, nos. 29–49; *Pastoral Statement for Catholics on Biblical Fundamentalism*, National Conference of Catholic Bishops, March 26, 1987.

CHAPTER OUTCOMES

See general note on page 18 of this resource.

Learning Outcomes
As a result of studying this chapter and exploring the issues raised, the young people should be able to:

- understand that the Bible is a source of wisdom and truth;
- appreciate that this wisdom is often couched in symbolic language;
- read and discuss examples of how metaphor and simile are used in the Bible;
- understand the function of metaphor in the Bible, in particular in relation to the 'Kingdom of God';
- recognize and name different literary genres in the Bible;
- understand and articulate the importance of recognizing literary genres when reading the Bible;
- identify the significance of some extracts from the Bible for their lives;
- differentiate between the literary and the spiritual meanings of the sacred texts;
- explain the three senses of Sacred Scripture: the *allegorical* sense; the *moral* sense; the *anagogical* sense;
- understand the concept of exegesis;
- understand the concept of fundamentalism;
- know the Catholic teaching on reading and interpreting Scripture;
- understand the symbolic meaning in the parable of the Sower.

Faith-formation Outcomes
As a result of studying this chapter and exploring the issues raised, the young people should also:

- appreciate that the Bible contains wisdom for their lives;
- grow in confidence in their ability to read the Bible;
- be aware of symbols in their lives that have a spiritual meaning;
- come to a deeper appreciation of the layers of meaning in the biblical texts;
- reflect on their lives in light of the parable of the Sower;
- be aware of prophetic voices in their lives;
- choose a biblical passage that will have special significance in their lives and consider how their lives would change if they were to live in accordance with its message.

Teacher Reflection

In all spiritual wisdom and understanding, God,
Fill me with knowledge of your will,
That I may lead a life worthy of you.
Keep me from envy and selfish ambition.
Grace me with gentleness born of wisdom.
May my faith never rest on human wisdom
But on the power of your spirit,
The spirit of Jesus Christ.

Notes and Guidelines for Student Activities

ATTEND AND REFLECT

How does the Bible offer wisdom for life?

Learning Outcomes
That the young people would:
- understand that the Bible is a source of wisdom and truth;
- appreciate that this wisdom is often couched in symbolic language.

Faith-formation Outcome
That the young people would also:
- appreciate that the Bible contains wisdom for their lives.

Overview
Chapter 8 opens with a biblical story and questions based on the concept of wisdom. It explores how the symbolic meaning of words must be understood in order to appreciate the wisdom they contain. This leads to a discussion of how the biblical authors used stories and symbolic language to convey great spiritual wisdom.

Supplementary Activity for 'Attend and Reflect'

Worksheet 1: 'Words of Wisdom' (*page 159 of this resource*) invites the young people to reflect on a wise saying from the Book of Proverbs and then to compose their own wisdom statement in a similar fashion.

HEAR THE STORY

Approaching the different literary genres and writing styles in the Bible

Learning Outcomes
That the young people would:
- read and discuss examples of how metaphor and simile are used in the Bible;
- understand the function of metaphor in the Bible, in particular in relation to the 'Kingdom of God';
- recognize and name different literary genres in the Bible;
- understand and articulate the importance of recognizing literary genres when reading the Bible;
- identify the significance of some extracts from the Bible for their lives.

Faith-formation Outcomes
That the young people would also:
- grow in confidence in their ability to read the Bible;
- be aware of symbols in their lives that have a spiritual meaning.

Overview
Section two, 'Hear the Story', presents the young people with a number of Scripture passages written in different literary genres. It helps them to recognize the literary genres involved and leads them to reflect on how that knowledge is essential for correct interpretation of a particular passage.

Supplementary Activities for 'Hear the Story'

The exercises in **Worksheet 2: 'Writing Styles and Literary Genres (1)'** (*page 160 of this resource*) will help the young people become more familiar with some of the information on writing styles and literary genres that they have encountered so far in this chapter.

Worksheet 3: 'Writing Styles and Literary Genres (2)' (*page 162 of this resource*) offers the young people a practical exercise to test how well they can identify literary genres in the Bible.

EMBRACE THE VISION
The literal meaning is a basis for the broader interpretation of Scripture

Learning Outcomes

That the young people would:
- differentiate between the literary and the spiritual meanings of the sacred texts;
- explain the three senses of Sacred Scripture: the *allegorical* sense; the *moral* sense; the *anagogical* sense;
- understand the concept of exegesis.

Faith-formation Outcome

That the young people would also:
- come to a deeper appreciation of the layers of meaning in the biblical texts.

Overview

Section three, 'Embrace the Vision', explores the fact that there are layers of meaning in Sacred Scripture. It goes on to examine the unity between the Old and the New Testaments and introduces the young people to the three spiritual senses of Sacred Scripture.

Supplementary Activity for 'Embrace the Vision'

In section three we introduce the young people to the term 'exegesis' and to the different 'spiritual senses' at work in the Bible. **Worksheet 4: 'Layers of Meaning in the Bible'** (*page 163 of this resource*) offers them an opportunity to explain these terms in their own words and so ensure that they have understood them correctly.

THINK IT THROUGH
How, then, should we read the Bible?

Learning Outcomes

That the young people would:
- understand the concept of fundamentalism;
- know the Catholic teaching on reading and interpreting Scripture.

Faith-formation Outcome

That the young people would also:
- come to a fuller understanding of how Catholics should approach reading the Bible.

Overview

Section four, 'Think It Through', explains why Catholics avoid fundamentalism in their interpretation of Sacred Scripture.

Supplementary Activities for 'Think It Through'

In section four the young people learn that some interpretations of the Bible are not in line with the teaching of the Church. **Worksheet 5: 'Interpreting the Word of God'** (*page 165 of this resource*) serves to consolidate this learning.

Teacher Tip for the 'Class Project' on page 143 of the students' text: The Church has a very specific teaching on how the theory of evolution can be explained as not in contradiction to the biblical accounts. The following are suggestions for research in this area:

- Under John Paul II's papacy, 'Communion and Stewardship: Human Persons Created in the Image of God' (International Theological Commission). See especially paragraphs 62, 64, 67 and 70.
- Pope Pius XII, *Humani Generis*.
- Pope John Paul II, 'Message to the Pontifical Academy of Sciences: On Evolution', delivered October 22, 1996.
- Under Benedict XVI's papacy, Vatican-sponsored Conference on Evolution.

Further suggestions for Group Activity/Discussion:
Galileo (1564–1642), Italian philosopher, physicist and inventor, was ordered to Rome to stand trial on suspicion of heresy in 1633, 'for holding as true the false doctrine taught by some that the sun is the center of the world'.

Encourage the young people to research 'Galileo's trial' and use the information gathered to prepare their own script for such a trial. (If you decide to have the students re-enact the trial in class, you could use the 'In the Spotlight' technique as outlined in the 'Student Activity Tool Kit' on page 273 of this resource.)

Or

The Catholic Church makes clear that there is no conflict between the truths of faith and the discoveries of science. Why do you think the Church takes this position? Do you agree? Why or why not?

Teacher Tip: If time permits, allow the young people to watch the movie *Inherit the Wind* starring Spencer Tracey for a lively presentation of the Scopes Trial.

JUDGE AND ACT

Learning Outcome
That the young people would:
- understand the symbolic meaning in the parable of the Sower.

Faith-formation Outcomes
That the young people would also:
- reflect on their lives in light of the parable of the Sower;
- be aware of prophetic voices in their lives;
- choose a biblical passage that will have special significance in their lives and consider how their lives would change if they were to live in accordance with its message.

Overview
In section five, 'Judge and Act', we introduce the young people to the literal and symbolic meanings of the parable of the Sower and we encourage them to work out the significance of this parable for their lives.

In this final section of the chapter the young people hear the story of Oscar Romero, the Archbishop of San Salvador who was killed for his defense of the poor. We hope that this story will challenge them to recognize the prophetic voices in their own lives.

Supplementary Activities for 'Judge and Act'

Worksheet 6: 'The Romero Prayer' (*page 167 of this resource*) offers the young people an opportunity to reflect on Romero's legacy.

Teacher Tip: Show a clip from the movie *Romero* (directed by John Duigan, 1989).

Directives for the Prayer Reflection at the end of the chapter
Divide the class into small groups (of no more than eight); elect a Reader and a Leader in each group.

After the reading of the extracts from Psalm 145, make sure that everyone who wishes to give a response has a chance to do so.

Additional Prayer Suggestion

Scripture Reflection
(*See instructions for the use of doodling in prayer in the 'Student Activity Tool Kit', page 274 of this resource.*)

Remind the young people of the words of Jesus, quoted in this chapter: 'You are the light of the world' (Matthew 5:14). Invite them to use this statement of Jesus as the basis for a prayer:

I am the light of the world.

JOHN 8:1

CHAPTER 8 | WORKSHEET 1

NAME:

Words of Wisdom

Read this wisdom saying from the Book of Proverbs:

At the end of your life you will groan . . .
and you say, 'Oh, how I hated discipline,
 and my heart despised reproof!
I did not listen to the voice of my teachers
 or incline my ear to my instructors.
Now I am at the point of utter ruin
 in the public assembly.'

– Proverbs 5:11–14

Consider for a moment what the writer of this piece wanted the readers to think about.

Now compose your own statement of wisdom focusing on the relationships between teachers and students.

_____
_____
_____
_____
_____
_____
_____
_____

NAME:

Writing Styles and Literary Genres (1)

Using the information in chapter 8 of your theology text, write a definition of the following words and give one example of each from the Bible.

A simile is

_____

_____

_____

Example from the Bible:

_____

_____

_____

_____

A metaphor is

_____

_____

_____

Example from the Bible:

_____

_____

_____

_____

CHAPTER 8 | WORKSHEET 2 (CONTD.)

Literary Genres

Match each literary genre named in the left column with the description in the right column that fits best.

History books	likely to be written in an ornate style, with the emphasis as much on language as on the storyline.
A short story is	read as an account of the faith experiences of some of the disciples of Jesus.
The Song of Songs is	circular letters to the first Christian communities.
The Gospels are	tend to be written in a direct, factual and concise manner.
The Epistles are	a love poem.

CHAPTER 8 | WORKSHEET 3

NAME:

Writing Styles and Literary Genres (2)

Fill in the grid with examples of the different literary genres in the Bible.

Type of writing	Bible references	Type of writing	Bible references
Stories		Letters	
Prayers		Historical accounts	
Hymns		Proverbs	
Parables		Prophetical texts	
Poetry		Myths	

CHAPTER 8 | WORKSHEET 4

NAME:

Layers of Meaning in the Bible

In your own words, write definitions of the following terms, giving examples where appropriate.

Exegesis:
_____
_____

The literal sense:
_____
_____

The allegorical sense:
_____
_____

The moral sense:
_____
_____

The anagogical sense:
_____
_____

CHAPTER 8 | WORKSHEET 4 (CONTD.)

Now read the parable of the Sower in Luke 8:5–15. In its literal sense, this could be understood as a story describing farming practices at the time of Jesus. However, biblical scholars have helped us to see deeper meanings in this parable. On the lines below, identify what you think is the deeper allegorical, spiritual and eternal meaning of this parable.

Allegorical meaning:

_____
_____
_____
_____

Spiritual/Moral meaning:

_____
_____
_____
_____

Eternal/Anagogical meaning:

_____
_____
_____
_____

CHAPTER 8 | WORKSHEET 5

NAME:

Interpreting the Word of God

Explain the following terms, giving examples, and discuss the effect of each on one's interpretation of Scripture.

Symbolic reading:

_____

_____

_____

_____

Example:

_____

_____

_____

_____

How this affects one's interpretation of Scripture:

_____

_____

_____

_____

_____

_____

Literalist/Fundamentalist reading:

_____
_____
_____
_____

Examples:

_____
_____
_____
_____

How this affects one's interpretation of Scripture:

_____
_____
_____
_____

Explain, in your own words, the Church's teaching on how Catholics should read the Bible.

_____
_____
_____
_____
_____
_____
_____
_____

NAME:

The Romero Prayer

This prayer was composed by Bishop Kenneth Untener, Bishop of Saginaw, Michigan, in November of 1979. On March 24, 2004, the anniversary of the martyrdom of Bishop Romero, Bishop Untener included in a reflection a passage entitled 'The mystery of the Romero Prayer'. The mystery is that he attributed these words to Oscar Romero, though they were never spoken by him. Bishop Untener died a few days later, on March 27, 2004.

It helps, now and then, to step back and take a long view.

The kingdom is not only beyond our efforts,
it is even beyond our vision.

We accomplish in our lifetime only a tiny fraction
of the magnificent enterprise that is God's work.
Nothing we do is complete, which is a way of saying
that the kingdom always lies beyond us.
No statement says all that could be said.
No prayer fully expresses our faith.
No confession brings perfection.
No pastoral visit brings wholeness.
No program accomplishes the church's mission.
No set of goals and objectives includes everything.

This is what we are about.
We plant the seeds that one day will grow.
We water seeds already planted,
knowing that they hold future promise.

We lay foundations that will need further development.
We provide yeast that produces far beyond our capabilities.

We cannot do everything, and there is a sense of liberation
in realizing that. This enables us to do something,
and to do it very well. It may be incomplete,
but it is a beginning, a step along the way,
an opportunity for the Lord's grace to enter and do the rest.

We may never see the end results, but that is the difference
between the master builder and the worker.

We are workers, not master builders; ministers, not messiahs.
We are prophets of a future not our own.
Amen.

CHAPTER 8 | WORKSHEET 6 (CONTD.)

REFLECT AND DISCUSS
- Think for a few moments about some of the messages in this prayer and how they apply to you in your own life.
- Discuss what you find most meaningful in this prayer.
- On the basis of what you have learned about the life of Oscar Romero, discuss why you think this prayer was attributed to him.

Inspirational quotations to add to your **WORDS OF WISDOM** collection:

'Aspire not to have more but to be more.'

OSCAR ROMERO

'We plant the seeds that one day will grow.'

BISHOP KEN UNTENER

Review of Chapter 8

I. True or false. Mark the true statements 'T' and the false statements 'F'. Cross out the words that make the false statements false. Write the words that make the false statements true under each false statement.

_____ 1. The biblical authors used a wide variety of styles of writing.

_____ 2. The written Word of God has only one layer of meaning—the literal sense or meaning of the words.

_____ 3. The use of literary genre distorts the meaning of Revelation.

_____ 4. A proverb is an example of a literary genre.

_____ 5. A metaphor compares one thing to another.

_____ 6. Exegesis is a form of storytelling.

_____ 7. The writings of the New Testament can only be fully understood in light of their connection to the writings of the Old Testament.

_____ 8. A fundamentalist interpretation of the Bible focuses solely on the historical context in which the sacred authors wrote.

_____ 9. We can only fully understand the meaning of the Bible with the help of the Magisterium.

_____ 10. The Church is the source and foundation of the unity of God's plan and of Sacred Scripture.

CHAPTER 8 | CHAPTER REVIEW (CONTD.)

II. Name and describe the three spiritual senses at work in the Bible.

_____

_____

_____

_____

_____

_____

_____

_____

III. Write a paragraph. Explain this statement with reference to the different literary genres used by the authors of Sacred Scripture: 'The fact is that truth is presented and expressed in various types of writing . . . and forms of literary expression.'

_____

_____

_____

_____

_____

_____

_____

_____

IV. How would you respond? An eighth grader says to you, 'My dad is not a Catholic. He is a Christian and he says that the words in the Bible mean exactly what they say.' Illustrate your answer with an example from everyday life.

_____

_____

_____

_____

_____

_____

_____

_____

_____

_____

V. Make a 'disciple decision'.
   1. What is the most important wisdom for life that you discovered in this chapter?

_____

_____

_____

_____

_____

_____

_____

_____

_____

2. Name several ways you can put that wisdom into practice. Choose one of the ways you identify and describe how you will make that wisdom part of your life right now.

CHAPTER 9

The Old and New Testaments
God's Faithfulness over Time

INTRODUCTION

Chapter 9 explores the unity between the Old Testament and the New Testament. In order to understand the writings in the New Testament we need to have some understanding of the Old Testament. The New Testament fulfills what was begun in the Old Testament. 'The unity of the two Testaments proceeds from the unity of God's plan and his Revelation. The Old Testament prepares for the New and the New Testament fulfills the Old; the two shed light on each other; both are true Word of God' (*Catechism of the Catholic Church* [CCC], no. 140).

Chapter 9 is developed under five major headings:

- **ATTEND AND REFLECT**: Why be trustworthy and faithful?
- **HEAR THE STORY**: The story of the Old and New Testaments
- **EMBRACE THE VISION**: The Old Testament Covenant was fulfilled in Jesus
- **THINK IT THROUGH**: How the Old Testament promises came to be fulfilled
- **JUDGE AND ACT** (*Activities and exercises that encourage the young people to integrate what they have learned in the chapter into their daily lives*)

Theological Background for the Teacher

A brick does not make a house and neither does an individual text make the Word of God. Each text of the Bible must be read with an awareness of the context from which it emerged. Also, no one biblical text or passage can be seen and interpreted in isolation from the rest of the Bible. As we read the Bible, we will become aware of how the inspired authors' insight and understanding of what they were trying to communicate grew over time. (See CCC, no. 110.) This development did not proceed smoothly. Cul-de-sacs were explored and rejected and wrong emphases corrected. For example, the command to wipe out one's enemies and their families in Deuteronomy 7:2; 20:16–17, in Joshua 6:17–18 and in 1 Samuel 15:3 must be read against Jesus' words about loving one's enemies.

The Bible is the Revelation of God's faithfulness through time. The Old Testament is the backdrop against which the Word of God can be seen in the light of all the searching, hopes and losses of the Israelite people. The books of the New Testament continue and fulfill the Old Testament's Revelation of God's saving work in the world. At the center of all Sacred Scripture is the living Word of God, Jesus Christ. (See CCC, no. 134.) He is the promised and hoped-for Messiah, the Savior. Jesus Christ is the 'Word made flesh', the incarnate Son of God, fully human and fully divine. He is the New Covenant for all people, not just the Jewish people. In Jesus lies the forgiveness of sins and a new life for everyone.

The *Catechism of the Catholic Church* states:

> The Church, as early as apostolic times, and then constantly in her Tradition, has illuminated the unity of the divine plan in the two Testaments through typology, which discerns in God's works of the Old Covenant prefigurations of what he accomplished in the fullness of time in the person of his incarnate Son.
>
> Christians therefore read the Old Testament in the light of Christ crucified and risen. Such typological reading discloses the inexhaustible content of the Old Testament; but it must not make us forget that the Old Testament retains its own intrinsic value as Revelation reaffirmed

by the Lord himself. Besides, the New Testament has to be read in the light of the Old. Early Christian catechesis made constant use of the Old Testament. As an old saying put it, the New Testament lies hidden in the Old and the Old Testament is unveiled in the New.

— CCC, nos. 128, 129

Jesus knew the Jewish Scriptures (see Mark 14:49 and Luke 24:25–27), read them and proclaimed them in the synagogue (see Luke 4:16–20.) The people to whom he spoke were also familiar with the Scriptures. They were looking forward to the coming of the Messiah. And from the writings of the prophets they gradually recognized Jesus as the Promised One.

ADDITIONAL BACKGROUND READING
Catechism of the Catholic Church, nos. 124–125, 128–130, 140; Vatican II, *Constitution on Divine Revelation* [*Dei Verbum*], nos. 14–20; 'Aspects of Old Testament Thought' by John L. McKenzie in *The New Jerome Biblical Commentary*, copyright © 1990, 1968 (Prentice Hall: Englewood Cliffs, New Jersey), 77:3–98.

CHAPTER OUTCOMES

See general note on page 18 of this resource.

Learning Outcomes
As a result of studying this chapter and exploring the issues raised, the young people should be able to:

- understand the concept of faithfulness;
- through reading and reflecting upon the story of Abraham, come to a deeper understanding of God's faithfulness and how it is revealed in the books of the Old Testament;
- understand the concepts of hope and covenant;
- understand the significance of the Exodus and the Passover in the history of the Israelite people;
- understand that the New Testament is the faith account of Jesus Christ, who brought new hope to God's people;
- begin to have a clearer understanding of the stages in the development of the four accounts of the Gospel;
- articulate how the coming of Jesus in the New Testament was the fulfillment of God's promise in the Old Testament;
- understand that the disciples gradually became aware of and after the Resurrection were convinced that Jesus was the promised Messiah;
- give examples of how the promises of the Old Testament were fulfilled in the New Testament;
- understand the consequences of being a faithful follower of Jesus.

Faith-formation Outcomes
As a result of studying this chapter and exploring the issues raised, the young people should also:

- reflect on their experience of faithfulness and of being faithful;
- be more aware of God's faithfulness in their lives;
- articulate how Jesus is a source of hope for them in their lives;
- as they learn more about who Jesus is, allow that knowledge to enhance their personal relationship with Jesus;
- be aware of the implications of God's promises in Scripture for the world today;
- reflect on how God's promises have been fulfilled in their lives;
- appreciate the significance of their Baptismal Promises and Profession of Faith;
- renew their Baptismal Promises and Profession of Faith.

Teacher Reflection

God hath spoken by his prophets,
Spoken his unchanging word,
Each from age to age proclaiming
God the One, the righteous Lord:
Mid the world's despair and turmoil
One firm anchor holdeth fast;
God is King, his throne eternal,
God the first and God the last.

God hath spoken by Christ Jesus,
Christ, the everlasting Son,
Brightness of the Father's glory
With the Father ever one;
Spoken by the Word incarnate,
God of God, ere time began,
Light of Light, to earth descending,
Man, revealing God to man.

Notes and Guidelines for Student Activities

Note: *For the Prayer Reflection at the end of the chapter the young people will be invited to renew their baptismal promises. You might encourage them to collect some pictures and articles about water which can be displayed in the room before the prayer.*

ATTEND AND REFLECT

Why be trustworthy and faithful?

Learning Outcome

That the young people would:
- understand the concept of faithfulness.

Faith-formation Outcomes

That the young people would also:
- reflect on their experience of faithfulness and of being faithful;
- be more aware of God's faithfulness in their lives.

Overview

We begin chapter 9 by helping the young people to become aware of the importance of trust in our lives. We explore the implications of making, keeping or breaking promises. We then look at God's promise to Abraham and at the fact that God's promise demanded a response from Abraham.

Supplementary Activity for 'Attend and Reflect'

Teacher Tip: You might begin this chapter with a Trust Walk. This will involve bringing the young people outside or into a large area within the school. They divide up into pairs, and one person is blindfolded while the other leads them around. The blindfolded person must trust that the 'sighted' person will lead them safely and help them avoid any obstacles. After a while they swap roles. At the end of the exercise they talk about how they felt in each role.

HEAR THE STORY

The story of the Old and New Testaments

Learning Outcomes

That the young people would:
- through reading and reflecting upon the story of Abraham, come to a deeper understanding of God's faithfulness and how it is revealed in the books of the Old Testament;
- understand the concepts of hope and covenant;
- understand the significance of the Exodus and Passover in the history of the Israelite people;
- understand that the New Testament is the faith account of Jesus Christ, who brought new hope to God's people;
- begin to have a clearer understanding of the stages in the development of the four accounts of the Gospel.

Faith-formation Outcome

That the young people would also:
- articulate how Jesus is a source of hope for them in their lives.

Overview

Section two, 'Hear the Story', traces the story of Abraham and Moses, culminating in the Covenant on Mount Sinai. It then looks at how the people were frequently unfaithful to the Covenant. Yet God always kept his promise to be with them and he sent the prophets to remind them of their side of the Covenant. Finally God promised to send the Messiah, who would establish a New Covenant. This promise was fulfilled in Jesus Christ, the Son of God.

Supplementary Activities for 'Hear the Story'

The Bible is the story of God's relationship with his people throughout the ages. **Worksheet 1: 'God's Relationship with Humankind'** (*page 179 of this resource*) will help the young people to reflect further on the story of God's relationship with Abraham.

They will then give their personal responses to God's relationship with them.

In section two the young people learn about the Exodus of Moses and the Israelites from Egypt to the Promised Land. This event is still remembered and celebrated by Jewish people today at the festival of Passover (*Pesach*), also known as the Festival of Unleavened Bread, which takes place on the fifteenth day of the Jewish month of Nisan. The high point is the Seder meal eaten in the home on the first evening of the festival. During this ritual meal, special foods are eaten, cups of wine are drunk, songs are sung and the great story of freedom is shared once again. **Worksheet 2: 'A Class Seder Meal'** (*page 181 of this resource*) provides instructions for a class re-enactment of a Seder meal. The experience of taking part in a Seder meal will help the young people develop a greater understanding of the significance of the Exodus for the ancient Israelites as well as for Jewish people today. This activity will also be useful to reflect back on when they are studying the Last Supper and the Eucharist.

Worksheet 3: 'People of the Old Testament' (*page 184 of this resource*) invites the young people to work in groups to produce a storyboard telling the life story of a person from the Old Testament. Each group is asked to read specific biblical passages about their chosen person and produce their story in words or pictures. When the storyboards are complete, a representative from each group presents the group's work to the class and the storyboards are mounted on a wall of the classroom.

Worksheet 4: 'The Faith Story behind the New Testament' (*page 186 of this resource*) provides a timeline for the students to fill in when reading 'The faith story behind the New Testament—New hope for God's people' on pages 157–8 of their theology text.

EMBRACE THE VISION
The Old Testament Covenant was fulfilled in Jesus

Learning Outcomes
That the young people would:
- articulate how the coming of Jesus in the New Testament was the fulfillment of God's promise in the Old Testament;
- understand that the disciples gradually became aware of and after the Resurrection were convinced that Jesus was the promised Messiah.

Faith-formation Outcome
That the young people would also:
- as they learn more about who Jesus really is, allow that knowledge to enhance their personal relationship with Jesus.

Overview
Section three, 'Embrace the Vision', explores how the followers of Jesus gradually came to the realization that he was the promised Messiah. At first they wondered if he was one of the prophets, but after the Resurrection they finally came to believe that he was in fact the Messiah and the Son of God. We introduce the story of the two disciples on the road to Emmaus. 'Then beginning with Moses and all the prophets, he interpreted to them the things about himself in all the scriptures' (Luke 24:27). We will examine this story in greater detail in Book 2 of the *Credo* series, *Son of God and Son of Mary*.

Supplementary Activity for 'Embrace the Vision'

The Old Testament points toward the New Testament. The New Testament is the fulfillment of what was promised in the Old Testament. Most importantly, Jesus is the promised Messiah of the Old Testament. The exercise in **Worksheet 5: 'From Promise to Fulfillment'** (*page 187 of this resource*) reinforces and reaffirms this truth for the young people.

THINK IT THROUGH
How the Old Testament promises came to be fulfilled

Learning Outcome
That the young people would:
- give examples of how the promises of the Old Testament were fulfilled in the New Testament.

Faith-formation Outcome
That the young people would also:
- be aware of the implications of God's promises in Scripture for the world today.

Overview
In section four, 'Think It Through', we give examples of incidents in the Old Testament that influenced the people's expectations of a Messiah and we discuss how these expectations were fulfilled in Jesus.

Supplementary Activity for 'Think It Through'

In this section we quote from the famous passage in Isaiah that inspired the tradition of the Jesse tree (Isaiah 11:1–2). **Worksheet 6: 'The Jesse Tree'** (*page 188 of this resource*) provides some background and instructions for creating a Jesse tree in class. The young people will need some art materials for this activity. This is a wonderful opportunity to review the incidents in the Old Testament that lead to the anticipation of a Messiah and to make the connection to Jesus and the New Testament.

JUDGE AND ACT

Learning Outcome
That the young people would:
- understand the consequences of being a faithful follower of Jesus.

Faith-formation Outcomes
That the young people would also:
- reflect on how God's promises have been fulfilled in their lives;
- appreciate the significance of their Baptismal Promises and Profession of Faith;
- renew their Baptismal Promises and Profession of Faith.

Overview
In section five, 'Judge and Act', we invite the young people to reflect again on the implications for their own lives of the fact that God is trustworthy and always keeps his promises. We explore the implications for us, as followers of Jesus, of pledging to keep our side of the Covenant. In the story of St. Stephen the young people will see that, ultimately, such commitment can lead to martyrdom. Finally, we remind the young people of when they made their first commitment to be a follower of Jesus, at their Baptism, and we invite them to renew their baptismal promises.

Supplementary Activities for 'Judge and Act'

In section five the young people learn about St. Stephen, the first Christian martyr. **Worksheet 7: 'A Modern-Day Martyr'** (*page 190 of this resource*) tells the story of Sister Dorothy Stang, a martyr from this millennium, who was assassinated on February 12, 2005 in the Brazilian Amazon rainforest. This story and the follow-up discussion will help raise the students' awareness of people still being martyred for living their Christian faith.

Teacher Tip: You might like to show the class the documentary entitled *They Killed Sister Dorothy*, which was released by the American film-maker Daniel Junge in 2008 and is narrated by Martin Sheen.

Research Project
Encourage the young people to find out about places in our world today where people are still being martyred for giving faithful witness to their faith in Jesus Christ.

Afterward discuss:
- Why are they being killed?
- Why would they rather die than deny their faith in Jesus Christ?
- What can you learn from them?

Directives for the Prayer Reflection at the end of the chapter
You will need some small bowls containing holy water that may be passed around the room at the appropriate time during the ritual. If the young people have brought in pictures and articles about water (as suggested on page 176 of this resource), you might invite them to display these in the room in advance of the Prayer Reflection.

Before the ritual begins, place the bowls containing the holy water on a table in the center of the room.

CHAPTER 9 | WORKSHEET 1

NAME:

God's Relationship with Humankind

Complete the fact-file on Abraham and then answer the questions that follow.

Name	Abraham
Lived in:	
Married to:	
Uncle to:	
Best known for	
Known as:	

CHAPTER 9 | WORKSHEET 1 (CONTD.)

What personal qualities do you think Abraham displayed in the way he responded to God?

_____

_____

_____

_____

_____

_____

List some of the ways in which you respond to God in your life.

_____

_____

_____

_____

_____

_____

_____

Name some of the personal qualities that such a response to God requires of you.

_____

_____

_____

_____

_____

_____

NAME:

A Class Seder Meal

The Seder meal
At the festival of Passover *(Pesach)*, also known as the Festival of Unleavened Bread, which takes place on the fifteenth day of the Jewish month of Nisan, Jewish people today remember and celebrate the Exodus of Moses and the Israelites from Egypt to the Promised Land. The high point of the festival is the Seder meal eaten in the home.

In preparation for the Seder meal, the table is set with the best available table cloth, tableware, candles and flowers. At the place where the leader of the ceremony—the father of the family, for example—is to be seated, the most important Passover symbols are placed on an elaborately decorated plate. These include three pieces of **unleavened bread,** or matzo. (On every Jewish Sabbath, two loaves are placed on the table; the third piece that is added at Passover points to the special importance of this feast.) **Bitter herbs,** usually horseradish, are also used, a reminder of the bitterness of slavery in Egypt. A **vegetable,** such as parsley or lettuce, is dipped in salt water in the course of the meal. **Fruit purée,** called *charoseth* or *haroseth,* made from apples, walnuts, cinnamon and moistened with red wine, serves as a reminder of the mortar with which the Israelite slaves made bricks for their Egyptian masters. **Wine,** a symbol of joy, is drunk four times during the meal. **Salt water,** a reminder of the tears that the Israelites shed in Egypt, is placed in little bowls or saucers and the parsley or lettuce is dipped into it in the course of the meal. A **bone** on the leader's plate is a reminder of the Paschal lamb that was offered in the temple. A **hardboiled egg** is added as a sign of mourning for the destruction of the temple, since in Jewish communities eggs were traditionally eaten by mourners. The **Cup of Elijah,** a specially decorated goblet or glass, is set for the prophet Elijah, who is expected to return at Passover to announce the coming of the Messiah.

Simplified version of a Seder meal:

Requirements:
Jugs of fruit-juice
Unleavened bread (matzo)
Bitter herbs
Dishes of apple or horseradish sauce
Sandwiches, pastries, cheese dip . . . meal-fill
Small cups: egg cups or paper cups for all
Wash-bowl and towel(s)

Leader: Blessed are you, Lord our God, King of the Universe, creator of the fruit of the vine. (*A drink is poured for everyone, and taken.*)

All: Blessed are you, Lord our God, King of the Universe. You have preserved us and sustained us to this hour. (*A second drink is poured.*)

Youngest: Why is this night different from all other nights?

CHAPTER 9 | WORKSHEET 2 (CONTD.)

Leader: We were slaves in Egypt, and the Lord, our God, brought us forth from there with a mighty hand.

Student 1: For he brought us forth from Egypt.
Student 2: Sent judgment on the Egyptians and their gods.
Student 3: Slew their first born, divided the sea for us.
Student 4: Plunged our oppressors in the waters.
Student 5: Supplied us with food for forty years in the wilderness.
Student 6: And brought us safely home to the land of Israel.

Youngest: We are eating unleavened bread. Why is this so?

Leader: Because we left in haste.

Youngest: We are heating bitter herbs. Why is this so?

Leader: Because the Egyptians made bitter the lives of our foreparents. In each generation, everyone ought to experience the bitterness of those days.
(All raise the second cup.)

Leader: Therefore it is our duty:

Student 7: To give thanks and to bless.
Student 8: To glorify and to praise.
Student 9: To adore him who performed all these miracles.

Leader: He brought us:

Student 10: From slavery to freedom.
Student 11: From sadness to joy.
Student 12: From darkness to light.

Leader: Let us sing to him a new song, Alleluia.

Solo recitation of Psalm 113, verses 1–3:

> Praise, O servants of the Lord;
>   Praise the name of the Lord.
> Blessed be the name of the Lord
>   from this time on and forevermore.
> From the rising of the sun to its setting
>   the name of the Lord is to be praised.
> *(All drink the second cup, and then all wash hands before taking bread. Each one takes a piece and raises it.)*

Leader: Blessed are you, O Eternal, our God,
Who brings forth bread from the earth.
(All eat a little bread and then dip the remainder in the dish of sauce before eating it. A third drink is poured.)

The meal takes place now.

Leader: Let us say grace.

All: May the name of the Eternal be praised now and forever more.

Student 13: You nourish the whole world through your goodness.
Student 14: By your grace and loving kindness you give food to every creature.
Student 15: May we never be in want of food.
Student 16: Bless this house and all that are here present and all that belongs to them.
Student 17: May we be worthy of seeing the days of the Messiah and the life of the world to come.
Student 18: And may the Lord grant peace to all Israel.

All: Amen.
(All drink the third cup. The forth and final drink is then poured.)

Leader: Let us give thanks to the Lord.

Solo recitation based on Psalm 136, with group response: 'His love is everlasting.'

O give thanks to the LORD, for he is good. *(Response)*
O give thanks to the God of gods. *(Response)*
O give thanks to the Lord of lords. *(Response)*
He alone does great wonders. *(Response)*
His wisdom made the heavens. *(Response)*
He brought Israel out of Egypt. *(Response)*
He split the Sea of Reeds. *(Response)*
He led his people through the wilderness. *(Response)*
He gave us new lands to live in. *(Response)*
He provides for all living creatures. *(Response)*
Give thanks to the God of heaven. *(Response)*
(All drink the fourth cup.)

Leader: Praised by thou, O Eternal our God,
Ruler of the Universe,
for the vine and the fruit of the vine,
and for the produce of our land,
and let thy compassion pour out on thy people.

All: Amen.

CHAPTER 9 | WORKSHEET 3

NAME:

People of the Old Testament

Work in groups, each group choosing one person from the list below. Look up the corresponding biblical reference from the Old Testament and read about the person you have chosen. Then create a storyboard, telling their life story in words or pictures. A blank storyboard template is provided to help you plan your work. When you are happy with it, copy it on to poster pages. Finally, choose a representative from your group to introduce and briefly explain your presentation. Present the storyboards in the order given below and, as each story is told, hang them on a wall of the classroom.

PERSON FROM THE OLD TESTAMENT	SCRIPTURE REFERENCE
Abraham	Genesis 12:1–20 and 15:1–6
Sarah	Genesis 21:1–7
Isaac	Genesis 22:1–18
Rebekah	Genesis 24:10–20
Jacob	Genesis 28:1–22
Joseph	Genesis 37:1–36
Miriam	Exodus 2:3–10 and 15:20–21
Moses	Exodus 3:1–12
Joshua	Joshua 1:1–9
Ruth	Ruth 1:1–22 and 4:9–22
David	1 Samuel 16:17–23
Solomon	2 Chronicles 7:11–22
Esther	Esther 7 and 8
Isaiah	Isaiah 35:1–10
Jeremiah	Jeremiah 1:1–10
Ezekiel	Ezekiel 11:14–25

REFLECT AND DISCUSS
- What differences and similarities do you notice between the various stories?
- What common themes emerge?

CHAPTER 9 | WORKSHEET 3 (CONTD.)

People of the Old Testament

Storyboard Template

The story of _____

The story begins

The story ends

CHAPTER 9 | WORKSHEET 4

NAME:

The Faith Story behind the New Testament

Read 'The faith story behind the New Testament—New hope for God's people' on pages 154–6 of your theology text and, as you do so, write down the key people, events and dates that are mentioned on this timeline.

Date	Summary of Key People, Events and Dates
Years immediately preceding AD 28 or 29	
AD 28 or 29	
AD 30 to 70	
AD 70	

186 | CREDO | GOD'S WORD REVEALED IN SACRED SCRIPTURE

CHAPTER 9 | WORKSHEET 5

NAME:

From Promise to Fulfillment

Insert an image of Jesus in the center of this page. On one side of the image, write quotations from the Old Testament that promise the coming of the Messiah. On the other side, write quotations from the New Testament that point to Jesus being the Messiah—the Promised One.

Old Testament   New Testament

The Jesse Tree

The Jesse Tree is a unique tree that is often used during Advent. Symbols representing the family tree or genealogy of Jesus Christ hang on the tree. It tells the story of God's plan of Salvation from Creation and throughout the Old Testament to the coming of the Messiah. The image of the Jesse tree comes from Isaiah 11:1: 'A shoot shall come out from the stump of Jesse, and a branch shall grow out of his roots.' Jesse was King David's father and a very important part of Jesus' genealogy. The prophet Isaiah declared that even though the family appeared to have died out, there would be renewal (the shoot growing out from the roots) in the person of a Messiah, the Savior of the Israelite people.

Making a Jesse Tree

Work together to create a Jesse tree for your classroom. There are many ways to go about this. You could use a small real or artificial evergreen tree or a bare branch on which to hang your symbols. Alternatively, you could draw or paint a tree on cardboard or paper and attach it to a wall. Your choice of symbols will depend on how and where the project is being carried out; the guidelines offered below are merely suggestions. The most important thing is that your choice of symbols portray the lineage of Jesus through the Old Testament and into the New Testament, illustrating the connection between the two.

Suggested Old Testament readings and symbols for a Jesse Tree:

- Genesis 1:1–31: Creation. *Symbols*: Dove, Sun, Globe
- Genesis 2:4—3:24: Adam and Eve. *Symbols*: Apple, Man, Woman
- Genesis 6:11–22; 7:17—8:12; 8:20–9:17: Noah and The Flood. *Symbols*: Rainbow, Ark, Dove
- Genesis 12:1–7; 15:1–6: Abraham and the Covenant. *Symbols*: Stars, Camel
- Genesis 21: 1—7: Sarah. *Symbol*: Cradle
- Genesis 22:1–19: The sacrifice of Isaac. *Symbols*: Ram, Altar, Bundle of wood
- Genesis 24:10–20: Rebekah. *Symbol*: A Well
- Genesis 27:41—28:22: Jacob and the Promise. *Symbol*: Ladder
- Genesis 37, 39:1—50:21: Joseph's dream. *Symbols*: Coat, Bag of Grain
- Exodus 2:1—4:20: Moses called by God. *Symbol*: Burning bush
- Exodus 19:1—20:20: Moses and the Ten Commandments. *Symbols*: The tablets
- Joshua 1:1–11; 6:1–20: Joshua and the Fall of Jericho: *Symbol*: Ram's Horn Trumpet
- 1 Samuel 3:1–18: Samuel. *Symbols*: Lamp, Temple
- 1 Samuel 16:23—17:58; 2 Samuel 5:1–5; 7:1–17: David. *Symbols*: Harp, Sling, Crown
- 1 Kings 3:3–28: Wisdom of Solomon. *Symbol*: Crown
- Ruth 2:1–9: Ruth. *Symbols*: Wheat or Straw
- Isaiah 11:1: Jesse. *Symbol*: Stump with Branch or Shoot
- Jonah 3:1-5: Jonah and the whale. *Symbol*: Whale
- Isaiah 1:10–20; 6:1—13; 8:11—9:7: Isaiah called to holiness. *Symbol*: Hot Coal
- Daniel 6: Daniel in the lion's den. *Symbol*: Lion

Suggested New Testament readings and symbols for a Jesse Tree:

- Luke 1:57–80; 3:1–20; 7:18–30: John the Baptist. *Symbols*: Scallop Shell, River
- Luke 1:26–38: Mary. *Symbols*: White Lily, Heart
- Luke 1:39–56: Elizabeth. *Symbols*: Mother and Child
- Luke 1:57–80: Zechariah. *Symbols*: Pencil and Tablet
- Matthew 1:19–25: Joseph. *Symbols*: Carpenter's Square, Hammer
- Matthew 2:1–12: Magi. *Symbols*: Star, Candle
- Matthew 2:1–12: Bethlehem. *Symbols*: Candle, Star
- Luke 2:1–20: Jesus. *Symbol*: Manger (Christmas Eve or Christmas Day)
- John 1:1–18: Christ. *Symbol*: Chi-Rho symbol (Christmas Day)
- Hebrews 1:1–14: Angels. *Symbol*: Angel

CHAPTER 9 | WORKSHEET 7

NAME:

A Modern-Day Martyr

SISTER DOROTHY STANG
American nun murdered in Brazil for her faith

Silver-haired American nun Dorothy Stang, who has died aged 73 after being shot by two gunmen on an Amazon road, looked more like an elderly American holidaymaker than a modern-day martyr. When the two gunmen intercepted her as she walked to a meeting of poor farmers, she must have known what was coming, but she opened her Bible and began reading to them. They shot her six times.

Sister Dorothy had been a worker for the CPT, the Roman Catholic Church's Pastoral Land Commission, since 1982, moving to a small town on the Transamazon Highway. The CPT had been created by the Brazilian bishops in 1975 in response to the mounting violence in the Amazon region, as landowners used gunmen to clear peasant farmers from disputed land. Sister Dorothy's particular interest was in teaching sustainable farming methods to poor settlers, most of whom were unfamiliar with Amazon soils.

Born in Dayton, Ohio, into a large Catholic family, she joined the Sisters of Notre Dame de Namur in 1948 and took her vows in 1956. The Order, founded in France at the end of the 18th century, was dedicated to 'taking our stand with poor people especially women and children in the most abandoned places'.

Like all CPT workers in the Amazon, Sister Dorothy knew her life was threatened. In 2004, although she knew she was putting her life even more at risk, she 'took her stand with poor people', naming logging companies who were invading and destroying state forests. Loggers reacted by calling her a terrorist and accused her of supplying peasant farmers with guns. She and other local leaders began to suffer direct death threats, but she refused to be intimidated and continued her work with the farmers.

Sister Dorothy Stang, nun and activist, born June 7, 1931; died February 14, 2005.

TALK IT OVER

- Reflect for a moment on the story of Sister Dorothy Stang.
- Talk about what you think of her story, what you admire about her and so on.
- Discuss why you think she continued to work in such extreme circumstances.
- Then bring some of your thoughts into a class discussion on the impact that people like Sister Dorothy have on our world and, most importantly, on you.

CHAPTER 9 | CHAPTER REVIEW

NAME:

Review of Chapter 9

I. **Multiple choice. Circle the letter next to the word(s) that best complete each statement so that it accurately states the teaching of the Catholic Church.**

1. The Old Testament is the faith story of _____.

   A. Abraham · B. Moses · C. the prophets · D. the Israelites · E. the Egyptians

2. God first entered the Covenant with _____.

   A. Abraham · B. Moses · C. the prophets · D. the Israelites · E. Christians

3. The descendants of Abraham, the Israelites, are named after the _____ of Abraham.

   A. son · B. grandson · C. wife · D. tribes · E. none of the above

4. God chose _____ to lead his people out of slavery in Egypt.

   A. Abraham · B. Israel · C. Jacob · D. Joshua · E. Moses

5. _____ were the first three kings of the Israelites.

   A. Abraham, Isaac and Jacob · B. Moses, Aaron and Joshua · C. Joshua, Samuel and Saul
   D. Samuel, Saul and David · E. Saul, David and Solomon

6. The Israelites were conquered and sent into exile by the _____.

   A. Egyptians · B. Canaanites · C. Assyrians · D. Babylonians · E. Assyrians and Babylonians

7. The _____ constantly reminded God's people of God's faithfulness and spoke about the coming of the Messiah.

   A. Apostles · B. prophets · C. kings of Israel · D. Evangelists · E. scribes

8. The word 'Messiah' means _____.

   A. Savior · B. Anointed One · C. Redeemer · D. Jesus · E. Son of God

CHAPTER 9 | CHAPTER REVIEW (CONTD.)

9. In AD 70 Jerusalem was captured by the _____ army, who destroyed the Temple.

   A. Assyrian · B. Babylonian · C. Roman · D. Greek · E. Egyptian

10. The Gospel came about in _____ main stage(s) of development.

    A. one · B. two · C. three · D. four · E. five

II. Define these terms. Use a complete sentence.

1. Hope _____

   _____

   _____

2. Covenant _____

   _____

   _____

3. Messiah _____

   _____

   _____

4. New Covenant _____

   _____

   _____

III. Write a paragraph. Choose either 1 or 2.

1. Explain the statement 'The faith story behind the Old Testament is "God keeps his promises"'.
2. Explain the statement 'The faith story behind the New Testament is "New Hope for God's People"'.

_____
_____
_____
_____
_____
_____
_____
_____
_____

IV. How would you respond? A Jewish friend says to you, 'Jesus was a Jew. Therefore, why do you need to have a religion that is different from the Jewish religion?'

_____
_____
_____
_____
_____
_____
_____
_____

V. Make a 'disciple decision'.
   1. What is the most important wisdom for life that you discovered in this chapter?

   _____

   _____

   _____

   _____

   _____

   _____

   _____

   _____

   2. Name several ways you can put that wisdom into practice. Choose one of the ways you identify and describe how you will make that wisdom part of your life right now.

   _____

   _____

   _____

   _____

   _____

   _____

   _____

   _____

   _____

   _____

   _____

   _____

   _____

CHAPTER 10

The Gospel Is Good News

INTRODUCTION

In this chapter we look at the Gospels as the Good News. We examine how the accounts of the Gospel came to be written and we begin to explore the Synoptic Gospels—the Gospels according to Mark, Matthew and Luke.

Chapter 10 is developed under five major headings:

- **ATTEND AND REFLECT**: What is good news?
- **HEAR THE STORY**: The formation of the Gospels
- **EMBRACE THE VISION**: Introduction to the Synoptic Gospels—Mark, Matthew and Luke
- **THINK IT THROUGH:** The greatest story ever told
- **JUDGE AND ACT** (Activities and exercises that encourage the young people to integrate what they have learned in the chapter into their daily lives)

Theological Background for the Teacher

THE ORIGINS OF THE TERM 'GOSPEL'

Today the term 'gospel'—from the Old English *godspel*, meaning 'good news'—is taken to refer to a book that narrates the story of Jesus, especially one of the canonical Gospels of Matthew, Mark, Luke and John. The term was originally used to translate the Greek word *euaggelion*, which means 'good news'. The Greek word used by the early Church did not, at first, refer to a written document but rather to the Good News that Jesus himself proclaimed: 'The time is fulfilled, and the kingdom of God has come near; repent, and believe in the good news' (Mark 1:15); and to the apostolic preaching about Jesus: 'And every day in the temple and at home they did not cease to preach and proclaim Jesus as the Messiah' (Acts of the Apostles 5:42).

Jesus lived in a pre-literary time, a time when books were not readily or easily produced. In Palestine, oral communication was the normal means of transmitting knowledge. Like every other gifted teacher of his time, Jesus used this method in his own teaching. His listeners had no paper to take notes and therefore they had to carry his message in their heads. So, at the end of a period of talking, he would tell a story or craft a saying that captured the essence of his teaching, which they could memorize. That is the origin and importance of the many stories, parables and sayings of Jesus that the Evangelists included in the Gospels.

The Apostles and other early disciples of Jesus used these sayings and stories again and again in their day-to-day lives. From repetition, the sharing of these sayings and stories emerged as the foundation for presenting various scenes from the life of Jesus and a standard collection of his sayings and teachings. The leaders and teachers of the early Church communicated and organized this material for practical use. As needed, the individual preacher used a saying or an account of an event from the early Church's rich and growing Tradition. Each of the Evangelists gathered these stories, sayings and teachings and arranged them to achieve the purpose for which they wrote their account of the Gospel.

HISTORICAL OR THEOLOGICAL?

The question is frequently asked: Are the Gospels historical or theological writing? The answer: They are a bit of both. As outlined in the students' text, there were three stages in thde formation of the Gospels: (1) the life and teaching of Jesus; (2) the oral tradition; and (3) the written Gospels. (*See Catechism of the Catholic Church* [CCC], no. 126.) There is no doubt but that the Gospel authors sought to present a real Person, the historical Jesus. The life of Jesus was itself a central focus of his preaching. His person was central to what he did. Theological insights were shaped by events and words that actually happened and were said. However, the history goes hand in hand with theology.

The Gospels were written to help us encounter the saving Christ Redeemer. Luke the Evangelist includes, in his introduction to his account of the Gospel, the words:

> Since many have undertaken to set down an orderly account of the events that have been fulfilled among us, just as they were handed on to us by those who were eyewitnesses and servants of the word, I too decided, after investigating

everything carefully from the very first, to write an orderly account for you, most excellent Theophilus, so that you may know the truth concerning the things about which you have been instructed.

– Luke 1:1–4

In John's account of the Gospel we read:

Now Jesus did many other signs in the presence of his disciples, which are not written in this book. But these are written so that you may come to believe that Jesus is the Messiah, the Son of God, and that through believing you may have life in his name.

– John 20:30–31

The main intent of the Evangelists was to pass on the apostolic faith of the Church in Jesus Christ, the incarnate Son of God, the Messiah and Savior of the world. The Good News that all the accounts of the Gospel proclaim is that God's plan of Salvation for the world has been brought to completion in the Person of Jesus of Nazareth, the Christ and Son of God, who suffered, died and was buried, and rose again.

The Risen Lord had completely changed the lives of the preachers, teachers and believers of the early Church. The inspired authors of the Gospels are not merely relating what Jesus said and that alone. Each Gospel is transmitting what Jesus once said to a believer whose life was radically changed by the Risen Lord. The Gospels are accounts of the life and teachings of Jesus, but accounts that preserve significant material at the expense of details that have no real relevance to the purpose of the writing: 'Now Jesus did many other signs in the presence of his disciples, which are not written in this book' (John 20:30). What remains are texts that speak to the lives of all believers, irrespective of time and place.

ADDITIONAL BACKGROUND READING
Catechism of the Catholic Church, nos. 101–133; *United States Catholic Catechism for Adults*, 21–33; Vatican II, *Constitution on Divine Revelation* [*Dei Verbum*], nos. 11–13; 'Gospel' in 'The Canon of the New Testament' by Raymond E. Brown, in *The New Jerome Biblical Commentary*, copyright © 1968, 1990 (Prentice Hall: Englewood Cliffs, New Jersey), 66:65.

CHAPTER OUTCOMES

See general note on page 18 of this resource.

Learning Outcomes
As a result of studying this chapter and exploring the issues raised, the young people should be able to:

- understand the meaning of the word 'gospel';
- understand why the Gospel is Good News;
- articulate why they think the early disciples answered Jesus' call to follow him;
- explain the three stages in the formation of the Gospels: the life and teaching of Jesus; the oral tradition; the written Gospels;
- understand the Gospels as faith accounts of the life and teachings, and Death and Resurrection of Jesus;
- compare accounts of the same event from the three Gospels; for example, the Feeding of the Five Thousand;
- understand the contexts of the three Synoptic Gospels;
- explore the reasons why Jesus had such an impact on humanity;
- know the story of Chiara Lubich.

Faith-formation Outcomes
As a result of studying this chapter and exploring the issues raised, the young people should also:

- reflect on their experience of good news in their lives;
- understand and articulate how the Gospels are Good News for their lives;
- consider the significance of Jesus for their lives and how that impacts on their choices, now and for the future;
- come to see more clearly for themselves why the story of Jesus is often called 'the greatest story ever told';
- choose a Gospel quotation as a motto for their lives;
- make a commitment to live according to their chosen motto;
- respond to the presence of the Risen Jesus in their lives.

Teacher Reflection

The One

Green, blue, yellow and red—
God is down in the swamps and marshes,
Sensational as April and almost incred-
ible the flowering of our catharsis.
A humble scene in a backward place
Where no one important ever looked;
The raving flowers looked up in the face
Of the One and the Endless, the Mind that has
baulked
The profoundest of mortals. A primrose, a violet,
A violent wild iris—but mostly anonymous
performers,
Yet an important occasion as the Muse at her toilet
Prepared to inform the local farmers
That beautiful, beautiful, beautiful God
Was breathing His love by a cut-away bog.

Notes and Guidelines for Student Activities

ATTEND AND REFLECT

What is good news?

Learning Outcomes
That the young people would:
- understand the meaning of the word 'gospel';
- understand why the Gospel is Good News;
- articulate why they think the early disciples answered Jesus' call to follow him.

Faith-formation Outcome
That the young people would also:
- reflect on their experience of good news in their lives.

Overview
Chapter 10 opens with a reflection on the impact of good news and encourages the young people to identify the role of good news in their lives. It then introduces the great truth that Jesus *revealed and was* the best news the world had ever heard.

Supplementary Activity for 'Attend and Reflect'

Group Work/Discussion
Encourage the young people to work in groups and search through a selection of newspapers—local, national or international—for 'good news' stories.
Follow this activity with a class discussion around the following questions:

- What did you discover?
- What kinds of stories dominate our newspapers?
- Why are there so few 'good news' stories? Is it because good news doesn't happen?
- When was the last time you heard really good news? Share some examples from your family, your school, your life.

HEAR THE STORY

The formation of the Gospels

Learning Outcomes
That the young people would:
- be able to explain the three stages in the formation of the Gospels: the life and teaching of Jesus; the oral tradition; the written Gospels;
- understand the Gospels as faith accounts of the life and teachings, and Death and Resurrection of Jesus;
- compare accounts of the same event from the three Gospels; for example, the Feeding of the Five Thousand.

Faith-formation Outcome
That the young people would also:
- understand and articulate how the Gospels are Good News for their lives.

Overview
Section two, 'Hear the Story', examines the three stages in the writing of the Gospels and explains that the Gospels are faith accounts of the life of Jesus rather than historical or journalistic accounts.

Supplementary Activities for 'Hear the Story'

Worksheet 1: 'Jesus and the People of His Time' (*page 201 of this resource*) contains role-cards to be photocopied and cut out for use in an 'In the Spotlight' role-play activity in which the students, acting as people who lived at the time of Jesus, have the chance to meet with 'Jesus' and tell him about their concerns and needs. We hope that this activity will give the young people some insight into the social and political world in which Jesus lived and will also help them to imagine themselves in the presence of the Risen Jesus. (*See the general instructions for 'In the Spotlight' activities in 'Student Activity Tool Kit', page 273 of this resource.*)

Have the class work in five groups, each group taking one role-card. For this activity, a representative from each group will 'become' a person from the time of Jesus, who will meet 'Jesus' (role-played by another student) and tell him about themselves and their situation.

In their groups, in advance of the role-play, the students read and discuss their role-card carefully so that they are clear about the person they will represent, what this person's concerns are at the moment and what good news he or she might be hoping to hear from Jesus.

When each group has had a chance to discuss their concerns and hopes, they then send one person from their group to meet with 'Jesus'.

All sit in a circle. 'Jesus' enters the group and says to each member, in turn: '*I am Jesus of Nazareth. What can I do for you?*'

Each group representative, in turn, tells 'Jesus' about themselves and what kind of good news they are hoping he will tell them.

At the end of the activity, you could facilitate further class discussion with questions such as:

- How did you feel acting in your role?
- How did others treat you in your role?
- How did you feel when Jesus appeared and put his question to you?
- How does this role-play give us an insight into the social and religious world into which Jesus was born?
- If Jesus were to say to you right now 'What can I do for you?', what would your answer be?

Graphic organizers are helpful for recording, organizing, summarizing and integrating information. The graphic organizer in **Worksheet 2: 'The Formation of the Gospels'** (*page 203 of this resource*) will help the young people to record and summarize what they have learned about how the written accounts of the Gospel in the New Testament were formed.

The graphic organizer in **Worksheet 3: 'Miracles of Loaves and Fish'** (*page 204 of this resource*) will help the young people to familiarize themselves with the details of the Gospel accounts of these miracles. This exercise will also prepare them for the related 'Group Work/Discussion' activity on page 177 of their theology text.

EMBRACE THE VISION

Introduction to the Synoptic Gospels—Mark, Matthew and Luke

Learning Outcome
That the young people would:
- understand the contexts of the three Synoptic Gospels.

Faith-formation Outcome
That the young people would also:
- consider the significance of Jesus for their lives and how that impacts on their choices, now and for the future.

Overview
Section three, 'Embrace the Vision', focuses on the three Synoptic Gospels. It explores the reality that while the aim of all three Gospels was to proclaim the Good News that Jesus, through his life, Death and Resurrection, brought to fulfillment God's plan of Salvation for the whole world, each evangelist wrote for a different audience and from a different perspective.

Supplementary Activities for 'Embrace the Vision'

Worksheets 4, 5 and 6 (*pages 206–208 of this resource*) provide revision exercises on the Synoptic Gospels based on the information given in this chapter.

THINK IT THROUGH

The greatest story ever told

Learning Outcome
That the young people would:
- explore the reasons why Jesus has had such an impact on humanity.

Faith-formation Outcome
That the young people would also:
- come to see more clearly for themselves why the story of Jesus is often called the 'greatest story ever told'.

Overview
Section four, 'Think It Through', explores why Jesus had such an impact on humanity. The text 'One Solitary Life' provides a backdrop for the discussion.

Supplementary Activity for 'Think It Through'

Group Work
The story of Jesus has been represented in various art forms for over two thousand years. Encourage the young people to work in groups and select one category from the following: films and songs or art and visual images or poetry and literature. In their chosen category they should research references and images that seek to represent Jesus' life on earth. Ask them to choose one and try to identify the kind of image of Jesus that the artist or author was seeking to convey. Afterward they can share their images, songs, poems or film clips with the class.

JUDGE AND ACT

Learning Outcome
That the young people would:
- know the story of Chiara Lubich.

Faith-formation Outcomes
That the young people would also:
- choose a Gospel quotation as a motto for their lives;
- make a commitment to live according to their chosen motto;
- respond to the presence of the Risen Jesus in their lives.

Overview
Chapter 10 has focused on the Gospel as Good News. In section five, 'Judge and Act', we introduce the young people to Chiara Lubich as someone who showed how the Good News of the Gospel can shape a person's life.

Supplementary Activities for 'Judge and Act'

Worksheet 7: 'Living the Good News' (*page 209 of this resource*) invites the young people to think of and describe people they know or have heard about whom they consider to be living the Good News of the Gospel.

Directives for the Prayer Reflection at the end of the chapter
You will need a Bible and a candle. Place the opened Bible in a prominent position in the room.

As the young people reflect on the questions asked during the Prayer Reflection, you might like to play some quiet background music.

Additional Prayer Suggestion

Scripture Reflection
(*See instructions for the use of doodling in prayer in the 'Student Activity Tool Kit', page 274 of this resource.*)

Use the following Scripture verse to engage the young people in prayer:

> **The kingdom of God has come near; repent and believe in the good news.**
>
> **MARK 1:15**

CHAPTER 10 | WORKSHEET 1

NAME:

Jesus and the People of His Time

The following are role-cards for an 'In the Spotlight' role-play activity. Students in the 'role' of people who lived at the time of Jesus have the chance to meet with 'Jesus' and tell him what kind of good news they are hoping for.

With the members of your group, in advance of the role-play, read and discuss your role-card carefully so that you are clear about who the character is, what his or her concerns are at the moment and what good news he or she might be hoping for from their meeting with 'Jesus'.

PHILIP THE PHARISEE

I am a Pharisee, a member of a Jewish religious group. We help to run the synagogues. The most important thing in our lives is God's Law, and all other laws that have been created around that Law. We strictly obey that Law and we want others to do the same. We spend much of our time studying God's Law so that we can guide others in their lives and help them to live the Law in all the details of their lives as well. People have a lot of respect for us because we are people of influence. We help others by pointing out how they can avoid breaking the Law in their everyday lives; for example, by not working on the Sabbath day. We fast regularly and expect everyone else to do the same. Being holy means keeping God's Law and keeping away from those who are sinners. Therefore we teach that those who break the Law are to be avoided at all costs by good religious people. We would like the Roman occupiers to leave our land because they are pagans who do not obey the Law of God. They are a bad influence on the people, but I suppose we have to live with them for the present.

SAMUEL THE SADDUCEE

I am a priest and I work in the Temple. My father was a priest too, as was his father was before him. We are considered to be a very powerful and blessed family because of this. We collect the Temple taxes, which must be paid by everyone who visits the Temple in Jerusalem. This money is used for the upkeep of the Temple and for the support of our families. My family lives well, but that is as it should be. When it comes to the Pharisees . . . well, they try their best but they are peasants after all, and in some ways they are not strict enough. We try to get along with the Romans because if we didn't they might close the Temple and that would be a disaster for the people and the Jewish religion. It wouldn't do us any good either.

CHAPTER 10 | WORKSHEET 1 (CONTD.)

ZACHARY THE ZEALOT
I try to keep a low profile. It's important that people don't find out too much about me because you never know who will betray you. We Zealots have one goal in mind—to get the Romans out of our country at any cost. We will use any means necessary, including violence, to achieve this goal. After all, the Roman army isn't interested in peaceful methods. We are often called Iscariots, a word that comes from the name given to the small daggers we sometimes use. We try to be good Jews and to keep the Jewish race pure; in other words, we have no time for foreigners. This is God's land and we are God's people. That is what we struggle for.

BARTHOLOMEW, A BEGGAR
I beg every day at the entrance to the Temple for a few coins or some scraps of food. My family once owned some land but they had to sell it to pay taxes, so all that is left for me is to live as a beggar. It is not an easy life. People don't like seeing the likes of me and are always trying to move us on. They tell us that we must have sinned to be so poor, but I know some sinners who are rich! It is hard to have faith in a God who seems to be so unfair.

LORENZO, A LEPER
I am a leper and I live on the edge of town with all the other sick and disabled people. I was a prosperous merchant and lived in a fine house until the first signs of the disease appeared. In the beginning I denied what was happening to me. I was a good man, after all! I had been blessed by God with good health and fortune. I prayed regularly and fulfilled all the requirements of the faith. I paid my taxes. I gave to the poor. Yet, in spite of all this, along came this horrible disease, advertising to all that I was a sinner! To this day I have no idea what I did to offend God, that he should punish me in this way. My family and associates no longer have anything to do with me and I depend on the charity of those who leave food at the outskirts of the town for people like me to collect. I find it hard to pray now. I am not allowed into the synagogue, of course, but that is not the reason. The truth is, I feel that God has let me down.

CHAPTER 10 | WORKSHEET 2

NAME:

The Formation of the Gospels

Fill in the graphic organizer, outlining the chain of events that led to the writing of the four accounts of the Gospel in the New Testament.

CHAPTER 10 | WORKSHEET 3

Miracles of Loaves and Fish

Look up all the Gospel accounts of miracles of loaves and fish and compare the similarities and differences between them. Write up your findings in the grid.

	Matthew 14:13–21	Mark 6:30–44	Luke 9:10–17
Things that are different from the other accounts			
Things that are the same as in the other accounts			

CHAPTER 10 | WORKSHEET 3 (CONTD.)

	John 6:1–15	Matthew 15:32–39	Mark 8:1–10
Things that are different from the other accounts			
Things that are the same as in the other accounts			

CHAPTER 10 | WORKSHEET 4

NAME:

The Gospel According to Mark

Complete the following fact-file on Mark's account of the Gospel.

Author	
Time of writing	
Target audience	
Main sources	

How Mark presents Jesus in his Gospel: _____

_____

_____

_____

Main point of Mark's Gospel: _____

_____

_____

Favorite story from Mark's Gospel: _____

_____

CHAPTER 10 | WORKSHEET 5

NAME:

The Gospel According to Matthew

Complete the following fact-file on Matthew's account of the Gospel.

Author	
Time of writing	
Target audience	
Main sources	

How Matthew presents Jesus in his Gospel: _____

_____

_____

_____

Main point of Matthew's Gospel: _____

_____

_____

_____

Favorite story from Matthew's Gospel: _____

_____

CHAPTER 10 | WORKSHEET 6

NAME:

The Gospel According to Luke

Complete the following fact-file on Luke's account of the Gospel.

Author	
Time of writing	
Target audience	
Main sources	

How Luke presents Jesus in his Gospel: _____

_____

_____

_____

Main point of Luke's Gospel: _____

_____

_____

Favorite story from Luke's Gospel: _____

_____

NAME:

Living the Good News

Think of people whom you feel show the Good News of the Gospel in their life. They can be people you know or famous people. Then fill in as many examples as you can think of in the chart provided.

PERSON'S NAME	HOW THEY SHOW THE GOOD NEWS OF THE GOSPEL

NAME:

Review of Chapter 10

I. Fill in the blanks. Complete the following paragraph so that it correctly states the teaching of the Catholic Church.

Just over two thousand years ago Jesus, the incarnate **(1)** _____, revealed most fully the best good news the world has ever heard. Jesus himself was the Good News. Jesus was the **(2)** _____ and **(3)** _____ whom God had promised to send. The four Gospel accounts, of **(4)** _____, **(5)** _____, **(6)** _____ and **(7)** _____, proclaim Jesus' life and work among us. The English word 'gospel' is a translation of the Latin word **(8)** _____, which means 'good news'. At the beginning of his work among us Jesus proclaimed, 'The time is fulfilled and the **(9)** _____ has come near; repent and believe in the **(10)** _____.

II. Choose either 1 or 2.
   1. Name the three stages in the formation of the Gospels.
   2. Describe the meaning of the term 'gospel'.

_____
_____
_____
_____
_____
_____

CHAPTER 10 | CHAPTER REVIEW (CONTD.)

III. Write a paragraph. Name the three Synoptic Gospels and describe how each portrays Jesus.

_____

_____

_____

_____

_____

_____

_____

_____

IV. How would you respond? A classmate asks you, 'There are so many differences in the Gospels; how can we really believe they are true?'

_____

_____

_____

_____

_____

_____

_____

_____

_____

_____

_____

CHAPTER 10 | CHAPTER REVIEW (CONTD.)

V. Make a 'disciple decision'.
1. What is the most important wisdom for life that you discovered in this chapter?

_____
_____
_____
_____
_____
_____
_____
_____

2. Name several ways you can put that wisdom into practice. Choose one of the ways you identify and describe how you will make that wisdom part of your life right now.

_____
_____
_____
_____
_____
_____
_____
_____
_____
_____
_____
_____

CHAPTER 11

Jesus and His Message in the Gospels According to Matthew, Mark and Luke

INTRODUCTION

Chapter 11 takes a more in-depth look at the Synoptic Gospels. The chapter is developed under five major headings:

- **ATTEND AND REFLECT**: What influences our lives?
- **HEAR THE STORY**: Jesus begins his public ministry
- **EMBRACE THE VISION**: Jesus inaugurates the Kingdom of God
- **THINK IT THROUGH**: Exploring the notion of the Kingdom of God
- **JUDGE AND ACT** (*Activities and exercises that encourage the young people to integrate what they have learned in the chapter into their daily lives*)

Theological Background for the Teacher

GOD IS THE AUTHOR OF ALL SCRIPTURE

While the Evangelists passed on historical events, they were not writers of history as we define 'historians' today. Their primary purpose in writing their accounts of the Gospel was to give witness to and authentically pass on the faith of the apostolic Church. Each Evangelist wrote with a specific purpose and audience in mind. We can see this in the patterns and sequences, the seams or link passages, the alterations and emphases that Matthew, Mark, Luke and John put into the various texts and passages of their account of the Gospel. (See *United States Catholic Catechism for Adults* [USCCA], 26.)

Though the Evangelists wrote down the words, God, who inspired all the sacred authors, is the author of all Scripture, including the Gospels. 'To compose the sacred books, God chose certain men who, all the while he employed them in this task, made full use of their faculties and powers' (*Constitution on Divine Revelation [Dei Verbum]*, no. 11). To understand what God wanted to communicate, it is important for us to understand the times and culture in which the sacred authors lived and the literary genres in which they wrote.

Even when taking all this into account, we must remember that the four accounts of the Gospel and all of Sacred Scripture must be read and interpreted with the help and guidance of the same Holy Spirit who guided the Evangelists and other sacred authors. To help us in this task, the Church provides three criteria for us to follow:

1. Be especially attentive to 'the content and unity of the whole Scripture'.
2. Read the Scripture within 'the living Tradition of the whole Church'.
3. Be attentive to the analogy of faith; that is, the coherence of the truths of faith among themselves within the whole plan of Revelation.

THE 'SYNOPTIC PROBLEM'

When the Gospels were being written and assembled, there was a large body of material relating to Jesus from which the inspired authors could draw. There was great potential, therefore, for each of the accounts of the Gospel to be very different from one another, but this did not happen in regard to the essence of the Gospel message. (See Luke 1:1–4 and John 21:24.) Centuries of comparing the first three Gospels have revealed a remarkable measure of agreement between them. However, they also differ from one another. The challenge of explaining this is called the 'Synoptic Problem'.

The Synoptic Gospels—Matthew, Mark and Luke—share passages that are very similar. For example, much of Mark is found in Matthew and Luke; namely, 80 percent of the verses in Mark are found in Matthew and 60 percent are found in Luke.

There are many theories that try to explain the similarities and dissimilarities within Matthew, Mark and Luke. Then there is the fact that some stories occur in only two of the three (Matthew 3:7–10 and Luke 3:7–9, John the Baptist's exchange with the Pharisees and Sadducees); while other passages are found in only one of the Synoptics (Luke 3:10–14, Jesus appointing seventy-two and sending them off in pairs, in advance, to the towns and places he would be visiting). Moreover, when all three Synoptics share the same story, they sometimes give it in precisely the same wording and at other times they word it differently, or sometimes two of them will word it the same way and the third will word it differently.

THE RESOLUTION OF THE SYNOPTIC PROBLEM
Biblical scholars have offered a number of theories to explain these similarities in the Synoptics. They suggest that all three Synoptics drew their accounts from a common source. But what was that source? Many scholars have named that source Q. (For further discussion of the Synoptic Problem, see 'Synoptic Problem' by Frans Neirynck in *The New Jerome Biblical Commentary*, copyright © 1990, 1968. Published by Prentice Hall, Englewood Cliffs, New Jersey.)

This chapter explores some of the key moments and teaching in the life of Jesus as presented in the Synoptic Gospels; namely, the birth of Jesus, the baptism and temptation of Jesus, Jesus' teaching on the Kingdom of God, and the parables of Jesus.

ADDITIONAL BACKGROUND READING
Catechism of the Catholic Church, nos. 512–667, 709, 763, 1323, 1329, 1337, 1366, 1412, 1521–1522, 1532, 1708, 1992, 2020, 2816, 2819; *Jesus of Nazareth: From the Baptism of Jesus in the Jordan to the Transfiguration* by Benedict XVI: 'The Gospel of the Kingdom of God', pages 46–63, and 'The Sermon on the Mount: The Beatitudes', pages 64–98, copyright © The Broadway Doubleday Publishing Group, New York, 2007.

CHAPTER OUTCOMES

See general note on page 18 of this resource.

Learning Outcomes
As a result of studying this chapter and exploring the issues raised, the young people should be able to:

- recall their earliest memories and be aware of how those memories impact on who they are today;
- explain the facts surrounding the birth and early life of Jesus;
- understand how the people and events in the early life of Jesus influenced him;
- consider the similarities and differences between the accounts of the birth, early life, baptism and temptations of Jesus in the Synoptic Gospels;
- articulate what Jesus meant by 'the Kingdom of God';
- understand how the values in the Beatitudes are the values of the Kingdom as articulated by Jesus;
- read and discuss a number of parables and be aware of how they explore the meaning of the Kingdom;
- understand that the miracles of Jesus manifest that the Kingdom of God is present in him, which is especially emphasized by his ministry with the poor, the sick and outcasts;
- list the Corporal Works of Mercy and connect them to the Kingdom of God.

Faith-formation Outcomes
As a result of studying this chapter and exploring the issues raised, the young people should also be able to:

- consider how they can resist temptations in their own lives, in light of what they have learned from the Gospel accounts of the temptations of Jesus;
- appreciate how their practice of Lent will be influenced by what they have learned from the temptations of Jesus;
- compare the values of the Beatitudes with their own values, and realize how the Beatitudes challenge them to live and work to build the Kingdom of God;
- appreciate more fully the meaning of the Our Father;
- reflect on what they have learned for their own lives from the parables and miracle stories they have read;
- decide how they will bring God's love into people's lives today.

Teacher Reflection

Your Father Knows Well You Need Them (Luke 12:30)
A loving hand guides our lives,
a loving force guides our world,
a loving and personal God is involved
in the past, present and future of our lives.

God knows each of us by name,
by the history of our lives, by our hopes.
Our peace and freedom from worry
comes partly from the love God has for each.
And then we have more space to solve problems.

A love which touches us
when we are worried, anxious, fearful.
Like the sparkle in the middle of a diamond,
like the color in the middle of a thread,
like the rain in the middle of a cloud.
Always there, essential
to the diamond, thread or cloud,
but not itself the diamond, cloud or thread.

Being involved in the love of God
brings the deepest happiness—
could the desert be happy without sand
or the sun happy without light?

All else will then be viewed in this light.
Our anxiety about past, present or future
is lived within the environment
of the love of God.

Notes and Guidelines for Student Activities

ATTEND AND REFLECT
What influences our lives?

Learning Outcomes
That the young people would:
- recall their earliest memories and be aware of how those memories impact on who they are today;
- explain the facts surrounding the birth and early life of Jesus;
- understand how the people and events in the early life of Jesus influenced him.

Overview
Chapter 11 begins by asking the young people to consider how the circumstances surrounding their birth and early life have influenced the people they are today. It then explores the events surrounding the birth and early life of Jesus and asks the young people to consider how these influenced Jesus' later life and the kind of person he became.

Supplementary Activity for 'Attend and Reflect'

Worksheet 1: 'Fact-file on Jesus' (*page 219 of this resource*) is a completion and comparison exercise based on the information given in section one. It will help the young people to remember the circumstances surrounding the birth of Jesus.

HEAR THE STORY
Jesus begins his public ministry

Learning Outcome
That the young people would:
- consider the similarities and differences between the accounts of the birth, early life, baptism and temptations of Jesus in the Synoptic Gospels.

Faith-formation Outcomes
That the young people would also:
- consider how they can resist temptations in their own lives, in light of what they have learned from the Gospel accounts of the temptations of Jesus;
- appreciate how their practice of Lent will be influenced by what they have learned from the temptations of Jesus.

Overview
Section two, 'Hear the Story', begins by exploring the significance of the baptism of Jesus as presented in all three Synoptic Gospels. It then presents the account of the temptation of Jesus in the desert and explains its significance not only for the people of the time but for us today.

Supplementary Activities for 'Hear the Story'

Worksheet 2: 'The Baptism of Jesus' (*page 220 of this resource*) gives references for the Gospel accounts of Jesus' baptism and provides a graphic organizer to help the students identify the points these accounts have in common and the points on which they differ. This exercise will not only familiarize the young people with the accounts of the baptism of Jesus from the Synoptic Gospels but it will also give them a greater insight into the similarities and differences between the Synoptic Gospels.

Teacher Tip: You could introduce the section 'The temptation of Jesus' (*page 198 of students' text*) by showing a film clip or TV documentary of someone surviving in the wilderness. You might show and discuss the National Geographic program called *Alone in the Wild*.

Worksheet 3: 'Reflection on the Temptation of Jesus' (*page 221 of this resource*) encourages the young people to connect the temptation of Jesus with their own lives.

Drama/Discussion
Students form small groups and create a short drama depicting the temptation of Jesus—imagining that it is taking place in our country in the present century.

Questions to consider: Where might Jesus be standing? What might the devil look like? What temptations might the devil offer?

Afterward, students name and discuss some of the temptations they face in the world today.

Research Project
Invite the young people to research the Church's practice of Lent. How does it connect with the time Jesus spent in the desert?

EMBRACE THE VISION

Jesus inaugurates the Kingdom of God

Learning Outcomes
That the young people would:
- articulate what Jesus meant by 'the Kingdom of God';
- understand how the values in the Beatitudes are the values of the Kingdom as articulated by Jesus.

Faith-formation Outcomes
That the young people would also:
- compare the values of the Beatitudes with their own values, and realize how the Beatitudes challenge them to live and work to build the Kingdom of God;
- appreciate more fully the meaning of the Our Father.

Overview
Section three, 'Embrace the Vision', presents Jesus' teaching about the Kingdom of God as a central theme in the Synoptic Gospels and a fulfillment of the teachings of the prophet Isaiah. We explain the Beatitudes as a summary of the values and way of life that Jesus taught as being central to the Kingdom of God. We encourage the young people to examine their own lives in light of this teaching of Jesus.

Supplementary Activities for 'Embrace the Vision'

The poem in **Worksheet 4: 'Reflection on the Beatitudes'** (*page 222 of this resource*) will help the young people to think about the meaning for their own lives of the values of the Kingdom that Jesus preached and inaugurated.

Worksheet 5: 'Living the Values of the Beatitudes' (*page 223 of this resource*) invites the young people to work in groups to prepare a presentation describing how life would change in the United States today if everyone lived according to the Beatitudes.

THINK IT THROUGH

Exploring the notion of the Kingdom of God

Learning Outcomes
That the young people would:
- read and discuss a number of parables and be aware of how they explore the meaning of the Kingdom;
- understand that the miracles of Jesus manifest that the Kingdom of God is present in him, which is especially emphasized by his ministry with the poor, the sick and outcasts.

Faith-formation Outcome
That the young people would also:
- reflect on what they have learned for their own lives from the parables and miracle stories they have read.

Overview
Section four, 'Think It Through', introduces the parables as stories in which Jesus further expanded on his teaching about the Kingdom of God and how it would take shape in our world. It also explores the miracles of Jesus as one of the most powerful ways in which Jesus revealed the Kingdom of God. Once again we encourage the young people to think about how these stories challenge them in their own lives.

Supplementary Activities for 'Think It Through'

Worksheet 6: 'The Parables of Jesus' (*page 224 of this resource*) will help the young people to revise what they have learned about Jesus' parables, to reflect on what one parable means for them in their daily lives and to check their understanding of the messages behind five well-known parables of Jesus.

Worksheet 7: 'The Kingdom of God' (*page 226 of this resource*) offers the young people an opportunity to examine the parables in chapter 13 of Matthew's Gospel. This exercise will give them further insight into the Kingdom of God.

The story in **Worksheet 8: 'The Challenge of the Gospel'** (*page 227 of this resource*) seeks to develop the young people's awareness of the challenge that is involved in living the values of the Gospel. It invites them to reflect on where they might find the help they will need to live in this way.

JUDGE AND ACT

Learning Outcome
That the young people would:
- list the Corporal Works of Mercy and connect them to the Kingdom of God.

Faith-formation Outcome
That the young people would also:
- decide how they will bring God's love into people's lives today.

Overview
In this section we continue to explore how we can live out the Beatitudes in our lives today. In the story of the *Nothing But Nets* campaign, the young people see an example of how the values that Jesus spoke of can be brought to bear on people's lives today.

Supplementary Activities for 'Judge and Act'

Media Project
Encourage the students to research articles in the local, national or international press, or on the internet, about people in our world today who work tirelessly to bring much-needed love and care to others against all the odds. Then see if they can find Gospel stories that mirror some of these articles.

Additional Prayer Suggestion

Scripture Reflection
(*See instructions for the use of doodling in prayer in the 'Student Activity Tool Kit', page 274 of this resource.*)

Use the following Scripture verse to engage the young people in prayer:

> One does not live by bread alone, but by every word that comes from the mouth of God.
>
> **MATTHEW 4:4**

CHAPTER 11 | WORKSHEET 1

NAME:

Fact-file on Jesus

Using the information in section one, 'Attend and Reflect', of chapter 11, complete the following fact-file on Jesus.

Name:	
Father:	
Mother:	
Place of birth:	
Date of birth:	
Place of residence:	
Close relatives:	
Education:	
Early history, according to Matthew and Luke	
Luke's account: What details are different from Matthew's account?	
Matthew's account: What details are different from Luke's account?	
What details do the two accounts have in common?	

CHAPTER 11: JESUS AND HIS MESSAGE IN THE GOSPELS | WORKSHEET 1 | 219

CHAPTER 11 | WORKSHEET 2

NAME:

The Baptism of Jesus

Read and compare the Gospel accounts of the baptism of Jesus by John the Baptist in the river Jordan in Matthew 3:13–17, Mark 1:9–11 and Luke 3:21–22. Then, on the graphic organizer, identify and write the points that the three accounts have in common and the points on which they differ.

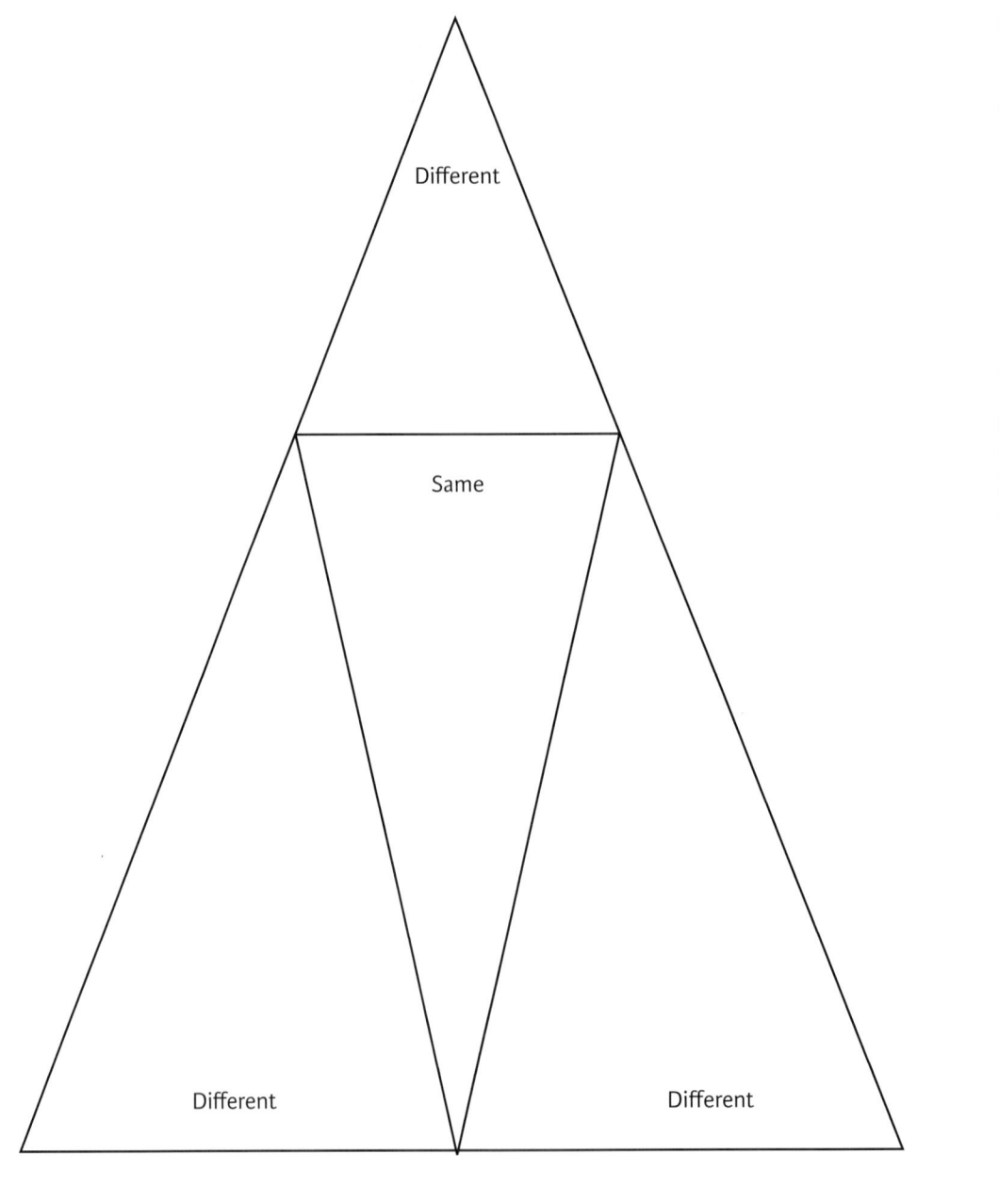

CHAPTER 11 | WORKSHEET 3

NAME:

Reflection on the Temptation of Jesus

Read Matthew 4:1–11 and then complete the following exercise.

Temptation	What the devil said	How Jesus responded
First		
Second		
Third		

TIME FOR REFLECTION
Now think about a time when you were tempted to do something wrong but you didn't give in to the temptation.

CHAPTER 11 | WORKSHEET 4

NAME:

Reflection on the Beatitudes

BEATITUDES

If you can hold great riches
Never letting them hold you;
If you can hear your praises sung
And still give God his due;
If you can help the slow and weak
And raise the one who falls,
And quickly come with helping hand
When anybody calls;
If you can have a heart that's free
From selfishness and sin,
And keep that heart so God's great light
May shine more strongly in;
If you can give forgiveness
To the one who hurts your heart;
If you can build a bridge and bring
Together those apart;
If you can say—this thing is wrong
Or that is right to do,
And stand your ground though other hearts
Would pain and punish you;
If you can be a friend to all,
To all be strong and true,
Then God who made the world
Will make his Kingdom come in you.

TIME FOR REFLECTION
- Ponder the questions in this poem in your heart.
- What do your answers say about how well tuned you are in your life to the values of the Beatitudes?

CHAPTER 11 | WORKSHEET 5

NAME:

Living the Values of the Beatitudes

Read and reflect on this statement:

The reign of God is the situation that results when God's will is really done. What is God's will? As revealed in Jesus, God's will is our well-being. God wants the wholeness, the healing and the salvation of every creature and of all of us taken together. The reign of God, then, involves justice and peace among everyone, healing and wholeness everywhere, fullness of life enjoyed by all.

GROUP ACTIVITY
- Work in groups of four.
- Your task is to prepare a presentation in which you will describe how life would change in the United States or in your neighborhood or in your school today if everyone lived according to the above statement.
- Try to be as specific as possible; for example, mention what life would be like for the poor, for children, for young people, for sick people, for families, for immigrants, for prisoners, for old people, and so on. Use pictures, photographs, posters and newspaper cuttings to illustrate your presentation.
- Finally, describe what you would be doing if you were to take seriously the message of the above statement.

NAME:

The Parables of Jesus

Complete the following sentences.

A parable is _____
_____
_____

Jesus told parables because _____
_____
_____

In the space provided below or on a separate sheet of paper, draw an image to represent your favorite parable. Write a few sentences to explain your reason or reasons for choosing this parable and the image that you have used. Then write about what this parable challenges you to do in your own life.

CHAPTER 11 | WORKSHEET 6 (CONTD.)

Match each parable with its message.

Parable

- The Parable of the Sower
- The Parable of the Mustard Seed
- The Parable of the Good Samaritan
- The Parable of the Prodigal Son /Loving Father
- The Parable of the Wedding Feast

Message

- We must treat everyone with kindness, regardless of race, color, gender, status in society and so on, as every person is our neighbor.
- God is loving and merciful and will welcome us back even if we have failed in the past.
- The Kingdom of God is open to all who wish to share in it by living according to God's will.
- The coming of the Kingdom of God will be successful despite all obstacles.
- The Kingdom of God may start very small but it will grow to become the greatest of all kingdoms, where everyone is welcome.

CHAPTER 11 | WORKSHEET 7

NAME:

The Kingdom of God

In Matthew's account of the Gospel, Jesus tells us that the Kingdom of God

- has small beginnings;
- grows to huge proportions;
- is worth giving up everything for;
- has good and bad people within it.

Look up the parables in chapter 13 of Matthew's account of the Gospel and match them with the statements given below.

The Kingdom. . . .	Parables in chapter 13 of Matthew's Gospel that match these statements
Has small beginnings	
Grows to huge proportions	
Is worth giving up everything for	
Has good and bad people within it	

NAME:

The Challenge of the Gospel

Catherine and the Winter Wheat

This is the winter wheat that is being hauled along the roads in late July or early August in southern Ontario, the winter wheat, the fall wheat—have it how you will.

It is sown in September, about the time of the equinox, when the wind blows northwesterly, or used to, across Star-of-the-Sea, and the heavy rain has not come. It stands through the winter, withering under the snow like common grass, blazing emerald in spring, and by early June it is breast-high, fading in color and heading up, as the farmers say, looking to their binders, against July, when the field will be yellow gold and heavy with grain.

It was our sole cash crop, and the brief season when we hauled wheat to the mill was always associated with new clothes and toys and coins in our pockets when my sisters and I were children.

One year before the war we carried our wheat, as we always did, to the mill at Streetsville on the Credit River. I was in my first teens. Before the war, the 1914 war, long ago now, I rode on the sacks sitting beside my sister Catherine, who was sixteen now, or nearly, while my father drove the team, and Emily, the oldest of us, seventeen, sat beside him and spelled him with the reins.

That way the trip took hours, though you'd cover it in a few minutes today in a car. But the sun was bright and the day fresh and beautiful after all the rain and the humid heat of the summer, and I talked away to Catherine and thought of the delight to come, of lying under the trees at the miller's while we waited our turn to unload and my father chatted with the men and smoked his pipe, and the greatest delight of all, when the wagon was empty and my father would give us money and tell us to get about our shopping.

This summer, this trip to the Credit River, this harvest, are special in my memory. There was the wetness of the July and the heat. My father was unusually preoccupied, worrying about the condition of the wheat he carried, for grain is sensitive to the weather in which it is matured and been harvested.

We knew that a good deal of wheat had been turned away at the mill in the last week for toughness, which is a matter of moisture content and difficult to deal with, though they do have drying equipment now at the mills which takes care of a lot of doubtful stuff. You daren't bin it though. Heating and spoilage is an ever-present risk.

At the time you hauled it home again, and you might dry it out with untold labor by spreading it out on the floor in the threshold of the barn, and keep it or sell it degraded for feed. Then, too, your barn was stuffed with hay and with straw from the threshing so you hadn't any floor to spread it on.

My father pondered the matter as he drove, and Emily, sensitive to the moods of others, was quiet. Catherine was wrapped in her thoughts. Only I was possessed of the high spirits proper to the occasion.

There wasn't much waiting around at the mill. Some years all the farmers seemed to arrive together and you might be four or five hours in line, and other times the season was strung out so you could get a load in when you brought it. We all went into the miller's office together.

Old Mr. Jonathan remembered all our names, inquired for my mother, and complained of his rheumatism, the hard times, the cost of labor, the bad wheat he'd been brought and how much he'd had to refuse. It was the same each year, but this year it was the toughness of the wheat he grumbled about most.

'Well, William,' he said at last, 'dump her off. No need to sample Laughlin's wheat, anyway.'

The girls and I looked at each other with relief. I felt like jumping up and down, for there is no doubt the worry about selling the wheat had been urgent in the last hour. My father and his father, the old Laughlin who bought Star-of-the-Sea from the O'Rourkes who built it in '69, were staunch men, and men of substance, but the substance was seldom cash.

My father stood there quite still, and the rest of us, starting for the door of the office, halted when he did not turn to go.

'No, Jonathan,' he said, after a little pause, 'I guess we'd better sample this. It's not been a good summer.'

The miller got up, a little surprised. 'H'm. All right. Thought it mightn't have been so bad your way.'

They went out together, and we followed without speaking to each other, and my father and the miller opened a lot of sacks, and talked as they pushed their hands into the wheat. Then they carried a couple of sample tins into the office and remained there for what seemed hours to us. At last my father came out and when we saw his face, our hearts sank. He didn't say anything but climbed back onto the wagon, and we got up beside him and around behind him, and he worked the wagon around and we started back toward the road.

At the road, he swung the team down toward the town and halted under the trees in front of the post office. Then he pulled a dollar out of his pocket and told Emily to get something for her mother and some ice cream for us while the horses were rested and watered.

But we didn't move at once. The blow had been heavy. Then suddenly there were tears in Emily's eyes and she turned on my father, hurt and passionate.

'Oh, why couldn't you have unloaded the wheat when he told you to? Why haven't you got the money for it? What did you say it had to be tested for?'

My father looked at her and us. Three pairs of eyes were upon him, wide-open, puzzled, accusing, in that moment or two before he spoke. Actually he said very little by way of answer. Only, 'Children, you'd better remember this all your lives.'

I think we must have stared at him a long time before we turned away, ashamed, realizing the enormity of what had been on our minds, of what Emily had expressed. We got down slowly off the wheat, leaving Father, and went into the shop and ate ice cream cones, not talking and not looking at each other.

Emily and I went and got some bit of something for Mother, and eventually we all got back on the wagon and went home with the sun sitting in front of us, and that is all there was to that day—but I have remembered.

TIME FOR REFLECTION
- Describe the effect this story has had on you.
- How do you think the children would have felt when they thought back on this event later on in their lives?

TALK IT OVER
- Think about a time when you were tempted to do something that you really knew was not in keeping with the teaching of Jesus in the Gospels. Maybe you ended up doing whatever it was, or perhaps you decided not to do it.
- Pair up with a partner and talk about what might help both of you to follow the values of the Gospel in your lives in the future.

NAME:

Review of Chapter 11

I. True or false. Mark the true statements 'T' and the false statements 'F'. Cross out the words that make the false statements false. Write the words that make the false statements true under each false statement.

_____ 1. The Bible accounts of Jesus' birth and early life are recorded only in the Gospels of Matthew and Luke.

_____ 2. Matthew tells us that the birth of Jesus took place during the reign of Caesar Augustus.

_____ 3. Matthew portrays Jesus as the new Abraham.

_____ 4. The baptism of Jesus is typically seen as the beginning of his public ministry.

_____ 5. The Beatitudes are the central theme of the Synoptic Gospels.

_____ 6. The writings of the prophet Isaiah help us understand the ministry of Jesus.

_____ 7. In Luke's Gospel the Beatitudes are part of Jesus' Sermon on the Mount.

_____ 8. The Church is the seed and the beginning on earth of the Kingdom of God.

_____ 9. The 'Woe' statements in Matthew's Gospel point to ways of not living for the Kingdom of God.

_____ 10. Luke teaches that wealth and prosperity are blessings from God.

CHAPTER 11 | CHAPTER REVIEW (CONTD.)

II. Write a paragraph describing how the parables and miracles of Jesus help us understand the meaning of the Kingdom of God.

III. Choose either 1 or 2. Explain the meaning and significance of the event(s) in the life and ministry of Jesus.
   1. The baptism and temptation of Jesus.
   2. The proclamation of the Beatitudes.

IV. How would you respond? Your friend's older sister has just died of cancer. On the ride home after band practice your friend says to you, 'Jesus performed so many miracles. I prayed and prayed for my sister. I was waiting and waiting for a miracle. But nothing happened. My sister died. She was only twenty-two.'

_____

_____

_____

_____

_____

_____

_____

V. Make a 'disciple decision'.
   1. What is the most important wisdom for life that you discovered in this chapter?

_____

_____

_____

_____

_____

_____

_____

_____

2. **Name several ways you can put that wisdom into practice. Choose one of the ways you identify and describe how you will make that wisdom part of your life right now.**

CHAPTER 12

The Gospel According to John
Jesus Is God's Word to the World

INTRODUCTION

In this chapter we explore the Gospel according to St. John and discuss the identity of its author. The chapter is developed under five major headings:

- **ATTEND AND REFLECT**: How important are symbols in the search for meaning in life?
- **HEAR THE STORY**: The authorship and content of John's Gospel
- **EMBRACE THE VISION**: A different perspective on miracles
- **THINK IT THROUGH**: Exploring the meaning for us in John's Gospel
- **JUDGE AND ACT** (*Activities and exercises that encourage the young people to integrate what they have learned in the chapter into their daily lives*)

Theological Background for the Teacher

THE AUTHORSHIP OF JOHN'S GOSPEL

Biblical scholars place the writing of the Gospel of John, or the Fourth Gospel, toward the end of the first century AD. This account of the Gospel has long been associated with the early Church in the port city of Ephesus, which is on the west coast of the country we now call Turkey.

According to tradition, the author of the Fourth Gospel is John the Apostle. He was the younger son of Zebedee, whose family had a fishing boat on the Sea of Galilee. His mother was Salome. Along with his brother James, he followed the call of Jesus (Mark 1:20). It is likely that James and John were in some kind of partnership with Peter in the fishing trade. John was especially close to Jesus and he is frequently referred to in the Fourth Gospel as the 'disciple Jesus loved' (John 13:23, 19:26, 21:7 and 21:20). Peter, James and John were often the ones chosen to accompany Jesus.

SYMBOLIC LANGUAGE

In the first section of this chapter we spend some time introducing the young people to the language of symbol in order to prepare them for their reading of St. John's Gospel. John's account of the Gospel, more than any of the other three, is rich in symbolic language and imagery.

Much of our religious language is symbolic. It has to be because it deals with 'mystery' and with the human person in relation to what is not immediately perceived by the senses in ordinary experience. Symbolic language points to particular realities, of whose truth only a fragment is caught in our everyday language. For example, the Bible describes God as light, which he is, but not in the way we commonly experience or think of light.

Young people are constantly using symbols in their communication, in their celebrations and in their activities, such as sport, drama, dance and so on. In this chapter we encourage the students to explore their own experience of the use of symbols and symbolic language in their everyday lives.

This exploration of the use of symbols in the young people's own life experiences leads on to an exploration of the Prologue to John's Gospel (John 1:1–18), the language of which is, to a large extent, symbolic. Here John describes Jesus as the Word. The central theme of the Prologue is Revelation. It begins: 'In the beginning was the Word. . . .' The Word was there before Creation and was God's instrument in Creation. Now that Word, Jesus of Nazareth, is present among us.

DISTINCTIVE FEATURES

Section two of this chapter explores the ways in which John's Gospel differs from the Synoptic Gospels. While the essential message of John's account of the Gospel is the same as that of Matthew, Mark and Luke, it differs from them in many ways. For example:

- Some of the people who have not appeared in any of the Synoptics, such as Nicodemus and the Samaritan woman, are central to John's Gospel.
- John is less interested in telling us stories about the events of the life of Jesus and more interested in revealing the meaning of what Jesus did and said.
- There are few short pithy sayings from Jesus and more long teachings, or discourses, such as the Last Supper discourse, which we discuss in section four of this chapter.
- The language in John's Gospel frequently makes use of symbols and tends to be more theological than that of Matthew, Mark and Luke.

JOHN'S PRESENTATION OF JESUS

John's Gospel, from its opening words, emphasizes the 'divinity of Christ'. John declares: 'In the beginning was the Word, and the Word was with God, and the Word was God' (John 1:1). John frequently identifies Jesus to be 'The Word'. The wonder of the Incarnation is that God the Son, the Second Person of the Blessed Trinity, became man: 'The Word became flesh and lived among us' (John 1:14). Jesus is the living Revelation of God, and what he reveals is love (John 3:16). Christians are called to reflect that love in their own communities (John 17:11, 21).

The way in which the author teaches about the identity and ministry of Jesus and how God touches human life through Jesus is deftly conveyed in the seven 'I am' statements: John 6:35; 8:12; 10:9; 10:11; 11:25; 14:6; 15:5. These are dealt with in section two of the chapter.

THE ROLE OF THE HOLY SPIRIT

The Evangelist notes with particular care the role of the Holy Spirit in the life of Jesus' disciples. The Holy Spirit is the teacher of Jesus' disciples (the Church) and their advocate. According to John 14:16, the Holy Spirit is involved in the remembering of Christ's words and actions as they are pondered again with new levels of insight. Through the Spirit, Christ talks to the believers as, through the ages, they attempt to grasp the mystery in different situations (John 16:13, 14). There is a link between the Spirit and worship in John 4:24: 'God is Spirit and those who worship him must worship in Spirit and truth.' The disciples of Jesus (the Church) are temples of the Holy Spirit (1 Corinthians 6:19), a living prayer, moved by the Holy Spirit and directed by true teaching

ADDITIONAL BACKGROUND READING

Catechism of the Catholic Church, nos. 109–119, 456–460, 515; *United States Catholic Catechism for Adults*, 26–31; 'The Gospel According to John' in *The New Jerome Biblical Commentary*, copyright © 1968, 1990 (Prentice Hall: Englewood Cliffs, New Jersey), 61:2–20.

CHAPTER OUTCOMES

See general note on page 18 of this resource.

Learning Outcomes

As a result of studying this chapter and exploring the issues raised, the young people should be able to:

- recognize and explain symbols used in John's Gospel;
- understand the context in which John wrote his Gospel and how that influenced what he wrote;
- list some differences between John's Gospel and the Synoptic Gospels;
- through becoming familiar with the 'I am' statements of Jesus, list some of the images of Jesus in John's Gospel;
- understand the significance of the miracle (sign) stories in John's Gospel;
- appreciate the significance of a number of passages from the Last Supper discourse in John's Gospel;
- reflect upon chapters 18 and 19 of John's Gospel;
- understand Mary Magdalene's role in the Post-Resurrection Narratives;
- find and read in John's Gospel accounts of significant relationships Jesus had with people;
- understand the term 'Hypostatic Union';
- know the story of St. Maximilian Kolbe.

Faith-formation Outcomes

As a result of studying this chapter and exploring the issues raised, the young people should also:

- identify and appreciate the power of symbols in their own lives;
- reflect on their own belief that Jesus is the Messiah, and on how this impacts on their lives;
- reflect on the meaning of Jesus' words at the Last Supper for their lives;
- reflect on how the humanity of Jesus can help them in their efforts to live as disciples of Jesus;
- recognize people in their families and neighborhoods who make significant sacrifices for others.

Teacher Reflection

A Teacher's Prayer
God, our Master,
You are the Supreme Teacher
Who illumines human beings with truth.
Blessed be your word of love.
God, our Father,
Make me your echo,
And allow me to sow truth and goodness.
Blessed be your attitude,
So full of understanding.
God, our Master,
Let me be passionate about beauty
And truth,
And warm my heart with your commandments.

Blessed be your light of truth,
Filled with blessings for us.
Grant me the gift of conveying,
Teaching, correcting, and indicating your ways,
Your shining glorious kindness.
God, our Master,
Direct my mind to your truth,
My hands to kind acts.
I am small and frail in your light,
But allow me to fulfill my difficult mission.
Blessed be your mercy,
Which teaches us so much.
Amen.

Notes and Guidelines for Student Activities

ATTEND AND REFLECT

How important are symbols in the search for meaning in life?

Learning Outcome
That the young people would:
- recognize and explain symbols used in John's Gospel.

Faith-formation Outcome
That the young people would also:
- identify and appreciate the power of symbols in their own lives.

Overview
Chapter 12 begins by introducing the young people to the use and significance of symbols in their lives. We then take a brief look at the structure of John's Gospel and focus on the symbolic language in the Prologue.

Supplementary Activities for 'Attend and Reflect'

Teacher Tip: You might invite the young people to recall what they learned about literary genres in chapter 8 and identify the 'language of symbol' as a literary genre.

Worksheet 1: 'Symbols in My Life' *(page 239 of this resource)* encourages the young people to think about and name some of the important symbols in their lives and to articulate why they regard these symbols as important.

Worksheet 2: 'The Light of the World' *(page 241 of this resource)* helps the young people to explore the various 'lights' in their world. From this we encourage them to imagine what their life would be like if they really believed that 'Jesus is the light of my world'.

The Nicene Creed is referred to on page 213 of the students' text. **Worksheet 3: 'The Nicene Creed'** *(page 242 of this resource)* provides an opportunity for the young people to explore this Creed in more detail. While the Creed regularly professed at Mass is named by most as 'The Nicene Creed', in reality it is the revision of the Creed adopted at the Council of Nicaea (325) by the Council of Constantinople (381). Hence the name 'The Niceno-Constantinopolitan Creed'.

HEAR THE STORY

The authorship and content of John's Gospel

Learning Outcomes
That the young people would:
- understand the context in which John wrote his Gospel and how that influenced what he wrote;
- list some differences between John's Gospel and the Synoptic Gospels;
- through becoming familiar with the 'I am' statements of Jesus, list some of the images of Jesus in John's Gospel.

Faith-formation Outcome
That the young people would:
- reflect on their own belief that Jesus is the Messiah, and on how this impacts on their lives.

Overview
Section two, 'Hear the Story', begins by exploring the identity of John the Evangelist and the authorship of the Fourth Gospel. It goes on to examine the significance and meaning of the seven 'I am' statements and the relationship that Jesus had with his disciples as expressed in John's Gospel.

Supplementary Activities for 'Hear the Story'

Worksheet 4: 'The Seven "I Am" Statements of Jesus in John's Gospel' *(page 244 of this resource)* invites the young people to reflect on what Jesus meant by these statements, and then, in groups, to compose their own 'I am' statements based on the Gospel message. This exercise will help the young people to become more familiar with the message Jesus taught about himself and his identity.

Creative Activity
Encourage the young people to draw a picture or write a news report that would sum up John's portrait of Jesus. They could do this activity alone or in pairs.

EMBRACE THE VISION

A different perspective on miracles

Learning Outcomes
That the young people would:
- understand the significance of the miracle (sign) stories in John's Gospel;
- appreciate the significance of a number of passages from the Last Supper discourse in John's Gospel;
- reflect upon chapters 18 and 19 of John's Gospel;
- understand Mary Magdalene's role in the Post-Resurrection Narratives.

Faith-formation Outcome
That the young people would also:
- reflect on the meaning of Jesus' words at the Last Supper for their lives.

Overview
Section three begins with the seven signs in the second part of John's Gospel, the Book of Signs. It then explores the Last Supper discourse and helps the young people understand some of the passages from it. Finally it looks at the Death and Resurrection of Jesus and at the post-Resurrection stories in John's Gospel.

Supplementary Activities for 'Embrace the Vision'

Worksheet 5: 'The Miracles of Jesus (1)' *(page 245 of this resource)* will help the young people to become more familiar with the details of the miracle (sign) stories in John's Gospel.

Worksheet 6: 'The Miracles of Jesus (2)' *(page 247 of this resource)* invites the young people to find specific biblical references for Jesus' miraculous deeds in all four accounts of the Gospel.

THINK IT THROUGH

Exploring the meaning for us in John's Gospel

Learning Outcomes
That the young people would:
- find and read in John's Gospel accounts of significant relationships Jesus had with people;
- understand the term 'Hypostatic Union'.

Faith-formation Outcome
That the young people would also:
- reflect on how the humanity of Jesus can help them in their efforts to live as disciples of Jesus.

Overview
Section four, 'Think It Through', begins by focusing on the fact that John's Gospel emphasized that Jesus was true God and true man. It goes on to explore some of the significant relationships and encounters Jesus had with people. The section concludes by examining some of the images of Jesus from John's Gospel.

Supplementary Activities for 'Think It Through'

Teacher Tip: The 'Group Work/Discussion' activity on page 224 of the students' text asks the young people to identify accounts in John's Gospel of significant encounters Jesus had with others, apart from his meeting with the Samaritan woman. These could include Nicodemus (John 3:1–21) or the woman caught in adultery (John 8:1–11).

Worksheet 7: 'Images of Jesus in John's Gospel' *(page 248 of this resource)* offers the young people an opportunity to give their own artistic interpretations of some of the images of Jesus from John's Gospel. This activity will help the students to become more familiar with the character of Jesus as presented in John's Gospel.

Art Activity
Invite the young people to make a piece of artwork of an image for Jesus that appeals in a particular way to them. The class might like to organize an exhibition of these artworks.

JUDGE AND ACT

Learning Outcome
That the young people would:
- know the story of St. Maximilian Kolbe.

Faith-formation Outcome
That the young people would also:
- recognize people in their families and neighborhoods who make significant sacrifices for others.

Overview
John's Gospel emphasized that sometimes we have to be prepared to suffer if we want to count ourselves among the disciples of Jesus. In this final section we introduce the young people to Maximilian Kolbe as an example of someone who made the ultimate sacrifice for his faith.

Supplementary Activities for 'Judge and Act'

In the Spotlight
(See instructions for 'In the Spotlight' activities in the 'Student Activity Tool Kit', page 273 of this resource.)

By the end of chapter 12 the young people should be familiar with the four Evangelists. To recap and assess the students' knowledge, invite Matthew, Mark, Luke and John to 'sit in the spotlight' and answer questions about their accounts of the Gospel, who they wrote for and so on.

Additional Prayer Suggestion

Scripture Reflection
(See instructions for the use of doodling in prayer in the 'Student Activity Tool Kit', page 274 of this resource.)

Use the following Scripture verse to engage the young people in prayer:

> **For God so loved the world that he gave his only Son, so that everyone who believes in him may not perish but may have eternal life.**
>
> **JOHN 3:16**

CHAPTER 12 | WORKSHEET 1

NAME:

Symbols in My Life

List some important symbols in your life.

_____

_____

Now choose one symbol that has significance in terms of your **family life**.

What is this symbol?

_____

Why is it important to your family?

_____

_____

_____

What is its symbolic meaning?

_____

_____

_____

Where did this meaning come from?

_____

_____

Now choose a symbol that is significant in terms of your **relationships with friends**.

What is this symbol?

_____

CHAPTER 12 | WORKSHEET 1 (CONTD.)

Why is it important to you and your friends?

_____

_____

_____

What is its symbolic meaning?

_____

_____

_____

Where did this meaning come from?

_____

_____

Finally, choose a symbol that is significant for you in terms of your **relationship with God**.

What is this symbol?

_____

Why is it important for your relationship with God?

_____

_____

_____

What is its symbolic meaning?

_____

_____

_____

Where did this meaning come from?

_____

_____

CHAPTER 12 | WORKSHEET 2

NAME:

The Light of the World

In the Prologue to John's Gospel the writer uses the symbol of light to talk about the coming of Jesus into the world. Later in John's Gospel, Jesus describes himself in this way: 'I am the light of the world. Whoever follows me will never walk in darkness but will have the light of life' (John 8:12).

What is the 'light' of your world?

_____

What does this 'light' mean for your life?

_____

_____

_____

_____

If you were to describe someone as 'the light of my world', what would this say about your relationship with that person?

_____

_____

_____

_____

What do you think it would mean for you if you were to believe the following statement: 'Jesus is the light of my world'? How might it affect your faith, your actions, your sense of security?

_____

_____

_____

_____

_____

CHAPTER 12 | WORKSHEET 3

NAME:

The Nicene Creed

The Nicene Creed expresses the principal tenets of our Catholic faith. Read through this creed now and pick out the phrase that you believe is central to your own faith; in other words, the phrase that you believe means most to you in your life right now.

I believe in one God,
the Father almighty,
maker of heaven and earth,
of all things visible and invisible.

I believe in one Lord Jesus Christ,
the Only Begotten Son of God,
born of the Father before all ages.
God from God, Light from Light,
true God from true God,
begotten, not made, consubstantial with the
    Father;
through him all things were made.
For us men and for our salvation
he came down from heaven,
and by the Holy Spirit was incarnate of the
    Virgin Mary,
and became man.

For our sake he was crucified under Pontius
    Pilate,
he suffered death and was buried,
and rose again on the third day

in accordance with the Scriptures.
He ascended into heaven
and is seated at the right hand of the Father.

He will come again in glory
to judge the living and the dead
and his kingdom will have no end.

I believe in the Holy Spirit, the Lord, the giver of life,
who proceeds from the Father and the Son,
who with the Father and the Son is adored and glorified,
who has spoken through the prophets.

I believe in one, holy, catholic and apostolic Church.
I confess one Baptism for the forgiveness of sins
and I look forward to the resurrection of the dead
and the life of the world to come. Amen.

TALK IT OVER
- With a partner, discuss the phrase you chose and your reasons for choosing it.

CREATIVE ACTIVITY
- Rewrite your chosen phrase in your own words on a piece of card that you can use as a bookmark.

CHAPTER 12 | WORKSHEET 4

NAME:

The Seven 'I Am' Statements of Jesus in John's Gospel

Read the following 'I am' statements of Jesus from St. John's Gospel before moving on to the activity below.

> 'I am the bread of life. Whoever comes to me will never be hungry, and whoever believes in me will never be thirsty.' (John 6:35)

> 'I am the light of the world. Whoever follows me will never walk in darkness but will have the light of life.' (John 8:12)

> 'I am the gate. Whoever enters by me will be saved, and will come in and go out and find pasture.' (John 10:9)

> 'I am the good shepherd. The good shepherd lays down his life for the sheep.' (John 10:11)

> 'I am the resurrection and the life. Those who believe in me, even though they die, will live.' (John 11:25)

> 'I am the way, and the truth, and the life. No one comes to the Father except through me.' (John 14:6)

> 'I am the vine, you are the branches. Those who abide in me and I in them bear much fruit, because apart from me you can do nothing.' (John 15:5)

REFLECT, DISCUSS, COMPOSE

- Choose one of these 'I am' statements from John's Gospel.
- Think for a few moments about what Jesus meant when he made this statement.
- Pair up with a partner and discuss the statement (or statements, if your partner has chosen a different one) and share your thoughts on the message that Jesus was seeking to convey.
- Then, still working together, compose your own 'I am' statement for Jesus based on your reading and understanding of the Gospels. Write this statement on the lines provided below.

_____

_____

_____

CHAPTER 12 | WORKSHEET 5

NAME:

The Miracles of Jesus (1)

Complete the following exercise on the miracle stories in John's Gospel.

Miracle story	Where did it happen?	Who was there?	What happened?	What did Jesus do/say?
The wedding feast of Cana (John 2:1–11)				
The healing of an official's son (John 4:46–54)				
The cure of the paralytic man at the pool (John 5:1–47)				
The feeding of the five thousand (John 6:1–14)				

CHAPTER 12 | WORKSHEET 5 (CONTD.)

Miracle story	Where did it happen?	Who was there?	What happened?	What did Jesus do/say?
The walking on water (John 6:16–24)				
The restoration of sight to a man born blind (John 9:1–12)				
The raising of Lazarus to life (John 11:38–44)				

CHAPTER 12 | WORKSHEET 6

NAME:

The Miracles of Jesus (2)

Jesus' miracles were often seen as evidence that God's Kingdom had arrived. Complete the chart by giving one example from any of the Gospels for each of the miracles listed.

The Miracle	Gospel reference
The blind see....	
The deaf hear....	
The lepers are cleansed....	
The crippled walk....	
The sick are healed....	
The oppressed (demon-possessed) go free....	
The dead are raised....	

NAME:

Images of Jesus in John's Gospel

Match each of the references from John's Gospel below with the image of Jesus that it describes.

The Word made flesh		John 15:5
The Light of the World		John 10:11
The Good Shepherd		John 11:25
The Way, the Truth and the Life		John 1:29
The Lamb of God		John 14:16
The Vine		John 6:35
The Bread of Life		John 1:14
The Resurrection and the Life		John 8:12

Choose one of the images listed above and illustrate it in the space below. You may be as creative as you wish, reflecting your own interpretation of this image of Jesus.

NAME:

Review of Chapter 12

I. Complete the statements. Use the terms in the box to state correctly the faith of the Catholic Church. Not all of the words provided will be used.

> Mary Magdalene · humanity · vine · Paraclete
> Good Shepherd · 'I Am' · helper · Fourth · the Beloved disciple
> Glory · seven · divinity · Signs · eternal life · Synoptic

1. John's Gospel is also called the _____ Gospel.
2. The four distinct parts of John's account of the Gospel are the Prologue, the Book of Signs, the Book of _____ and the Epilogue.
3. John's Gospel teaches that the Word came into the world to bring _____.
4. John's Gospel focuses on the _____ of Christ.
5. John's Gospel uses the image of the _____ to describe Jesus' life-giving relationship with his disciples.
6. The author of John's Gospel includes seven _____ statements to teach that Jesus is truly God.
7. John's Gospel uses the image of the _____ to help us come to know God's caring love for us.
8. In John's Gospel, the miracles of Jesus are found in the Book of _____.
9. Jesus promised to send the Holy Spirit, the _____, to his disciples to be their helper.
10. According to John's Gospel, the Risen Jesus appeared first to _____.

II. Define and explain. Choose either 1 or 2.
   1. Define the term 'symbol' and explain the importance of symbolic language in John's Gospel.
   2. Define the term 'hypostatic union' and explain how it helps us understand the mystery of the Incarnation.

___

III. Compare and contrast. Discuss the similarities and differences between the Last Supper in John's Gospel and the Last Supper in the Synoptic Gospels.

___

IV. How would you respond? Several of your friends ask you, 'Why do you always volunteer for the service projects at school? What a waste of time. You'll never get a high paying job helping people!'

___

V. Make a 'disciple decision'.
   1. What is the most important wisdom for life that you discovered in this chapter?

   _____
   _____
   _____
   _____
   _____
   _____
   _____
   _____

   2. Name several ways you can put that wisdom into practice. Choose one of the ways you identify and describe how you will make that wisdom part of your life right now.

   _____
   _____
   _____
   _____
   _____
   _____
   _____
   _____
   _____
   _____
   _____
   _____

CHAPTER 13

Jesus' Death and Resurrection   Heralds a New Hope

INTRODUCTION

Chapter 13 leads the young people to accompany Jesus on his last days on earth. We help them to enter into the dispositions and intentions of Jesus during his Passion, his suffering and Death. We invite the young people to become keenly aware of Jesus' love for the Father, his determination to carry out his mission, his love for others, his prayer to the Father for his disciples (which includes them), his forgiving attitude and his readiness to lay down his life. We also encourage them to imagine the amazement of the disciples at Jesus' Resurrection from the dead.

Chapter 13 is developed under five major headings:

- **ATTEND AND REFLECT**: Can you believe it?—Always hope!
- **HEAR THE STORY**: The arrest, trial and Crucifixion of Jesus
- **EMBRACE THE VISION**: Reversing death into new life
- **THINK IT THROUGH**: Jesus' Resurrection: What really happened?
- **JUDGE AND ACT** (Activities and exercises that encourage the young people to integrate what they have learned in the chapter into their daily lives)

Theological Background for the Teacher

THE DEATH OF JESUS

The Death of Jesus was Jesus' ultimate choice and expression of his love for his Father and for all people. Jesus fulfilled his Father's will by denouncing sin, evil, hypocrisy, deceit and obstinacy. By doing so he made many enemies, especially among some of the religious leaders. They were infuriated when he rebuked them for their lack of faith and for their pride. They were scandalized by his association with sinners and outcasts. They were scandalized and angered by what they considered to be his blasphemous assertion to be the Son of God. They decided to silence him by putting him to death. It was in obedience to his Father's will that Jesus freely chose to suffer and to accept the sentence of 'death by crucifixion' to save all people from their sin.

THE RESURRECTION OF JESUS

The Resurrection is central to the faith and hope of Christians. It is both a historical and a transcendent event. St. Paul asserted the faith of the Church in the Resurrection when he wrote:

> I handed on to you as of first importance what I in turn had received: that Christ died for our sins in accordance with the scriptures, and that he was buried, and that he was raised on the third day in accordance with the scriptures, and that he appeared to Cephas, then to the twelve. Then he appeared to more than five hundred brothers and sisters at one time, most of whom are still alive, though some have died. Then he appeared to James, then to all the apostles. Last of all, as to one untimely born, he appeared also to me.
> – 1 Corinthians 15:3–8

The New Testament refers to the Resurrection in two ways: (1) Jesus was raised from the dead, as in 1 Corinthians 15:4, and (2) Jesus rose for the dead, as in John's Gospel where Jesus says, 'No one takes it from me, but I lay it down of my own accord. I have power to lay it down, and I have power to take it up again' (John 10:18). More often, however, the New Testament says that God the Father raised Jesus from the dead.

The Resurrection was the Father's response to the love, confidence and obedience of the Son. During his life and on the Cross, Jesus was united with the Father, the source of all life. Therefore, he could not remain in death and the Father raised him up to a new and glorified life. St. Paul passes on this apostolic faith, writing to the Church in Philippi:

> Christ Jesus . . . though he was in the form of God, did not regard equality with God as something to be exploited, but emptied himself, taking the form of a slave, being born in human likeness. And being found in human form, he humbled himself and became obedient to the point of death—even death on a cross. Therefore God also highly exalted him and gave him the name that is above every name, so that at the name of Jesus every knee should bend . . . and every tongue should confess that Jesus Christ is Lord.
> – Philippians 2:6–11

What does it mean that Jesus rose or was raised to new life? In presenting the Resurrection of Jesus, we must stress that it was not a return to the earthly life Jesus had lived before his Death and Resurrection. It is important not to equate Jesus' Resurrection with his raising of Lazarus (John 11:1–44), the young man at Nain (Luke 7:11–17) and Jairus' daughter (Luke 8:49–56) from death. They were all restored to the earthly life they lived before they died. They grew old and died again. Christ's Resurrection was essentially different.

The Gospels tell us that the tomb in which the dead body of Jesus was placed was empty after the Resurrection, indicating that the same body that once was dead was now alive again. (See *Catechism of the Catholic Church* [CCC], no. 646; Luke 24:30–31, 39–40, 41–43; John 20:20, 27; 21:4, 7, 13–15.) But the Gospels also tell us that the body of the Risen Jesus was no longer a physical body but a 'body of glory' (Philippians 3:21), a 'spiritual body' (1 Corinthians 15:44). Jesus was alive again, but in a new way. Luke's Gospel also teaches this truth in his well-known account of the Risen Jesus' conversation with his two disciples on the road to Emmaus. The two disciples do not at first recognize him and think he is a stranger who is totally unaware of the events of Jesus' Death and Resurrection (Luke 24:13–35).

The Risen Jesus was raised to an essentially new life that we cannot adequately imagine or describe in human language. He was raised to a life liberated from death: 'Christ, being raised from the dead, will never die again; death no longer has dominion over him' (Romans 6:9). The Risen Jesus whom the Apostles encountered after the Resurrection was the same Jesus whom they had known before his Death, but who had entered into a completely new kind of life. Therefore, the disciples on the road to Emmaus (Luke 24:13–35), Mary Magdalene at the tomb (John 20:11–14) and the disciples on the shore of the lake (John 21:1–14) had difficulty recognizing him.

POST-RESURRECTION

Our faith in the Resurrection rests on the eyewitness testimony of the Apostles, the disciples and the witness of the Church today. The Resurrection was an event that the Apostles could verify; an event to which they gave witness or attested to all their lives— and for which some of them gave their lives; an event in which Christians have always believed and in which we believe today.

The Gospels and the Acts of the Apostles tell us that, forty days after the Resurrection, Jesus ascended, or was taken up, into heaven, where he now 'sits at the right hand of God'. He was 'raised', 'exalted', 'glorified'. The Risen Jesus was established as Lord of the whole universe and all power was given to him.

> Christ's ascension marks the definitive entrance of Jesus' humanity into God's heavenly domain . . . . Jesus Christ, the head of the Church, precedes us into the Father's glorious kingdom so that we, the members of his Body, may live in the hope of one day being with him for ever.
> – CCC, nos. 665 and 666

The Risen Jesus now lives in the glory of the Father. But he is also with us: 'I am with you always, to the end of the age' (Matthew 28:20). While Jesus, the incarnate Son of God, lived on earth, he was limited by time and space. He is now liberated from these limitations imposed by his human, physical body. He is now present and active everywhere, without any restrictions.

The Risen Jesus remains present and active through his followers, the Church, of whom he is the Head. United with Christ and sharing in his Death and Resurrection through Baptism, we live in the power of the Holy Spirit, who is the Spirit of the Risen Jesus.

ADDITIONAL BACKGROUND READING

Catechism of the Catholic Church, nos. 571–682; United States Catholic Catechism for Adults, 89–100; Pope John Paul II, 'The Resurrection Is a Historical Event That Transcends History', General Audience, March 1, 1989 (available on Vatican website).

CHAPTER OUTCOMES

See general note on page 18 of this resource.

Learning Outcomes
As a result of studying this chapter and exploring the issues raised, the young people should be able to:

- understand the depth of faith of the members of the early Church in the Resurrection of Jesus and the hope it gave to them;
- connect this with the risks the members of the Church took and the hope with which they lived their lives;
- understand the term 'Paschal Mystery';
- connect Jesus' Last Supper with the Passover and with the Eucharist;
- recall the main events from the story of the Passion and Death of Jesus;
- understand the concept of sacrifice;
- having read the account of the Passion and Resurrection of Jesus, reflect on it through the experiences of those who were there, such as Peter and Mary Magdalene;
- having read the Post-Resurrection Narratives from the Gospels and the earliest New Testament text on the Resurrection from the First Letter to the Corinthians, recognize the difference between the Resurrection of Jesus and the raising of Lazarus or the daughter of Jairus;
- know the story of Jesus' Ascension into heavenly glory;
- understand the images of Jesus as Savior, Redeemer and Lord, and the contemporary metaphor for Jesus as Liberator.

Faith-formation Outcomes
As a result of studying this chapter and exploring the issues raised, the young people should also:

- be able to articulate the causes of fear, concern and worry in the lives of young people and in their own lives in particular and become aware of how the Resurrection of Jesus can be a source of hope for them in the midst of such anxieties;
- appreciate the Eucharist as a source of hope for their lives;
- reflect on Peter's denial and repentance and find there inspiration for repentance in their own lives;
- through taking part in the Stations of the Cross, relate the Passion of Jesus to situations in today's world;
- choose what they find to be the most moving part of the Passion Narratives and describe how they would present it in art or music;
- grow in their appreciation of the meaning of the Resurrection for their lives;
- create their own image to describe the meaning of the Paschal Mystery;
- consider how their faith in the Resurrection can make them agents of hope in the world.

Teacher Reflection

The Killing
That was the day they killed the Son of God
On a squat hill-top by Jerusalem.
Zion was bare, her children from their maze
Sucked by the demon curiosity
Clean through the gates. The very halt and blind
Had somehow got themselves up to the hill.

After the ceremonial preparation,
The scourging, nailing, nailing against the wood,
Erection of the main-trees with their burden,
While from the hill rose an orchestral wailing,
They were there at last, high up in the soft spring day. . . .

. . . Some
who came to stare grew silent as they looked,
Indignant or sorry. But the hardened old
And the hard-hearted young, although at odds
From the first morning, cursed him with one curse,
Having prayed for a Rabbi or an armed Messiah
And found the Son of God. What use to them

Was a God or a Son of God? Of what avail
For purposes such as theirs? Beside the cross-foot
Alone, four women stood and did not move
All day. The sun revolved, the shadow wheeled,
The evening fell. His head lay on his breast,
But in his breast they watched his heart move on
By itself alone, accomplishing its journey.
Their taunts grew louder, sharpened by the knowledge
That he was walking in the park of death,
Far from their rage. Yet all grew stale at last,
Spite, curiosity, envy, hate itself.
They waited only for death and death was slow
And came so quietly they scarce could mark it.
They were angry then with death and death's deceit.

I was a stranger, could not read these people
Or this outlandish deity. Did a God
Indeed in dying cross my life that day
By chance, he on his road and I on mine?

Notes and Guidelines for Student Activities

ATTEND AND REFLECT
Can you believe it? – Always hope!

Learning Outcomes

That the young people would:
- understand the depth of faith of the members of the early Church in the Resurrection of Jesus and the hope it gave to them;
- connect this with the risks the members of the Church took and the hope with which they lived their lives;
- understand the term 'Paschal Mystery';
- connect Jesus' Last Supper with the Passover and with the Eucharist.

Faith-formation Outcomes

That the young people would also:
- be able to articulate the causes of fear, concern and worry in the lives of young people and in their own lives in particular and become aware of how the Resurrection of Jesus can be a source of hope for them in the midst of such anxieties;
- appreciate the Eucharist as a source of hope for their lives.

Overview

In this opening section we introduce the young people to the fact that the Resurrection of Jesus was the fulfillment of all the promises of the Old Testament and of the promises that Jesus himself made in the New Testament. The Resurrection enabled the early disciples of Jesus to overcome all their fears. We help the young people to explore the difference their faith in the Resurrection can make to their own lives. We then take a fresh look at the story of the Passion and Death of Jesus, beginning with the triumphant entry into Jerusalem. We look also at the story of the Last Supper, emphasizing that in order to get the total picture, we need to read the accounts from all four Gospels.

Supplementary Activity for 'Attend and Reflect'

Worksheet 1: 'Passover Meal/Last Supper' (*page 261 of this resource*) provides the young people with an opportunity to compare the events of the Last Supper with the rituals involved in a traditional Passover meal.

HEAR THE STORY
The arrest, trial and Crucifixion of Jesus

Learning Outcomes

That the young people would:
- recall the main events from the story of the Passion and Death of Jesus;
- understand the concept of sacrifice.

Faith-formation Outcomes

That the young people would also:
- reflect on Peter's denial and repentance and find there inspiration for repentance in their own lives;
- through taking part in the Stations of the Cross, relate the Passion of Jesus to situations in today's world;
- choose what they find to be the most moving part of the Passion Narratives and describe how they would present it in art or music.

Overview

By combining material from all four Gospels, section two, 'Hear the Story', presents a step-by-step account of Jesus' journey to Calvary and his Death on the Cross. We take a particular look at Peter's denial of Jesus and consider the relevance of this for the students' own lives. We also introduce the Seven Last Words of Jesus. Finally, we explain the concept of sacrifice in the context of the sacrifice of Jesus on the Cross.

Supplementary Activities for 'Hear the Story'

Worksheet 2: 'The Seven Last Words of Jesus' (*page 263 of this resource*) invites the young people to look up and reflect on Jesus' last words from the Cross.

Teacher Tip: By drawing on all four accounts of the Gospel, the students' text seeks to give the young people an overview of the Passion (the suffering and Death) of Jesus. As a revision exercise at the end of section two, you might like to encourage the young people to use a graphic organizer or timeline to plot the events leading up to Jesus' death. (*See samples in 'Student Activity Tool Kit', pages 277–80 of this resource.*)

EMBRACE THE VISION
Reversing death into new life

Learning Outcome
That the young people would:
- having read the account of the Passion and Resurrection of Jesus, reflect on it through the experiences of those who were there, such as Peter and Mary Magdalene.

Faith-formation Outcome
That the young people would also:
- grow in their appreciation of the meaning of the Resurrection for their lives.

Overview
Section three, 'Embrace the Vision', begins by considering the situation of the close followers of Jesus after he had been crucified. It then introduces the young people to the Resurrection Narratives from all four Gospels, emphasizing always the impact these events would have had on the disciples.

Supplementary Activities for 'Embrace the Vision'

Worksheet 3: 'The Empty Tomb Stories in the Gospels' (*page 264 of this resource*) will help the young people to familiarize themselves further with the various accounts of the Empty Tomb in the four Gospels.

Role-play
Invite the students to imagine and discuss how each of the following people might have reacted on hearing that Jesus' body was no longer in the tomb: Pilate; Simon of Cyrene; Mary the mother of Jesus; A guard at the tomb.

The students then break up into pairs, with one person taking on the role of one of the people listed above.

Then, with their partner, they have the conversation they imagine this person might have had with a close friend on hearing of the discovery of the empty tomb.

Finally, they act out the conversation for the rest of the group.

Guided Meditation: 'Why don't we recognize him?'
(*This meditation would be most appropriate for use at the end of section three. See 'Student Activity Tool Kit', pages 274–6 of this resource, for further helpful suggestions in relation to conducting guided meditations.*)

Invite the young people to imagine themselves walking with the two disciples on the road to Emmaus. Read the story slowly, pausing at intervals to allow the young people to reflect and respond.

The Walk to Emmaus (Luke 24:13–35)
Now on that same day [Easter Sunday] two of them were going to a village called Emmaus, about seven miles from Jerusalem, and talking with each other about all these things that had happened. While they were talking and discussing, Jesus himself came near and went with them, but their eyes were kept from recognizing him. *(Pause)*

- *Why do you think they don't recognize him?*
- *Why do you not recognize him?*
- *Why doesn't he introduce himself?*

And he said to them, 'What are you discussing with each other while you walk along?' They stood still, looking sad. Then one of them, whose name was Cleopas, answered him, 'Are you the only stranger in Jerusalem who does not know the things that have taken place there in these days?' He asked them, 'What things?' *(Pause)*

- *How would you tell Jesus himself the story of what happened in Jerusalem?*
- *What would be your mood? The points to highlight?*

They replied, 'The things about Jesus of Nazareth, who was a prophet mighty in deed and word before God and all the people, and how our chief priests and leaders handed him over to be condemned to death and crucified him. But we had hoped that he was the one to redeem Israel. Yes, and besides all this, it is now the third day since these things took place. Moreover, some women of our group astounded us. They were at the tomb early this morning, and when they did not find his body there, they came back and told us that they had indeed seen a vision of angels who said that he was alive. Some of those who were with us went to the tomb and found it just as the women had said; but they did not see him.' *(Pause)*

- *They 'had hoped'. Had they now given up hope? Why?*
- *Have you lost hope too, like them?*
- *Why do you think they did not believe the women's report?*

Then he said to them, 'Oh, how foolish you are, and how slow of heart to believe all that the prophets have declared! Was it not necessary that the Messiah should suffer these things and then enter into his glory?' Then beginning with Moses and all the prophets, he interpreted to them the things about himself in all the Scriptures. *(Pause)*

- *What do you think of Jesus' first response? A bit harsh? Frustrated?*

- *What might the Risen Christ have highlighted from the Hebrew Scriptures, the Old Testament, about himself?*

As they came near the village to which they were going, he walked ahead as if he were going on. But they urged him strongly, saying, 'Stay with us, because it is almost evening and the day is now nearly over.' So he went in to stay with them. When he was at table with them, he took bread, blessed and broke it, and gave it to them. Then their eyes were opened, and they recognized him; and he vanished from their sight. *(Pause)*

- *Why did they offer him hospitality, to stay on?*
- *Why do you think they 'recognized him' in the breaking of the bread?*
- *When do you recognize him? What do you see?*
- *Why did he disappear, now that they knew who he was?*
- *Where did he go? (Might it be into them, into us, into what is now the body of Christ?)*

They said to each other, 'Were not our hearts burning within us while he was talking to us on the road, while he was opening the scriptures to us?' That same hour they got up and returned to Jerusalem; and they found the eleven and their companions gathered together. They were saying, 'The Lord has risen indeed, and he has appeared to Simon!' Then they told what had happened on the road, and how he had been made known to them in the breaking of the bread. *(Pause)*

- *As you take your leave of your two companions, what do you want to say to them?*
- *If you had been there, how do you think you would eventually describe to your friends what happened on the road to Emmaus?*

Worksheet 4: 'The Encounter at Emmaus' (*page 266 of this resource*) invites the young people to imagine themselves back in the time of Jesus, having heard rumors about the encounter between the Risen Jesus and the two disciples on the road to Emmaus, and to write the story of what happened in their own words.

THINK IT THROUGH

Jesus' Resurrection: What really happened?

Learning Outcomes

That the young people would:
- having read the Post-Resurrection Narratives from the Gospels and the earliest New Testament text on the Resurrection from the First Letter to the Corinthians, recognize the difference between the Resurrection of Jesus and the raising of Lazarus or the daughter of Jairus;
- know the story of Jesus' Ascension into heavenly glory;
- understand the images of Jesus as Savior, Redeemer and Lord, and the contemporary metaphor for Jesus as Liberator.

Faith-formation Outcome

That the young people would also:
- create their own image to describe the meaning of the Paschal Mystery.

Overview

In section four, 'Think It Through', we explore the Resurrection as a real event and as a mystery of faith. We look at a number of images used by St. Paul to describe the meaning of the Resurrection for the early Church. We review the images of Jesus as Savior, Redeemer and Lord, as well as the contemporary image of Liberator. Finally, we encourage the young people to create their own image to describe the meaning of the Paschal Mystery.

Supplementary Activity for 'Think It Through'

Jesus' Resurrection was not a return to the earthly life he had lived before his death. After the Resurrection Jesus was alive again, but in an essentially new way. The story in **Worksheet 5: 'Understanding the Resurrection'** (*page 267 of this resource*) should help the young people as they try to grapple with what this meant. We invite them to follow this up with a discussion on what the Resurrection means for us today.

JUDGE AND ACT

Faith-formation Outcome

That the young people would:
- consider how their faith in the Resurrection can make them agents of hope in the world.

Overview

In section five, 'Judge and Act', we introduce the young people to Mary Magdalene as a model of faith in the Risen Jesus. We end the chapter with a Prayer Reflection based on the Stations of the Cross.

Supplementary Activities for 'Judge and Act'

Media Project

Encourage the young people to work in groups and find some pictures or stories in recent local, national or international newspapers that show that the Risen Jesus is present in the world today. They should look for pictures and stories that reflect hope, love and solidarity. They could make a display of their findings in the classroom using suitable captions.

Teacher Tip: There are many films on the life of Jesus that can be used to illustrate the Passion and the Resurrection. The films mentioned below are particularly effective:

The Passion of the Christ
(Directed by Mel Gibson, 2004)

Jesus of Nazareth
(Directed by Franco Zeffirelli, 1977)

The Bible—Jesus
(Time Life, directed by Robert Young, 2004)

Matthew (International Bible Society and Pathway Media, directed by Van Den Bergh, 2006)

There is also a wide variety of artwork available on this topic.

Additional Prayer Suggestion

Scripture Reflection
(*See instructions for the use of doodling in prayer in the 'Student Activity Tool Kit', page 274 of this resource.*)

Use the following Scripture verse to engage the young people in prayer:

> **Jesus, remember me when you come into your kingdom.**
>
> **LUKE 23:42**

If available, you might play the Taizé chant 'Jesus, remember me when you come into your kingdom' while the young people are engaged in prayer.

CHAPTER 13 | WORKSHEET 1

NAME:

Passover Meal / Last Supper

Read about what happens at a typical Passover (Seder) meal and what happened at the Last Supper. Then discuss the questions below.

Outline of a Passover Meal	The Last Supper
Part 1: Preparation ⊙ The host blesses the feast and the first cup of wine. ⊙ Hands are washed. ⊙ Food is set in place: wild herbs, sauce, unleavened bread, lamb. ⊙ Bitter herbs are eaten.	⊙ Jesus sends Peter and John to prepare a room. (Luke 22:1–13) ⊙ Jesus takes his place as host and speaks with the Apostles of his desire to eat the Passover before he suffers. (Luke 22:14–16) ⊙ The first cup of wine is drunk. (Luke 22:17–18) ⊙ Bitter herbs are passed as Jesus says: 'One of you is about to betray me.' (Luke 22:21–23) ⊙ Jesus washes the Apostles' feet as a sign of love and service. (John 13:5)
Part 2: Pre-Meal Ritual ⊙ The youngest asks: 'Why?' ⊙ The host explains the meaning of the meal and says a Prayer of Thanksgiving. ⊙ All sing Psalm 112/113. ⊙ The second cup of wine is drunk.	⊙ Jesus instructs the Apostles to love one another. (John 13:34–35) ⊙ Peter questions Jesus: 'Why can't I follow you?' Jesus explains how Peter will deny him three times. (John 13:36–38) ⊙ Jesus promises to send the Holy Spirit. (John 14:1–27) ⊙ Jesus prays for his disciples. (John 16:32; 17:21)
Part 3: The Meal ⊙ Hands are washed. ⊙ Bread is eaten with sauce. ⊙ The third cup of wine is poured. ⊙ The lamb is eaten. ⊙ All sing Psalm 136.	⊙ Jesus breaks the bread and passes it to the Apostles, saying: 'This is my body that is for you. Do this in remembrance of me.' (1 Corinthians 11:24) ⊙ Jesus takes the cup of wine and says: 'This cup is the New Covenant in my blood. Do this, as often as you drink it, in remembrance of me.' (1 Corinthians 11:25) ⊙ The Passover lamb is prepared and passed around. ⊙ Jesus' self-surrender to death occurred as the Passover lambs were being sacrificed in the Temple. As St. Paul put it, 'Our Passover lamb, Christ, has been sacrificed.' (1 Corinthians 5:7).

Outline of a Passover Meal	The Last Supper
Part 4: Conclusion ⊙ All sing Psalms 114–118. ⊙ All drink the third cup of wine.	⊙ 'When they had sung the hymn they went out to the Mount of Olives.' (Mark 14:26; Matthew 26:30)

REFLECT AND DISCUSS
- In what ways is the traditional Passover meal similar to the Last Supper?
- In what ways do they differ?
- What do these similarities and differences reveal about the significance of the Last Supper?

CHAPTER 13 | WORKSHEET 2

NAME:

The Seven Last Words of Jesus

Look up the following biblical references and write out the last words of Jesus spoken from the Cross. Then take time to pause and reflect on these words.

Luke 23:34 _____

Matthew 27:46 _____

John 19:26–27 _____

John 19:28 _____

Luke 23:43 _____

John 19:30 _____

Luke 23:46 _____

CHAPTER 13 | WORKSHEET 3

NAME:

The Empty Tomb Stories in the Gospels

Using the various Gospel accounts of the women disciples finding the empty tomb, complete the following table.

Which Gospel?	Names of the women	Reason for going to the tomb	What the women found on arrival	Message of the angel(s) or young man	Reaction of the women
Mark					
Matthew					
Luke					

CHAPTER 13 | WORKSHEET 3 (CONTD.)

Read the story of the Empty Tomb in John's Gospel (20:1–18). Recall the details in your own words.

_____

_____

_____

_____

_____

_____

_____

_____

_____

_____

_____

_____

_____

_____

_____

_____

_____

NAME:

The Encounter at Emmaus

Imagine yourself back in the time of Jesus, having just heard rumors about the encounter between the Risen Jesus and the two disciples on the road to Emmaus. Write the story that you will pass on to the people in your family and village.

CHAPTER 13 | WORKSHEET 5

NAME:

Understanding the Resurrection

Look up and read from your Bible Luke 24:13–35. This well-know Gospel narrative of the appearance of the Risen Jesus to the disciples traveling on the road from Jerusalem to Emmaus is proclaimed at Mass every year on the Third Sunday of Easter. Imagine that you are one of the two disciples. Place yourself in the story.

REFLECT AND DISCUSS
- Think about how this Gospel narrative might help you come to a deeper understanding that Jesus was alive in a new way after the Resurrection.
- Why do you think the two disciples (one of whom is yourself) reacted the way they (you) did?
- How do you think the eleven (the Apostles) and their companions received the two disciples when they related their meeting and conversation with the Risen Jesus?
- Discuss your thoughts and insights.
- Then talk about what the Resurrection event means for us today.

Review of Chapter 13

I. **Fill in the blanks. Complete the following paragraph so that it correctly states the teaching in the Gospel.**

On the Sunday before his Passion Jesus entered (1) _____ for the annual celebration of the Passover. The Passion of Jesus is his (2) _____ and (3) _____. It was during Passover that Jesus celebrated the Last Supper with his disciples and gave us the (4) _____, the memorial of Christ's own (5) _____. After the Last Supper Jesus was arrested, falsely accused of committing the crime of (6) _____ and put on trial. After the trial Jesus carried a cross to a place called (7) _____, where he was crucified and died. Three days later Jesus was raised from the dead. We call this event the (8) _____. The Risen Jesus first appeared to (9) _____, who brought the Good News of the Resurrection to the other disciples. St. Paul wrote, 'If Christ has not been raised . . . then your (10) _____ has been in vain'.

CHAPTER 13 | CHAPTER REVIEW (CONTD.)

II. Choose either 1 or 2.
   1. Name the seven last words of Jesus.
   2. Explain the meaning of the term 'The sacrifice of the Cross'.

_____

_____

_____

_____

_____

_____

_____

_____

III. Compare and contrast. Explain the difference between Jesus raising Lazarus from the dead and the Resurrection of Jesus.

_____

_____

_____

_____

_____

IV. How would you respond? You and your friends are walking through the mall. A friend says, 'Look at all this stuff. Do you think that we need to wait until we die and get to heaven to be really happy?'

_____

_____

_____

_____

_____

_____

V. Make a 'disciple decision'.
   1. What is the most important wisdom for life that you discovered in this chapter?

   _____

   _____

   _____

   _____

   _____

   _____

   _____

   _____

   2. Name several ways you can put that wisdom into practice. Choose one of the ways you identify and describe how you will make that wisdom part of your life right now.

   _____

   _____

   _____

   _____

   _____

   _____

   _____

   _____

   _____

   _____

   _____

   _____

Student Activity Tool Kit

There is a wide range of activities for students offered throughout the *Credo* series. This 'tool kit' contains suggestions and instructions for getting the optimum benefit from these activities.

TOOLS FOR EFFECTIVE LEARNING
- Reflect and Discuss/Talk It Over (p. 271)
- Shared Reading Technique (p. 271)
- Jigsaw Reading (p. 271)
- Peer Teaching (p. 271)
- Graphic Organizers (p. 272)
- Mind Maps (p. 272)
- In the Spotlight (p. 273)
- Journal Exercises (p. 273)
- Faith Words Quiz (p. 273)
- Blogs/Blogging (p. 273)
- Vox Pops (p. 273)
- Walking Debates (p. 273)
- Words of Wisdom Collection (p. 274)

TOOLS FOR EFFECTIVE PRAYER
- Doodling as a prayer technique (p. 274)
- Meditations—A guide to facilitate successful meditations (p. 274)
- Sample formats for introducing and concluding guided meditations (p. 275)

Tools for Effective Learning

REFLECT AND DISCUSS/TALK IT OVER
The 'Reflect and Discuss' and 'Talk it over' activities that appear throughout the text may be approached in a variety of ways. The young people may discuss the topic in pairs, in small groups or as a single class group. Before they do so, they should take a few moments just to think about the question(s) to be discussed. Following their discussion they may compare their mental or written notes and identify the answers they think are best, most convincing or most unique. The teacher may then invite them to share their conclusions with others. The teacher may do this by going around each pair or group or by taking answers as they are called out (or as hands are raised). The teacher or a designated helper may record students' responses on the board or overhead.

SHARED READING TECHNIQUE
This technique is useful when students have to read and comprehend a long or difficult text. It is especially useful for reading a long Bible passage.

Step 1: Each student is assigned a reading partner; one will be reader A and the other reader B.

Step 2: Both students silently read the first section; for example, a selection of Bible verses or a paragraph.

Step 3: Student A is initially the summarizer and student B is the accuracy-checker. The summarizer explains in his or her own words the content of the first section. The accuracy-checker listens carefully and offers help or prompts if anything is left out.

Step 4: The students move on to the next section, switch roles and repeat the process until they have completed the text.

Step 5: At the end they summarize the key points.

JIGSAW READING
Step 1: Divide a text into different sections, say five paragraphs.

Step 2: Students split up into groups, each group getting one paragraph to read.

Step 3: In their group the students read the relevant text, discuss the key points and prepare to teach the others in the class what they have learned.

Step 4: Students move around so that one student from each group joins a new group.

Step 5: In the new group they share and teach what they learned in the first group.

This continues until all the information has been shared.

PEER TEACHING
Peer teaching is a fun activity, as young people enjoy taking on the role of 'teacher'. It prompts them to think about their own understanding of a topic and

how they can enhance their peers' understanding. It also encourages them to take more responsibility for their learning. In addition, it develops their skills in communication and teamwork.

Step 1: Organize the class into mixed-ability groups of three or four students. Divide the section of the course or chapter into different areas, and give each group an area to teach. It is important to give clear guidelines at the start; for example, concerning roles within the group, timing of the exercise, giving and taking peer feedback and so on.

Step 2: Give students time in class to brainstorm on how they will teach the area. The teacher may allocate roles within the group or the group members may do this. The roles assigned might involve collecting information, creating a visual display of the information, or teaching the topic to the whole class. If there are four in a group, one role could be that of question-taker; this student anticipates possible questions from the class and prepares answers to them with the team.

Step 3: Students then research their topic for homework and come up with ideas to teach the topic.

Step 4: Give the students time in class to put together their ten-minute teaching session. In addition, they will need time to decide on questions to ask the other groups on their areas.

Step 5: Give each team time to teach their section and five minutes for questions from the class.

Step 6: At the end of the process, the class evaluate each team's performance. If sections were left out or not covered sufficiently, if notes were unclear or if information was not accurate, they should inform the team of this. They also share what helped them remember the material.

Note: Peer teaching can also be done in small groups of three or four, where each group member reads or revises a different section and they teach the other people *within* that group.

GRAPHIC ORGANIZERS

Graphic organizers help students in recording, organizing, summarizing and integrating information. They can take many forms, from Venn diagrams to mind-maps. They may be used for note-making, for revision, for brainstorming a topic and so on. A number of graphic-organizer templates are provided on pages 277–80 of this resource, which may be photocopied and used for a variety of topics.

MIND MAPS

A mind map is a diagram used to represent words and images linked to and arranged around a key theme or idea. Mind maps can be used to generate, visualize, structure and classify ideas, and as an aid in study, organization, problem-solving, decision-making and writing. Mind maps may also aid recall of existing memories. The process of mind-mapping can be divided into three steps:

Step 1: *Getting Started*
Take a sheet of plain paper and some colored pens. Turn the page so it is in landscape position. In the center of the page draw an image that represents the topic you are working on, and then label the image. Always start in the middle of the page, as this gives you space to spread your ideas in all directions, without being limited by the boundaries found in linear note-making.

Step 2: *Expanding Your Thinking*
The next step entails creating thick colorful branches radiating out from the central image. These branches will represent your main stream of thoughts. There is no limit to the number of main branches, but five or six might be adequate. On each branch, clearly state in bold colorful capitals your main thoughts using a single key word. Use your imagination.

It is important to use colors as they will add energy to your mind map and enhance your creative thinking. To get your thoughts flowing, you may need to ask yourself a few questions. The two main things that make mind-mapping so effective are imagination and association. The brain's thinking processes are naturally image-filled, so in order to incorporate this natural process into the activity it is important to include images and pictures on your mind map. Not only will images save you time in comparison to note-taking, but they are also easier to remember.

Step 3: *Ideas, Thoughts and Associations*
You can use 'association' to expand your mind map to the final stage. Look at the key words on the main branches—these key words should spark off further ideas. Draw smaller branches stemming from the key words to accommodate the associations you make. The number of sub-branches is limitless; it is dependent upon the number of ideas you can think of. The sub-branch may then trigger more thoughts and ideas associated with the key word of that branch, leading to the development of the next level of sub-branches. Continue this process until all your thoughts and ideas are on your mind map.

IN THE SPOTLIGHT

Throughout this text, students will learn about many famous people; for example, Abraham and St. Thomas Aquinas. The 'In the Spotlight' activity will help to bring their stories to life. This activity should be used after the class is familiar with the person's story. One student takes on the role of the person being studied. The class must think of questions to ask the person relating to the topic being explored, and the student 'in the spotlight' answers the questions from the famous person's perspective. A number of people can be 'in the spotlight' at the same time to form a panel of experts; for example, the Evangelists Matthew, Mark, Luke and John could lead a discussion on the content of the four Gospels.

Step 1: Begin by asking each student to write a question that they would like to ask the famous person.

Step 2: Select a student or panel of students to be the person(s) 'in the spotlight'. They should sit or stand at the top of the class and answer the questions in character.

JOURNAL EXERCISES

Suggestions for Journal exercises are given throughout the students' text. These allow students to write answers to questions that they might consider too personal to answer in class. They can be particularly valuable because they give students time to pause, reflect and then record their ideas and feelings on a topic. Journal writing can also be a form of prayer. If the Journal activity takes place during class time, you could light a candle (if local fire regulations permit) and/or play some soft music to create a prayerful atmosphere.

FAITH WORDS QUIZ

Faith words are highlighted throughout the text to enable students develop their religious vocabulary. A good way of reviewing the text at the end of the semester is to have a quiz based on these words.

Step 1: Organize the students into teams. Each team divides up the chapters to be reviewed between them. They each take flash cards and write the faith words from the assigned chapters on one side and an explanation on the other side. They may include diagrams or pictures—anything that will help their teammates understand and remember the definitions.

Step 2: Each student takes a turn at explaining the faith words to the rest of their team members.

Step 3: The teacher can lead an end-of-semester quiz based on the faith words, with prizes for the best team!

BLOGS/BLOGGING

'Blogging' is another form of journaling. The term 'blog' is a shortened form of 'weblog'. A blog is a type of website, similar to an online journal. It is usually maintained by the writer and can provide commentary or news on a particular subject or it can function as a more personal diary. Entries are commonly displayed in reverse-chronological order; that is, the last entry is listed first. The word 'blog' can also be used as a verb, meaning 'to maintain or add content to a blog'. Most blogs are set up in such a way as to allow readers to add comments. There are numerous internet sites that provide instructions for setting up and maintaining blogs.

VOX POPS

Vox populi is a Latin phrase that literally means 'voice of the people'. It is a term often used in broadcasting for interviews with members of the general public. Students may use this technique to put a question to other young people in the school or to people in a parish or local club; for example 'Do you believe in God? Why?/Why not?' They could use a video recorder or mobile phone to record the responses and then watch or review them in class.

WALKING DEBATES

A 'walking debate' can be a useful and exciting strategy for helping young people to engage with decision-making, morality and justice issues.

Step 1: Begin by clearing the tables and chairs out of the way to create space in the classroom.

Step 2: Place a sign bearing the word 'Right' on one wall, a sign with the word 'Wrong' on the opposite wall, and a third sign in the middle of the room saying 'Not sure'.

Step 3: According as you read out a list of statements relating to moral decisions, the students move around and position themselves beside whichever sign corresponds with their choice of answer.

Step 4: After each statement, one student standing at each position must say why they have chosen their position. Students can be offered the option of changing their position as they listen to one another. In directing the discussion, you may also invite the young people to consider what factors influence their discernment of what is right and wrong.

WORDS OF WISDOM COLLECTION

There are quotations from Scripture or inspirational people highlighted throughout the *Credo* series. Students are invited to create a personal collection of their favorite words of wisdom in their journal, which they may add to throughout the year. You might like to organize a class project to create a collection of inspirational quotations that could be presented as a class gift at the end of the year.

Tools for Effective Prayer

DOODLING AS A PRAYER TECHNIQUE

The doodle is a ubiquitous feature of teenage culture. Many people doodle without even being aware of what exactly they are doing. For example, students in class will often begin to make shapes on a page while the teacher is talking, which they then decorate and embellish. Generally there is no end in mind, but the very act of doodling focuses the student's attention. Doodling can be used in an imaginative way by the teacher to provide a focus for contemplation. Many high school Theology teachers and other teachers of Religious Education have begun to employ the act of doodling as a technique used in prayer, which young people are very happy to engage in.

Doodling has long been a means for fostering deep reflection, invoking the use of the gift of one's inner imagination as a source of reflection. Recent research clearly indicates that there are a wide variety of 'learning styles' or 'intelligences' by which people learn best and express themselves best. Doodling, in one sense, is a means of expression that particularly suits people whose preferred 'learning style' or 'intelligence' is more visual than verbal. While the use of words is the most common form of learning and expression, for many the use of words is not the most effective and comfortable way of discovering truth and expressing themselves. Employing art and architecture as an expression of faith attests to the power of the 'visual' in passing on one's personal faith in Christ as well as the faith of the Church. The use of doodling in the *Credo* series recognizes the power of simple drawing (or doodling) to be a basic form of reflection on and artistic expression of the faith life for many young people.

In each chapter of the teacher's resource we provide a suggestion for the use of doodling during a prayerful reflection on Scripture.

Preparation:
Each student will need:
- Gel pens, markers or crayons
- A black marker, pen or sharp pencil
- A plain sheet of paper

Note: No erasers are required, as every mark made is part of the entire prayer! The end product will serve as a visual reminder of time spent in prayer.

General Guidelines:
Step 1: Begin by lighting a candle (if the fire regulations of your school permit) to symbolize the presence of God. Say the prayer suggested for the lesson, repeating it slowly a number of times.

Step 2: Play a recording of some soft background music and encourage the young people to become relaxed and calm.

Step 3: Ask the students to write on their page the words of the prayer that they have just heard.

Step 4: Slowly, with their minds focused on the words, they begin to doodle around the words, adding design and color as they like.

Step 5: When they are finished, repeat together the words of the prayer.

Invite the students to take their artwork with them as a reminder of their prayer time.

MEDITATIONS—A GUIDE TO FACILITATE SUCCESSFUL MEDITATIONS

There are opportunities and suggestions for meditative prayer throughout the *Credo* series. The following points are worth noting:

Preparation: It is strongly recommended that you read through each meditation before doing it in class. When you are familiar with it, the piece will flow better, allowing for suitable emphases and pauses as necessary.

Atmosphere: A lighted candle (if local fire regulations permit) and soft background music will help create a relaxed, prayerful atmosphere. You might also like to use incense or some other aroma. It is also worth putting a 'Do Not Disturb' notice on the door.

Remind the young people that this a special time for them to get in touch with themselves and to connect with the presence of God. They should therefore be attentive and avoid becoming distracted or distracting other students.

Pace: Pace is crucial—a good meditation should be slow, with plenty of appropriate pauses.

Posture: The best posture is the one that helps you pray. However, for the purposes of a facilitated meditation at school, the preferred option is for students to sit erect in a chair, with their back straight, both feet flat on the floor and hands on lap or on the desktop.

Breathing: Encourage the young people to breathe smoothly, deeply and slowly. Such a pattern, once achieved, inevitably leads to more effective and deeper meditation.

Awareness: Awareness, an essential element of meditation, can best be achieved by learning to listen: to one's own body, thoughts and feelings. Begin by encouraging the young people to listen to the sounds outside the room, then the ones inside the room, then the very slight sounds in their own body (small movements of breath, stomach, heart). By focusing initially on outside sounds, these will eventually cease to be a distraction and can be simply 'let go'.

Centerpiece/Focal point: It is often helpful to have a centerpiece for the young people to focus on, such as a candle, icon or image, or indeed any object or image from nature.

Mantra: Another useful technique is the use of the mantra. Mantras are sacred words or phrases which, when repeated either out loud or in the mind, help to bring the pray-er into a deeper sense of self, or into a higher state of consciousness, or more closely into a sense of the presence of God. A suitable mantra might be a short scriptural phrase such as 'My Lord and My God'. It is often beneficial to say the mantra on the inward or outward breaths or on both.

Sacred Scripture: The Bible is used as a source for many of the meditations in the *Credo* series. A number of mediations are based on Bible stories. Students are often encouraged to place themselves imaginatively in the Bible story. Another form of scriptural prayer that is explored is *lectio divina*, which focuses on four basic movements in praying the Scriptures; namely, *lectio* (reading), *meditatio* (meditation), *oratio* (prayer) and *contemplatio* (contemplation), and sometimes a fifth, *actio* (action).

Personal meditation: The young people should be encouraged to attempt meditation on their own too; for example, in their bedroom or in a little-used room in their home, or even in a secluded place outdoors.

Sample Formats for Introducing and Concluding Guided Meditations

All the meditations in the *Credo* series can be introduced and concluded in a similar pattern. You should adapt the following to suit your own situation and circumstances.

SAMPLE INTRODUCTION
Leader
Times of silence are precious. Our aim during this meditation is to enter into silence—the silence of our own hearts. In order to become still in our innermost heart we must first become still in our body.

And so, we begin by relaxing our bodies. . . . Just close your eyes gently. . . . Sit straight in the chair or desk, leaning comfortably against the back, with both feet flat on the floor. . . . Rest your hands gently on your knees or hold them together loosely. . . .

Bring your attention to your neck and shoulders. . . . Notice any tension you experience there, and just imagine that tension flowing gently down your arms and out of your body through your fingers. . . .

Become aware of your back against the seat. . . . and then, further down, feel your weight pressing against the seat. . . . You are becoming more and more relaxed. . . .

Become aware of your breathing. . . . Don't breathe any more heavily or deeply than you normally do. . . . Notice the colder air at the bottom of your nostrils as you breathe in . . . . and the warmer air as you breathe out. . . . You are now breathing gently and easily. . . . The breath you are breathing now is the breath of life; the breath that God breathed into your body when you were born. . . . Give thanks for this breath, this gift of life. . . .

Now we are going to relax the mind. . . . Images and thoughts and feelings will come into your mind—just let them come and go gently. . . . Don't focus on any thought or image in particular. Just let them come and go of their own accord. . . . Allow all tension or stress to evaporate. . . . You are becoming more and more relaxed. . . .

SAMPLE ENDING

The meditator is totally relaxed and at a deeper level of consciousness, so he or she has to be brought back gently to an awareness of the room and the surroundings.

Leader
Return your attention now to your breath. . . . Notice how peacefully you are breathing. . . . Become aware of your body and your posture as you sit in your seat. . . . Notice how calm and relaxed and peaceful it is. . . .

Begin now to stretch your arms and your legs. . . . Open your eyes gently and become aware of the room and the people around you. . . .

GRAPHIC ORGANIZER TEMPLATE

GRAPHIC ORGANIZER TEMPLATE

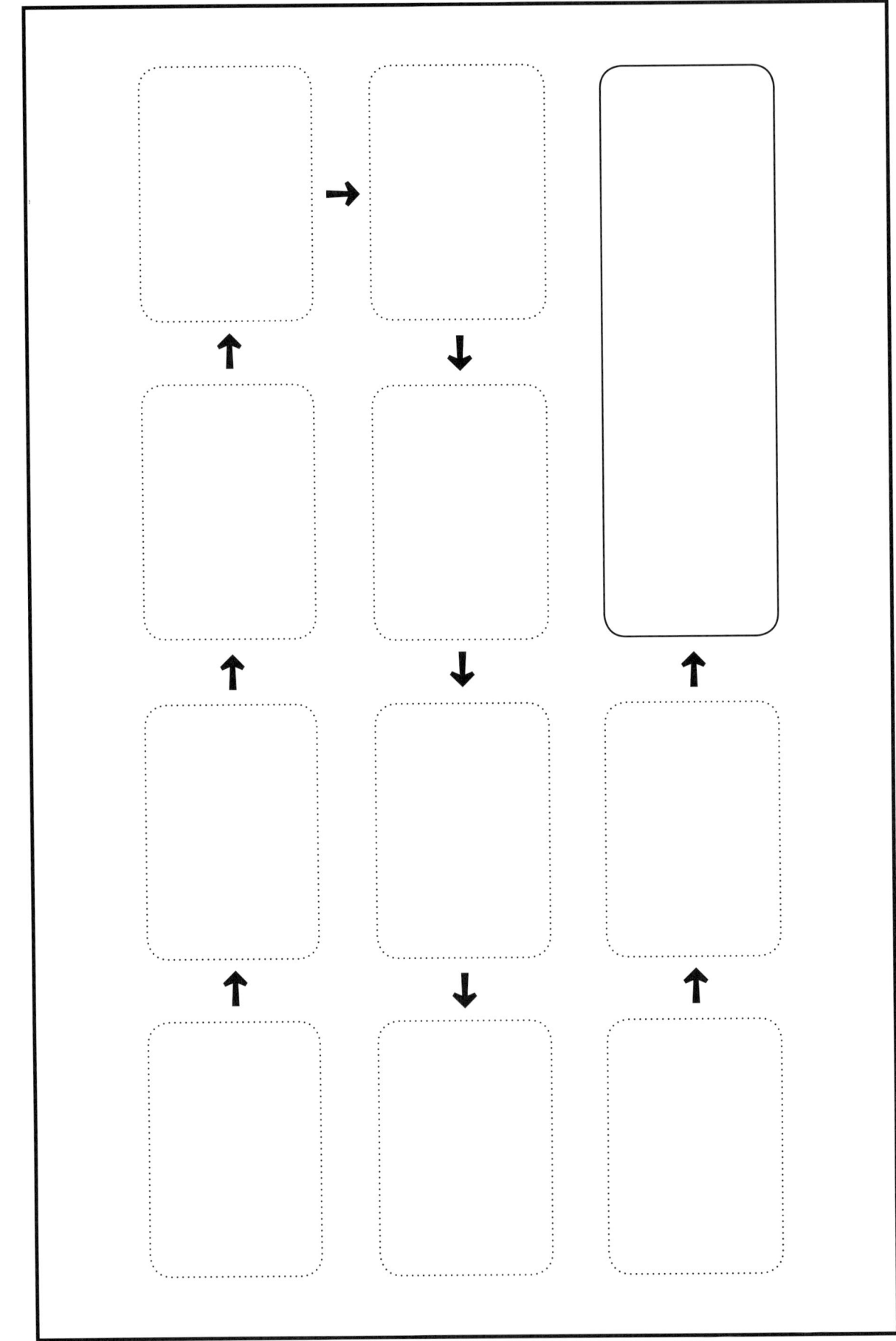

GRAPHIC ORGANIZER TEMPLATE

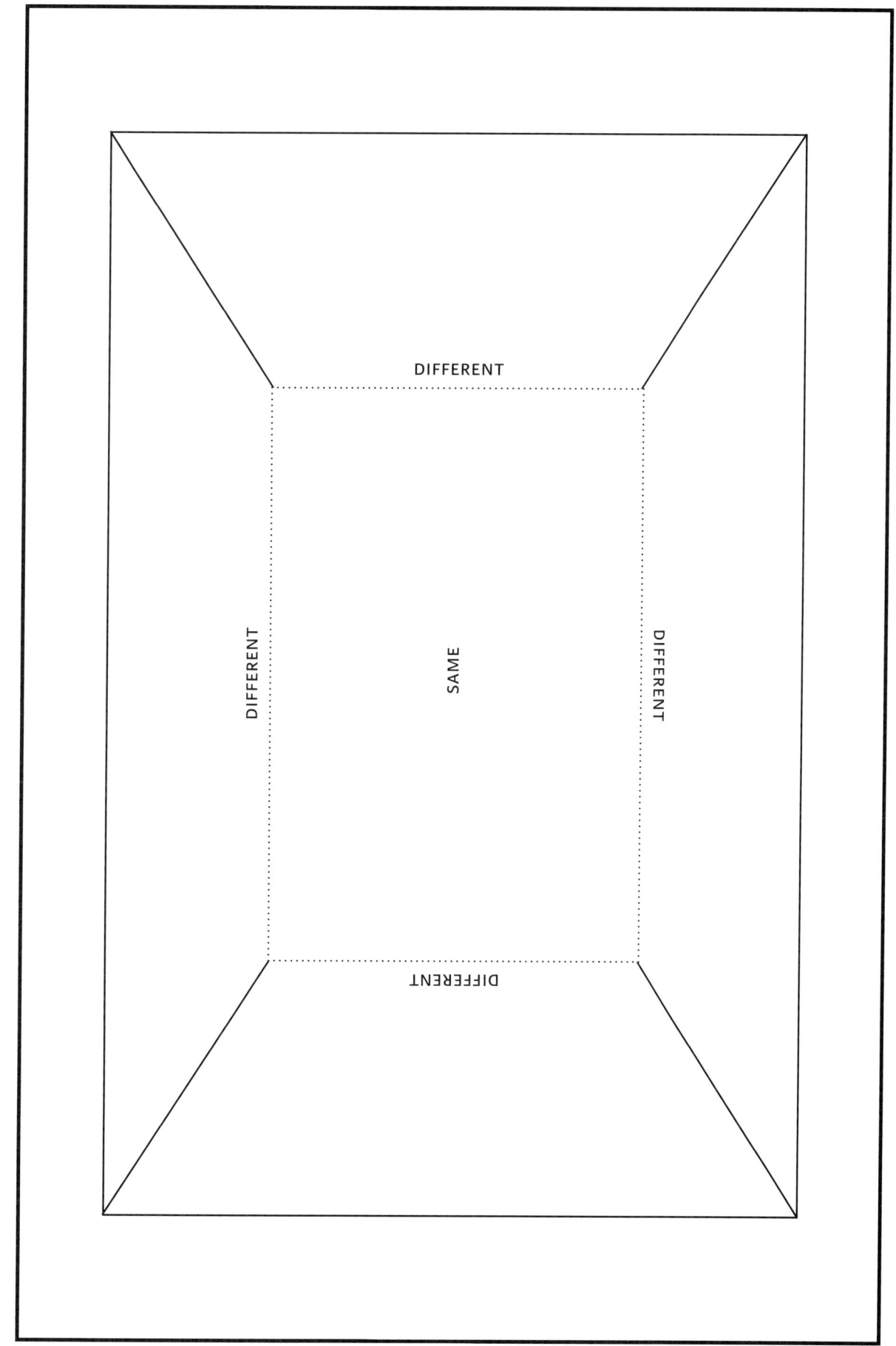

STUDENT ACTIVITY TOOL KIT | GRAPHIC ORGANIZER TEMPLATE | 279

GRAPHIC ORGANIZER TEMPLATE

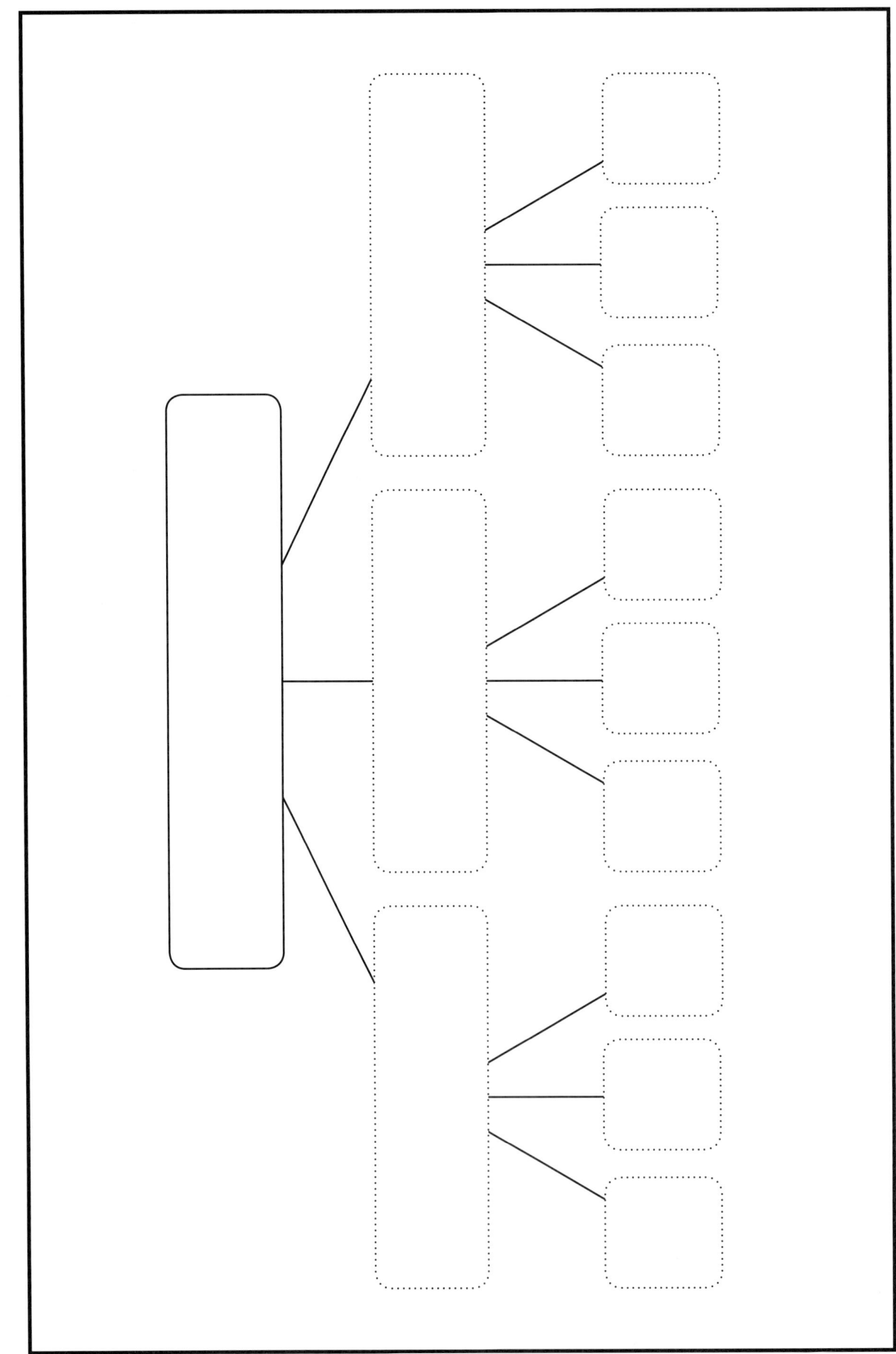

Answer Key to Chapter Reviews

Chapter 1 Review

I. **1.** God; heart; **2.** scientific; faith; **3.** dominion; stewards; **4.** God's; **5.** gift; human; revealed.

II. **Appropriate responses** will develop the revelation that God created human beings in the image and likeness of God, to share in the life and love of God, to live in happiness with him, and to have responsibility for all of creation.

III. **Key truths:** Appropriate responses will include: human life is an expression of God's life; humans share the very life (breath) of God; humans are created to live in community; we have been created to love and be loved; every person is unique; man and woman are equal partners.
Importance for daily living: Appropriate responses will center around respect for the dignity of every person and the goodness of all creation.

IV. **Accept all responses that** present the teaching of the Church that the search for happiness does not wait until life after death.

V. **Accept all appropriate responses.**

Chapter 2 Review

I. **1.** T; **2.** T; **3.** T; **4.** F (The *Catechism* presents **three** paths though which every person can come to know God. These are creation and the human person **and Revelation**); **5.** T; **6.** T; **7.** F (Atheists **do not believe that** God exists); **8.** F (Agnostics **argue that we cannot know of** the existence of God); **9.** T; **10.** F ('Transcendence' refers to the idea that God is the absolute other).

II. **Appropriate responses will include:** The five proofs of St. Thomas Aquinas for the existence of God are: (1) The existence of a *prime mover*. Nothing can move itself; therefore there must be a first mover. We call this first mover God.
(2) The existence of an *uncreated creator*. Nothing can create itself. There must be, at the beginning, an uncreated creator. We call this uncreated creator God. (3) The existence of a *necessary being*. Nothing created needs to exist. There must be a necessary being. We call this necessary being God. (4) The existence of a *perfect standard*. There are degrees of perfection for any given quality in created things, such as beauty. There must be a perfect standard by which all other qualities are measured. We call this perfect standard God.
(5) The existence of an *intelligent designer*. We can see that the universe works and is ordered so we can conclude that it was designed by an intelligent designer. We call this intelligent designer God.

III. **1. Appropriate responses will include** the key points from pages 28–30 of the students' text.
2. Appropriate responses will include the key points from pages 33–34 of the students' text.

IV. **Appropriate responses might include:** I also find it difficult to explain all the evil and suffering in the world. But I know that God doesn't cause it. There is also so much beauty and goodness in the world, our search for truth never seems to end; and our longings for happiness all point toward God's existence.

V. **Accept all appropriate responses.**

Chapter 3 Review

I. **1.** Word of God; **2.** covenant; **3.** Psalms; **4.** Abraham; **5.** prophets; **6.** Moses; **7.** Mount Sinai; **8.** Messiah; **9.** Kingdom of God; **10.** Great Commandment.

II. The two main parts of the Bible are the Old Testament and the New Testament.
With regard to what each book passes on to us, appropriate responses will include the key points on pages 45–49 of the students' text, which elaborates on how the *Old Testament* tells the story of God's covenantal relationship with the Israelites before the coming of Jesus and on how the *New Testament* is the story of Jesus Christ, the founder of the Church, of his life and teachings, Passion, Resurrection, and Ascension, and of the early Church after Jesus' Ascension.

III. **Appropriate responses will explain** the Church's teaching that Jesus is the Messiah whom God promised to send his people, and in Jesus God established and entered into the new and final Covenant with all humanity.

IV. **Appropriate responses will include:** While the Bible contains history, stories and teaching about

events of the past, Scripture is the living Word of God. While the content is rooted in a particular moment in history, the message is timeless and universal. God continues to speak to us through Scripture.
V. **Accept all appropriate responses.**

Chapter 4 Review

I. **(1)** interpretation; **(2)** written; **(3)** Tradition; **(4)** Magisterium; **(5)** Jesus; **(6)** Christ; **(7)** Pope; **(8)** bishops; **(9)** Scripture; **(10)** Tradition.

II. **Appropriate responses will include:**
  1. a. Biblical inspiration: To say that the biblical authors were inspired means that the Holy Spirit assisted them so that they wrote faithfully and without error the truth that God wanted them to write.
  b. Inerrancy: The Church teaches that the people who wrote the Bible were inspired by God and, therefore, that the Bible is the Word of God spoken through the words of human beings. This means that in matters of the truths of God's Revelation for our salvation, the Bible is without error because God is its author.
  c. Literary genre: The biblical authors were people of their time and culture. They wrote using the forms of writing with which they were familiar, for example, poetry, fiction, history, parables, hymns, sermons, letters and so on. We refer to these different forms of writing as 'literary genres'.
  d. Biblical translation: Biblical scholars decipher the words and meanings of the original languages in which the Bible was written so as to translate the Bible into other languages. The Bible is now available in most languages. The various translations of the Bible are constantly being updated in light of the new insights of scholars.
  2. Appropriate responses will include: The biblical authors were inspired by God to write without error the truth which God, for the sake of our salvation, wished to see confided to the Sacred Scriptures. The biblical authors were limited by the knowledge available to them in their time and culture. They wrote in their own language and used the forms of writing, or the literary genres, available to them at that time.

III. **Appropriate responses will include:** God is the primary author of the Bible. The human authors of the Bible were guided in their writing by the Holy Spirit to use their talents and abilities so that they wrote without error the truth that God wanted them to know for their salvation. While they could be mistaken about matters other than the truths that God inspired them to write, they wrote God's Word, about Revelation and Faith and Tradition, without error.

IV. **Appropriate responses will refer** to the fact that biblical scholarship is always growing in its understanding of the languages and cultures of the biblical authors, and to the role of the Magisterium, the teaching office of the Church, which, guided by the same Holy Spirit who guided the human authors to write the Bible, now guides the Church in authentically interpreting the Bible.

V. **Accept all appropriate responses.**

Chapter 5 Review

I. **1.** C; **2.** A; **3.** C; **4.** A; **5.** D; **6.** C; **7.** C; **8.** D. **9.** D; **10.** D.

II. **1. Appropriate responses will include:** The writings of Sacred Scripture pass on the faith of the People of God, of the Jews and of Christians. They pass on the people's understanding of God's presence and saving work among them. The writings of Sacred Scripture were first passed on by word of mouth—storytelling—by the community of believers from generation to generation until they were eventually written down under the inspiration of the Holy Spirit. This writing began during the time of King David.
  2. *Stage 1:* Life of Christ: The Apostles' and the first disciples' experience of Jesus.
  Stage 2: Oral Tradition: The passing on of the memories and understanding of the meaning of the life, Death, Resurrection and Ascension of Jesus and of his teachings.
  Stage 3: Writing of the New Testament: With the death of the Apostles, the writings that are now included in the New Testament began to be written down.

III. **Appropriate responses will reflect an understanding that:** God has revealed himself fully by sending his own Son, in whom he established his Covenant. The Son is the Father's definitive Word; so there will be no further Revelation after him.

IV. **Appropriate responses will reflect an understanding that:** The biblical authors wrote using literary genres of their time, including such sayings as 'an eye for an eye and a tooth for a tooth'—which seems to teach that it is okay to get revenge or to harm others in the same way as they harm you. Biblical and other scholars are continuously discovering new insights into the meaning of the language used by the sacred authors. This tells us that we need to be careful not to interpret the words of Scripture in a very literal way. We need to know the meaning of the words and sayings that the sacred authors used to teach the truth God revealed.

V. **Accept all appropriate responses.**

Chapter 6 Review

I. **1.** Sacred Tradition; **2.** Acts of the Apostles; **3.** Liturgy; **4.** Liturgy of the Word; **5.** Lectionary; **6.** three; **7.** Liturgical; **8.** Divine Office; **9.** Breviary; **10.** Plainchant.

II. **Appropriate responses will include** references to and briefly describe the Lord's Prayer, the Liturgy of the Word, the Divine Office, the Psalms, the tradition of plainchant and the practice of *lectio divina*.

III. **Appropriate responses will include:** The seasons of the Liturgical Year are Advent, Christmas, Lent, the Sacred Triduum and Easter. *Advent* celebrates our preparation for the coming of Jesus. *Christmas* celebrates the birth of Jesus as the Son of God and the Savior of the world. *Lent* challenges us to live out the commitments of our Baptism and prepares us for the celebration of the Passion (suffering and Death) and Resurrection of Jesus. The *Sacred Triduum* celebrates the events of the Paschal Mystery of Jesus. *Easter* is the fifty-day celebration of the Resurrection of Jesus. **Accept all appropriate Bible passages.**

IV. **Appropriate responses might include:** The Bible has always been important in the life of Catholics. We have always loved the Bible as we love the Eucharist. It is true that Catholics have not always personally read the Bible as much as other Christians may have. We have come to realize that this was not a good thing. Today our Church encourages all Catholics to read the Bible prayerfully every day and give it a central place in our daily life. Today more and more Catholics are reading and studying the Bible, praying with its texts and sharing their faith in Bible study groups.

V. **Accept all appropriate responses.**

Chapter 7 Review

I. **Appropriate definitions will include:**
1. The *Magisterium* is the living teaching office, or teaching authority, of the Catholic Church, made up of the Pope and the bishops, guided by the Holy Spirit, whose responsibility and task it is to give authentic interpretation to the Word of God contained in both Sacred Scripture and Sacred Tradition.

2. *Sacred Tradition* is the body of teaching of the Church, expressed in her beliefs, doctrines, rituals and Scripture, that has been handed down from the Apostles to their successors, the Pope and the bishops, through the ages, in an unbroken line of succession.

3. *Apostolic Tradition* refers to those things that Jesus taught to the Apostles and early disciples, which were passed on to us first by word of mouth and only later were written down.

4. The *historical context of a biblical passage* refers to the fact that the sacred authors were people of their time. The time and culture in which they lived influenced how and what they wrote.

5. The *faith context of a biblical passage* refers to the sacred authors' experience of God and God's relationship with them. The Bible is a book of faith written for a people of faith.

II. **1. Accept all appropriate responses.**
2. Appropriate responses will include: Both Sacred Scripture and Sacred Tradition transmit Revelation, the Word of God, to us under the guidance of the Holy Spirit. Nothing taught through Sacred Tradition ever contradicts Scripture, since both Sacred Scripture and Sacred Tradition come to us under the guidance of the Holy Spirit.

III. **Appropriate responses will include** the roles of historical context, political context and faith context.

IV. **Appropriate responses might include:** God is the primary author of Sacred Scripture. The Church is guided by the same Holy Spirit who inspired the sacred authors in their writing of the Bible. Nothing taught through Sacred Tradition ever contradicts Scripture since both Sacred Scripture and Sacred Tradition come to us under the guidance of the Holy Spirit.

V. **Accept all appropriate responses.**

Chapter 8 Review

I. **1.** T; **2.** F (The written Word of God has **several layers** of meaning); **3.** F (The use of literary genre **helps us understand** the meaning of Revelation) **4.** T; **5.** T; **6.** F (Exegesis is **a process that helps us understand the meaning of a biblical text**); **7.** T; **8.** F (A fundamentalist interpretation of the Bible focuses solely on the **literal meaning of what** the sacred authors wrote) **9.** F (We can **never** fully understand the meaning of the Bible, **even** with the help of the Magisterium); **10.** F (**Jesus Christ** is the source and foundation of the unity of God's plan and Sacred Scripture).

II. **Appropriate responses will include:** (1) The *allegorical* sense is at work when a particular story stands for something in the life of Christ or of the Church. For example, the miracle at the Red Sea prefigures Christ's victory over death and the Christian's new life through the waters of Baptism. (2) The *moral* sense is at work when the biblical passage suggests things that we ought to do. For example, the love of God for Israel, and then for the Church, suggests that married love should be similarly faithful, supportive and forgiving. (3) The *anagogical* sense is at work when the biblical events are a sign of something eternal. For example, the feeding of the Israelites with manna in the desert and the multiplication of the loaves and fish all foreshadow the heavenly banquet in the Kingdom of God.

III. **Appropriate responses will include:** The inspired human authors of the Bible used the forms of expression commonly used by the people of their time to convey the truth that God wanted to reveal to us. These forms of expression are called literary genres. They include stories, poems, psalms, letters, proverbs, historical accounts and so on. If we want to understand the message in the biblical writings, then we need to know what literary genre is being used in any given piece of Scripture. Many parts of the Bible can appear like a coded text to us. It is not that the biblical authors were trying to hide or obscure their message. Rather, they wrote in language suitable to their audience and culture, which may seem coded to us.

IV. **Appropriate responses might include:** What your Dad says is true but not the whole truth. People can use words in many ways to communicate their message. For example, when you hear that the mall is having a 'fire sale', it does not mean that the stores are selling fire. It means that they are trying to sell as much of their merchandise as they can. The writers of the Bible used words in the same way. We need to know how they were using their words before we can really understand the meaning of the message the Bible is communicating to us.

V. **Accept all appropriate responses.**

Chapter 9 Review

I. **1.** D; **2.** A; **3.** B; **4.** E; **5.** E; **6.** E; **7.** B; **8.** B; **9.** C; **10.** C.

II. **Appropriate responses will include: 1.** *Hope* is the desire for and expectation of the Salvation God promised, which is based on God's unwavering fidelity to keeping and fulfilling his promises.
2. A *covenant* is a solemn agreement made between human beings or between God and a human being or human community involving mutual commitments or guarantees.
3. The *Messiah* is the 'Anointed One' or 'Christos' whom God promised to the Israelites to be the Savior of all peoples.
4. The *New Covenant* is the final and everlasting Covenant in Jesus Christ between God and all people.

III. **1. Appropriate responses will include** the key points from pages 155–156 of the students' text.
2. Appropriate responses will include the key points from pages 157–158 of the students' text.

IV. **Appropriate responses will include** references to the relationship between the Old Testament and the New Testament, to the Covenant with Israel and the New and Everlasting Covenant (Jesus Christ), and to the Messiah.

V. **Accept all appropriate responses.**

Chapter 10 Review

I. **1.** Son of God; **2.** Messiah; **3.** Savior; **4.** Matthew; **5.** Mark; **6.** Luke; **7.** John; **8.** *evangelium*; **9.** Kingdom of God; **10.** good news.

II. **1.** The three stages in the formation of the Gospels are (1) the life and teaching of Jesus, (2) the oral tradition, and (3) the written Gospels.
2. Appropriate responses will include: The term 'gospel' comes from the Old English word *godspel*, meaning 'good news'. *Godspel* was originally used to translate the Greek word *euaggelion* (Latin *evangelium*), a term the early Church used for the Good News of Jesus Christ. The Church uses the term 'Gospel' to refer to the four New Testament books that proclaim the life, teaching, Death and Resurrection of Jesus. More generally, the term refers to the proclamation of the entire message of faith revealed in and through Jesus Christ.

III. **Appropriate responses will include:** The Synoptic Gospels are the Gospels according to Matthew, Mark and Luke. The *Gospel of Mark* portrays Jesus as an active healer and miracle worker, who accepts loneliness and suffering as the cost of obedience to his Father's will. The *Gospel of Matthew* emphasizes that Jesus is the Messiah promised to the Jewish people. The *Gospel of Luke* emphasizes Jesus' mercy, compassion and concern for all people, especially the poor and others marginalized by society in his time.

IV. **Appropriate responses might include:** True, there are differences, but there are also similarities and they agree on many key points. It is important to remember that the Gospels are not biographies as we understand biographies today. The Gospels are really telling the faith story of the Church. The

main intent of the four Evangelists was to pass on the faith of the Church in Jesus and his teachings and his work in the world. The details are not the issue. What matters is the message.
V. **Accept all appropriate responses.**

Chapter 11 Review

I. **1.** T; **2.** F (Matthew tells us that the birth of Jesus took place during the reign of **King Herod**); **3.** F (Matthew portrays Jesus as the new **Moses**); **4.** T; **5.** F (The **Kingdom of God** is the central theme of the Synoptic Gospels); **6.** T; **7.** F (In Luke's Gospel the Beatitudes are part of Jesus' Sermon on the **Plain**); **8.** T; **9.** F (The 'Woe' statements in **Luke's** Gospel point to ways of not living for the Kingdom of God); **10.** F (Luke **does not teach** that wealth and prosperity are blessings from God).

II. **Appropriate responses would include:** Jesus used parables to help people understand what the Kingdom of God is like. In his parables he compared things that the people were familiar with to the Kingdom of God, about which the people knew very little. The people of Jesus' time truly believed in miracles as the work of God. The miracles of Jesus pointed to the fact that the Kingdom of God had come. God was at work among his people.

III. **Appropriate responses would include:**
1. The baptism of Jesus is seen as the beginning of his public ministry. The Spirit coming down refers back to the Old Testament and the descent of the Spirit on the Israelites during their Exodus from slavery in Egypt. The baptism of Jesus marks the beginning of a new Exodus, the journey of freedom out of sin to new life in Christ.
2. The proclamation of the Beatitudes presents a profile of a believer who is truly living the values of the Kingdom of God. These values take up the promises to Abraham, the Israelites and the prophets, fulfilling them in the Kingdom of God.

IV. **Appropriate responses might include:** Jesus performed miracles to help people believe that God is always at work among his people. This was an important message for people who thought illness was a punishment from God for their sins. We also believe that people who have died are still alive in a new way. It is very difficult for us when someone we love dies. Our faith in God and living in a new way can really help.

V. **Accept all appropriate responses.**

Chapter 12 Review

I. **1.** Fourth; **2.** Glory; **3.** eternal life; **4.** divinity; **5.** vine; **6.** 'I Am'; **7.** Good Shepherd; **8.** Signs; **9.** Paraclete; **10.** Mary Magdalene.

II. **1. Appropriate responses will include:** A symbol points to something beyond itself and helps us discern and make meaning out of life and express and share the meaning we discover. Symbols communicate experience where words are not enough. Symbols convey meaning when an experience is so profound that it is difficult to find the words to communicate its meaning. In John's Gospel we encounter a symbol-laden world of meaning; deciphering symbols in the Fourth Gospel will help to shed light on the meaning of God's Revelation for our lives.

2. Appropriate responses will include: 'Hypostatic union' is the term used to state the fact that Jesus, the Son of God, became man in the Incarnation and that Jesus possesses two natures, the divine nature and a human nature, united in one divine Person. The Son of God became man without giving up being God. The one divine Person, Jesus, is true God and true man. Jesus is fully divine and fully human.

III. **Appropriate responses will include:** John's Gospel and the Synoptic Gospels both present an account of the Last Supper. The Synoptic Gospels focus on the details of the Passover Meal and the institution of the Eucharist. The washing of the feet is only found in John's Gospel and John's Gospel does not give an account of the Last Supper (Passover) meal and the institution of the Eucharist. John's Gospel contains Jesus' last discourse with his disciples and his prayer to the Father for them, which the Synoptic Gospels do not.

IV. **Appropriate responses will include:** At the Last Supper Jesus washed the feet of his disciples. Through this symbolic act Jesus gave away the secret for living a successful and happy life. We are to follow his example by loving and serving others. This is the highest paying of all jobs because, through this 'way of living', we are blessed by God with a happiness that money could never buy.

V. **Accept all appropriate responses.**

Chapter 13 Review

I. **(1)** Jerusalem; **(2)** suffering; **(3)** Death; **(4)** Eucharist; **(5)** sacrifice; **(6)** blasphemy; **(7)** Calvary *or* Golgotha; **(8)** Resurrection; **(9)** Mary Magdalene; **(10)** faith.

II. **Seven Last Words: (1)** 'Father, forgive them; for they do not know what they are doing.' **(2)** 'My God, my God, why have you forsaken me?' **(3)** 'Woman, here is your son.' 'Here is your mother.' **(4)** 'I am thirsty.' **(5)** 'Truly, I tell you, today you will be with me in Paradise.' **(6)** 'It is finished.' **(7)** 'Father, into your hands I commend my spirit.'
Sacrifice of the Cross: The 'Sacrifice of the Cross' refers to Jesus freely offering his life for us on the Cross. A sacrifice is a free offering, a gift, made by a person for the welfare of others. It is a sincere sign of the love of one person for another. The greatest sacrifice is to give one's life for another.

III. **Appropriate responses** will make the distinction between resuscitation and Resurrection. *Resuscitation* is bringing physical life back to the same body of the person who has experienced death. *Resurrection* is experiencing death and coming to new life—a radically new life. The body of the Risen Jesus was so transformed that it had properties that were not limited by space and time and 'his humanity can no longer be confined to earth, and belongs henceforth only to the Father's divine realm' (CCC, no. 645).

IV. **Appropriate responses** would be developed around the faith of the Church in the resurrection of the body. There is no contradiction between happiness on earth and eternal happiness. But focusing on material possessions as the source of happiness leads to a dead end. *(Note: This would be a good time to have the young people revisit chapter 1 and answer the opening question: 'Where do we find meaning in life?')*

V. **Accept all appropriate responses.**

Acknowledgments

Grateful acknowledgement is made to the following holders of copyright material:

Scripture quotations are taken from the *New Revised Standard Version Bible: Catholic Edition* copyright © 1993 and 1998 by the Division of Christian Education of the National Council of Churches of Christ in the United States of America. All rights reserved.

Excerpts from the English translation of the *Catechism of the Catholic Church* for use in the United States, second edition, copyright © 1997, United States Catholic Conference, Inc.— Libreria Editrice Vaticana. All rights reserved.

Excerpts from the *United States Catholic Catechism for Adults*, Washington, DC, USCCB, copyright © 2006 USCCB. All rights reserved.

Excerpts from the English translation of the *Rite of Baptism for Children* © 1989 International Committee on English in the Liturgy, Inc (ICEL); the English translation of *The Roman Missal* © 2010 ICEL. All rights reserved.

Excerpts from documents of Vatican II are from A. Flannery (ed.), *Vatican Council II: Constitutions, Decrees, Declarations* (New York/Dublin: Costello Publishing/Dominican Publications, 1996).

Excerpts taken from *Catholic Household Blessings & Prayers*, Revised Edition © 2007, Bishops Committee on the Liturgy, United States Conference of Catholic Bishops, Washington, DC.

Extract on p. 23 from *Keepers of the Story* by Megan McKenna (New York: Seabury, 2005), copyright © Megan McKenna, 2005.

Worksheet 3 on pp. 29–30 adapted from an article by Professor E. Just in *Celebrating One World: A Worship Resource on Social Justice* edited by Linda Jones, Annabel Shilson-Thomas and Bernadette Farrell (London: HarperCollins and CAFOD, 1998), copyright © E. Just, 1998.

'Surprise Surprise!', p. 66, by Clare Maloney, from *Alive-O 8* (Dublin, Ireland: Veritas, 2004), copyright © Clare Maloney, 2004.

'Researching the Riddle', p. 84, by Reason A. Poteet, copyright © Reason A. Poteet.

Extract on p. 88 from Pope Benedict XVI's Homily on the occasion of Marian Vespers with the Religious and Seminarians of Bavaria, 2006, copyright © Libreria Editrice Vaticana, 2006.

Excerpt on p. 95 from Dr. Martin Luther King's Jr.'s 'I have a dream' speech, copyright © Estate of Dr. Martin Luther King, Jr.

Extract on p. 105 from *Storytelling, Imagination and Faith* by W.J. Bausch (New London, CT: Twenty-Third Publications, 1984), copyright © W.J. Bausch, 1984.

'It Is Not Enough', p. 123, by David Whyte, from *Where Many Rivers Meet*, copyright © Many Rivers Press, 2004. Printed with permission from Many Rivers Press, Langley, Washington. www.davidwhyte.com.

Extract on p. 127 from *150 Stories for Preachers and Teachers* by Jack McArdle (Mystic, CT: Twenty-Third Publications, 1993), copyright © Jack McArdle, 1993.

Extract on p. 142 from *Send My Roots Rain: A Spirituality of Justice and Mercy* by Megan McKenna, copyright © 2003 by Megan McKenna. Used by permission of Doubleday, a division of Random House, Inc.

Extract on p. 146, as told by Joan D. Chittister, OSB in *Reimagining the Catholic School*, N. Prendergast and L. Monahan (eds), (Dublin, Ireland: Veritas, 2003), copyright © Joan D. Chittister, 2003.

Adapted extract on p. 155 from *Psalming the New Testament* by Desmond O'Donnell and Maureen Mohan (Dublin, Ireland: Veritas, 2001), copyright © Desmond O'Donnell and Maureen Mohan, 2001.

Prayer on p.167 by Bishop Kenneth Untener of Saginaw.

Prayer on p. 175 by G.W. Briggs, from *Daily Prayer from the Divine Office* (London: Collins, 1974), copyright © G.W. Briggs, 1974.

'A Class Seder Meal', p. 181, adapted from Raymond Brady, *Christian Way*, Book One, Teacher Guide (Dublin, Ireland: Veritas, 1980), copyright © Raymond Brady, 1980.

Extract on Sister Dorothy Stang, p. 190, adapted from an article by Jan Rocha in *The Guardian* newspaper (London, February 2005), copyright © Jan Rocha, 2005.

'The One', p. 197, by Patrick Kavanagh is reprinted from *Collected Poems*, edited by Antoinette Quinn (Allen Lane, 2004), by kind permission of the Trustees of the Estate of the late Katherine B. Kavanagh, through the Jonathan Williams Literary Agency.

Instructions on p. 198 and 'In the spotlight' activity, p. 201, adapted from *Junior Cert Religious*

Education Guidelines for Teachers, National Council for Curriculum and Assessment/Department of Education and Science (Dublin, Ireland: The Stationery Office, 2001), copyright © Government of Ireland, 2001.

'Your Father Knows Well You Need Them', p. 215, from *Who Do You Say That I Am?: And Other Gospel Questions* by Donal Neary SJ (Dublin, Ireland: Veritas, 2001), copyright © Donal Neary, 2001.

'Beatitudes', p. 222, by Christy Kenneally, from *Workers for the Kingdom* (Dublin, Ireland: Veritas, 1987), copyright © Christy Kenneally, 1987.

Extract on p. 223 from *Consider Jesus* by Elizabeth Johnson (London: Geoffrey Chapman, 1990), copyright © Elizabeth Johnson, 1990.

'Catherine and the Winter Wheat', p. 227, by F. B. Hughes, from *Workers for the Kingdom* (Dublin, Ireland: Veritas, 1987), copyright © F. B. Hughes, 1987.

'A Teacher's Prayer', p. 235, by Hugo Schlesinger, from *Prayers of Blessing and Praise for All Occasions* (Mystic, Connecticut: Twenty-Third Publications, 1987), copyright © Hugo Schlesinger, 1987.

'The Killing', p. 255, by E. Muir, from *Daily Prayer from the Divine Office* (London: Collins, 1974), copyright © E. Muir, 1974.

Outline of the Passover Meal, p. 261, adapted from the Religious Education Support through the Second Level Support Service/Department of Education and Science, Ireland/National Development Plan, Ireland, copyright © Religious Education Support Service. http://www.ress.ie.

Note on 'Shared reading technique', p. 271, based on Johnson, Johnson and Holubec.

'Mind Maps', p. 272, © ThinkBuzan Ltd. http://www.thinkbuzan.com.

Notes on facilitating successful meditations, pp. 274–6, adapted from Tim Quinlan, *Still Point Meditations for School and Parish* (Dublin, Ireland: Veritas, 2002), copyright © Tim Quinlan, 2002

Front cover
Main image: The face of Christ (mosaic) by Byzantine School (6th century). Sant'Apollinare Nuovo, Ravenna, Italy/The Bridgeman Art Library.
Top left: Photo by Nancy Honey.
Center: Ethiopian monk holding a fifteenth-century illuminated Bible, © Christophe Boisvieux/Corbis.

Every effort has been made to contact the copyright holders of the material reproduced in *God's Word Revealed in Sacred Scripture*. If any infringement has occurred, the owners of such copyright are requested to contact the publishers.